AF668904

Playing Techniques of Tabla: Banaras Gharana

Playing Techniques of Tabla: Banaras Gharana

Pandit Chhote Lal Misra

KANISHKA PUBLISHERS, DISTRIBUTORS
NEW DELHI-110 002

KANISHKA PUBLISHERS, DISTRIBUTORS
4697/5-21A, Ansari Road, Daryaganj
New Delhi -110 002
Phones : 2327 0497, 2328 8285
Fax : 011-2328 8285
E-mail : kanishka_publishing@yahoo.co.in
kanishkabooks@gmail.com

Playing Techiques of Tabla: Banaras Gharana

First Published-2007

Edition-2023

© Author

ISBN : 978-81-7391-929-1

PRINTED IN INDIA

Published by Madan Sachdeva for Kanishka Publishers, Distributors, 4697/5-21A, Ansari Road, Daryaganj, New Delhi-110002, Typeset by Sunshine Graphics, Delhi, and Printed at G.S. Printers, Delhi.

A Memorable Name in Music Gharana
of *Banaras* Tabla Wizard

THE LEGEND PT. ANOKHE LAL MISHRA

Presented with Great Honour to the Holy Feet of My Respected Gurudev

–Chhote Lal Misra

Preamble

There are so many books available on the subject of Tabla whose writers have written focusing their own areas. No doubt these books are useful for students, but some specific terms are left viz. controversy in technical words and some specific clarifications in practical/experimental aspect which is very important for the students. Proper knowledge of Gharana (style) is very important in the initial stage, likewise 'A for apple, B for ball, C for cat, D for doll... and so on, is necessary for primary students, otherwise they will go astray without knowledge of direction.

In the interest of the students, I would like to give a message that no student can establish him as a successful artist by the help of books only. Music is the science of traditional learning, and therefore, guidance of a Guru (tutor) is very necessary. By making efforts to comply with the instructions given by Guruji, keeping real devotion and good feelings of respect for music and music teachers, a student can touch the top of music, otherwise there will be no effect in his performance and in the field of music he will loose his entity. A student of music can make his future bright by devoting to music and get the social status and thus, can become immortal by adding his name in the history of music. My blessings goes to one of my disciples Mr. Om Prakash Srivastava who devoted his time and support in presenting this book in English language.

Chhote Lal Misra

B–27/64, Kushmanda Apartments
Durga Kund,
Varanasi–221 005
U.P. (INDIA)

BY THE SAME AUTHOR

• तबला ग्रन्थ 2006	Rs. 995	ISBN 81-7391-844-9
• ताल प्रबन्ध 2006	Rs. 450	ISBN 81-7391-843-0
• ताल प्रसून 2004	Rs. 450	ISBN 81-7391-642-X

Contents

Part–II

PRACTICAL

Part–I

THEORY

1

Music/Gharana

What is Music and its Gharana, a brief introduction is given below:

It is very difficult to understand a great and deep subject like music. Its explanation and prevalence is infinite. Shaaranga Deo has defined the music in *'Sangeet Ratnaakar'* as under:

> *'Geetam Vadyam Tatha Nrityam Trayam Sangeet Muchyate'* means, the mixture of song, instrument and dance, is known as music (Sangeet). Right from the ancient period, the learned persons in the field of music, agreed on the above three arts in music. But song (vocal) has been accorded supremacy among the above three.

Pt. Bhaatkhande has also narrated that in limited sense, the word 'music' represents vocal music, even then, in Hindu hearts the vocal music, instrumental music and dance are so closely related to each other that the writers of olden times have used the word 'music' as consolidated form of these concurrent arts. That's why, the co-ordination of all the three arts has been adopted in Indian music.

Gharana

When an art, after being developed and purified, becomes so cultured and prosperous that it gets a special recognition and honour, a tradition of that particular art takes birth. This tradition comprises the history and achievements of artists. On the basis of the practical improvement of the art, the creation of different style and its development is also entered in the tradition. In this way, the traditions of vocal, instrumental and dance in Indian music were brought forward in different forms at different times and after a period of time, these traditions were developed as different Gharanas of music.

Six Gharanas are Prevalent Named of Tabla

1. Delhi Gharana—started by Ustad Siddhar Khan.
2. Ajrada Gharana—started by Ustad Kallu Khan and Ustad Meeru Khan.
3. Lucknow Gharana—started by Ustad Modu Khan and Ustad Bakhshu Khan.

4. Farrukhabad Gharana—started by Ustad Hajee Vilayat Ali Khan.
5. Banaras Gharana—started by Pandit Ram Sahaiji and
6. Punjab Gharana—started by Lala Bhawani Das.

The only base of the credit or validity of different Gharanas in Tabla, is their different playing style. The variety of these styles can be understood by two methods. First, by the compositions of 'Baaj' of Tabla and second, by method of sounding or playing the 'Bols' of Tabla.

As different subjects are written according to alphabet, in the same way one and the same 'Bol' is played on Tabla in different Gharanas by applying different fingers and by striking different fingers on Chanti, Lav & Syahi of Tabla's Pudi with variations. Therefore, in Tabla recital, the playing style with excellence of dexterity of hand in striking is called 'Baaj' and the word 'Baaj' is very prevalent in the field of musicians.

The credit for getting the respected name of 'Banaras' as a Tabla Gharana and generating a new style, goes to the great Tabla scholar the Legend **Pt. Raam Sahai Ji.** The names of his five disciples are fit to be inscribed here. They are given in seriatim, first Pt. Bhagat Ji, second Pt. Ram Sharan Ji, third Pt. Pratap Ji (Partappu Ji), fourth Baij Nath ji alias Baiju Ji and fifth Shri Yadu Nandan Ji.

Pt. Bhagat Ji (Gurudutt Ji), one of the best disciples of Pt. Ram Sahai Ji, was established as a great scholar of Tabla-recital and treasurer of the art of Tabla. It was Bhagat Ji whose disciple was Pt. Bhairo Prasad Ji, and gradually, among the best disciples of **Pt. Bhairo Prasad Ji**, a very glittering name rose, that established its place in the heart of each and every musician and music admirer, this name was *Pt. Anokhe Lal Mishra Ji.*

Tabla Wizard Pandit Anokhey Lal Mishra

Among the list of all-time-greats in Indian music Stands the name the legend Pt. Anokhey Lal Mishraji. He was regarded by many of the Leading musicians and critics as one of the greatest Tabla players of all time. Famous not only for his music but for his dedication, he remains a rare example of a musician whose entire being was devoted to his music.

Pt. Anokhey Lal ji was born in the year 1914 in Varanasi. Though many of his ancestors had been Tabla players, and his father a Sarangi player, his training did not begin at home due to the loss of his father at the age of 2 Tragically, his mother pasted away a few years later when Pt. Ankhey Lal ji was just six, Leaving him in the care of his paternal grandmother who had great difficalties in providing for him. At the age of 6th he started Tabla training under Pandit Bhairav Prasad ji, a famous exponent of the Banaras Gharana, with keen interest and great labour he began to go ahead in this field and always kept a smiling face during his practice in spite of any obstructions. He was highly disciplined in his practice and long before becoming a performing artist he developed a strict practice routine of 18 hours a day. As a result of his austere practice and receiving the blessings of his Guru ji (teacher), he began to be invited to various musical festivals at the age of 18 only. He established himself as a popular artist after accompanying the renowned musicians of those days. In a very short span he achieved the top-place in the world of music.

Tabla become his life and little else mattered to him. Even when he became famous he maintained 12 hours of practice a days and seemed to have no interest in becoming a star.

Pandit ji was very traditional as an heir to the Banaras Gharana yet he had great respect for the material of other Gharana, some of which he incorporated into his own solo repertoire. Though he could play complicated compoitions and Taals with ease, he maintained a simple style using basic traditional Bols (rhythmic syllables), applying his refined technique of using only the minimum required hand movement to produce a given sound clearly and properly. And while he was famous for his immense speed he used no gimmicks in his playing.

He was named as the wizard of "Naa Dhin Dhin Naa" in the world of music and accomplished 'Dhira Dhira Kita Taka' on Tabla so extra-ordinarily that it became memorable forever.

He would play a composition in high speed in exactly the same way as in slow speed. And even in increased speed. Each Bol was audible.

Infact, Pt. Anokhey Lal ji was the first Tabla player to maintain his top speed, while playing a particular composition in a solo, for unprecedented durations of time. Previously the style had been to play one's fastest compositions for a very short time at top speed before slowing down and moving on to the next. Pandit Mishraji endurance inspired others to pursue his standard and consequently the tradition of soling has since been widely accepted style of presentation.

He was the man of extra-ordinary personality. He was very simple, devotional temperament and pitiful by nature. He was having great respect to his elders and was affectionate to his disciples. That's why he has been placed in the category of saints and deity by the musicians and music lovers.

I would like to say in brief that such personality and performer will be long awaited. I am proud of being one of his close disciples.

He passed away on March 10, 1958 and left behind his lawful wife (our Guru Maa), two sons and two daughters. His eldest son Pt. Ram Ji Mishra followed his foot-mark and made his own identity by performing matchless Tabla recital, and youngest son Shri Kashi Nath Mishra is also doing good in the field of Tabla smoothly and regularly.

Pt. Mahapurush Mishra and Pt. Ishwar Lal Mishra are the best disciples of our respected Guruji Who made bright the name of our Guruji as well as the name of our Country in abroad also. Apart from them, there is a number of other disciples who are doing better and going ahead.

Banaras Gharana

Pandit Ram Sahai

Brothers

Pt. Gauri Sahai Pt. Janki Sahai Pt. Ishwari Sahai

Pt. Bhairav Sahai (Son)

Pt. Baldev Sahai (Son)

Pt. Bhagwati Sahai (Son)

Pt. Sharda Sahai (Son)

Sanjay Sahai (Nephew)

5-Main Disciples

1. Pt. Bhagat Ji (Gurudatt ji)
2. Pt. Ram Sharan Ji
3. Pt. Pratap Ji (Partappu Ji)
4. Pt. Baij Nath ji (Baiju Ji)
5. Pt. Yadu Nandan Ji

Pt. Durga Sahai 'Nannhu Sahai' (Son)

Pt. Kanthe Maharaj (Disciple)

Pt. Kishan Maharaj (Nephew)

Pooran Maharaj (son)

Shubh Shankar (Grand son)

Pt. Dargahi ji (Son)

Pt. Vikramaditya 'Bikkuji Maharaj (Son)

Pt. Gamaji (Son)

Prof. Rangnath Mishra (Son)
Pt. Vijay Shankar Mishra (Son)

Pt. Bacha Maharaj (Grand Son)

Pt. Samta Prasad 'Godai Maharaj' (Son)

Pt. Kumar Lal Mishra (Son)

Pt. Bhairo Prasad Mishra (Disciple)

Pt. Anokhe Lal Mishra (Disciple)

Pt. Ramji Mishra (Son)
Pt. Mahapurush Mishra (Disciple)
Pt. Chhote Lal Misra (Disciple)
Pt. Ishwar Lal Mishra (Disciple)

Disciples of Pt. Ramji Mishra

Sanjaya Mishra] Pooran Mishra, Kuber Nath Mishra, Dev Kishor Benarji, Kishanram Dohakar, Homnath (Nepal), Somyakanti Mukharji, Harprit Singh Sonu, Chandra Prakash, Piolal (Kolkata), Stifen (U.S.A.), Najayan Mishra, Lalit Kumar and others.

Disciples of Pt. Chhote Lal Misra

Ramkumar Mishra (Varanasi) Sanjay Kumar Mishra, Surendra Chandra Pathak, Girindra Chandra Pathak, Avinash Kumar Ratanman (Mongher-Bihar), Sanjay Kumar Mishra, Dhnanjay Mishra, Deepak Mishra, Udaya Singh, Dr. Parth Chakravorty, Dr. Prem Narayan Singh, Dr. Rishitosh Kumar. Dhananjaya Kumar Mishra, Deepak Kumar Mishra. Somya Kanti Mukharji, Dr. Mahendra Sharma (Bam-Bam), Dr. Narendra Pathak (Jaunpur), Ajay Pathak, Shivendra Pratap Tripathi, Dev Kishor Benarji, Somyakanty Mukharji, Rahul Bhatt, Govind Shukla, Aroop Chatarji, Rohit Mishra, Shiva Kumar Shukla, Om Prakash Srivastava, Akash Srivastava, Manish Panday, Jagarnath Singh, Jagdamba Singh, Pankaj Rai, Rajneesh, Deepak Singh, Achyut Ram Bhandari (Nepal), Daniel, Klemo (Switzarland), Henary Ritzman, Daniel, Charly, Wintarmayar, Petar (Germany), Adriyan (England), Masa, Sainio, (Japan), Mariyastarlin, Mathew (U.S.A.), Naresh Kumar Pandit, Roopak (Holand), Omary, Gill (Isrial), Petar (Sweden), Chandra Lal, Ranjan, Pradeep (Shrilanka) Omprakash Panday, Siddharth Chakravorty and others.

Disciples of Pt. Ishwar Lal Mishra

Kashinath Mishra, Pundalik Krishna Bhagwat, Gyanendra, Purnendu, Dhananjaya Kumar Mishra, Deepak Kumar Mishra, Sanjaya Mishra, Aamat Fredrik (French), Stiven Slavek (U.S.A.), Steve (Switzarland), Sandip Bhattacharya and others.

2

Tal Lipi (Tal Script)

There are two popular systems in Northern Indian Music known as Bhatkhande System and Vishnu Digambar System.

Bhatkhande System

The symbol in Bhatkhande System is as under:

There is no symbol for one Matra in this system.

Symbol for 'Sum' – ×

Symbol for 'Khali' – S

To extend any Matra, the symbol for 'Avagraha' (impediment) – S

Symbol for speaking/reading two 'Bols' in

One Matra (Beat) ⌣ or ⌊ ⌋ ⌊1 2⌋

(It is called 'Dugun')

Symbol for reading/speaking three 'Bols'

In one Matra (Beat) ⌣ or ⌊ ⌋ ⌊123⌋

(It is called 'Tigun')

Symbol for reading/speaking four 'Bols'

In one Matra (Beat) ⌣ or ⌊ ⌋ ⌊1234⌋

(It is called 'Chaugun')

Symbol for reading/speaking six 'Bols'

In one Matra (Beat) ⌣ or ⌊ ⌋ ⌊123456⌋

(It is called 'Chhaigun')

Symbol for reading/speaking eight 'Bols'

In one Matra (Beat) ⌣ or ⌊ ⌋ ⌊12345678⌋

(It is called 'Athgun')

There is no symbol for reading/speaking one 'Bol' in one Matra, therefore, 'Dha' will be 'Ekgun'.

Symbol for different Bols will be as under:

Dha ge	1/2	i.e. Dugun
Dha ge na	1/3	i.e. Tigun
Dha ge ti te	1/4	i.e. Chaugun
Ti ra ki ta ta ka	1/6	i.e. Chhaigun
Dha S ti ra ki ta ta ka	1/8	i.e. Athgun
Dha S	2/1	

i.e. 'Dha' will remain paused for one Matra more.

Since there is 'Dha' of one Matra in two Matras, it will be called 'Adhagun'.

In Bhatkhande System Tal Deepchandi and Tal Jhumra will be shown as under:

Tal Deepchandi

Matras-	1	2	3	4	5	6	7	8	9	10	11	12	13	14
Theka-	Dha	Dhin	S	Dha	Dha	Tin	S	Ta	Tin	S	Dha	Dha	Dhin	S
Symbol-	×			2				0			3			

Both of the above Talas are of 14 Matras. Both are having four 'Vibhag' and three 'Tali' (clap) & one 'Khali' (empty).

Tal Jhumra

Matras-	1	2	3	4	5	6	7
Theka-	Dhin	S Dha	Tirakita	Dhin	Dhin	Dhage	Tirakita
Symbol-	×			2			
Matras-	8	9	10	11	12	13	14
Theka-	Tin	S Ta	Tirakita	Dhin	Dhi	Dhage	Tirakita
Symbol-	0			3			

In Bhatkhande System the first 'Vibhag' (division) is meant for 'Sum' and it is indicated with '×' whereas next coming vibhagas will be numbered and the vibhag of Khali will be indicated with '0', it is not numbered. The 'Vibhag' following 'Khali' will be numbered in sequence as cited above.

Vishnu Digambar System

In this system, figure '1' is used for 'Sum' and symbol '+' is used for Khali. Bols are numbered in serial. Different Matras and fraction of Matras are indicated as under:

Matra	*Symbol*	*Bol*							
One 1	–	Dha							
Two 2	~ or	Dha or Dha S ~							
Half ½	0	Dha 0	Ge 0						
One fourth ¼	◡	Ti ◡	Ra ◡	Ki ◡	Ta ◡				
1/8	◡ ‿	Ki ◡ ‿	Ta ◡ ‿	Ta ◡ ‿	Ka ◡ ‿	Ti ◡ ‿	Ra ◡ ‿	Ki ◡ ‿	Ta ◡ ‿
1/3	~~	Dhe ~~	Ti ~~	Te ~~					
1/6	≈≈	Ta ≈≈	Ka ≈≈	Di ≈≈	Na ≈≈	Ta ≈≈	Ka ≈≈		

In this system, Tal Deepchandi and Tal Jhumra will be narrated as under:

Deepchandi:

Dha	Dhin	S	Dha	Dha	Tin	S
	1				6	
Ta	Tin	S	Dha	Dha	Tin	S
	+			11		

Jhumra:

Dhin	S	**Dha**	**Ti** ◡	**Ra** ◡	**Ki** ◡	**Ta** ◡	**Dhin**	**Dhin**	**Dha**	**Ge**	**Ti** ◡	**Ra** ◡	**Ki** ◡	**Ta** ◡
1	0	0					4		0	0				
Tin	S	**Ta**	**Ti** ◡	**Ra** ◡	**Ki** ◡	**Ta** ◡	**Dhin**	**Dhin**	**Dha**	**Ge**	**Ti** ◡	**Ra** ◡	**Ki** ◡	**Ta** ◡
+	0	0					11		0	0				

Therefore, '1' is written for 'Sum'. Where there is Tali, the number of that Matra will be written and Khali will be indicated by the symbol '+'.

3

Tabla and its Parts

The Tabla is the most popular Percussion instrument of North India, representing a great and long tradition. The Tabla is found in many kinds of music including folk, light classical and classical.

Technically, Tabla refers only to the smaller of the two drums with the larger being called the Duggi or Bayan meaning 'Left'. The Tabla proper also called Dayan (right), is made of wood and shaped like a large cup closed at the bottom, about 30 cm. high. In Common usage, however, Tabla refers to both. Bayan is usually similar in height to the Dayan though much wider in the center and at its mouth, the latter measuring around 25 cm. Some where Tabla is known as 'Nargha' and in Saurashtra it is called 'Dukkad'. But at Present Tabla has become very popular and the instruments right and left are known as Tabla and Bayan or Duggi. Both drums are coverd with goat skin and upon each skin is fastened a Syahi, the most significant feature of the Tabla. It is a kind of circular pad fastened firmly to the skin. When making the Syahi it is first applied as a paste made from a ground mixture of iron powder, glue, wheat powder and charcoal. It is applied Layer by Layer and then polished dry with a smooth stone. Its thickness and evenness must be correct in order for the skin's sound to be balanced.

On the Dayan the overtone created by the presence of the Syahi is tuned with the vocalist's pitch or the tonic of the instument being accompanied.

The teachnique of the Tabla is quite developed with a large number of sounds being produced. Most of the strokes on the Dayan are made with the fingers and occasionally with the palm. The Bayan uses mostly the fingertips with inflection being made by the base of the wrist.

Each sound on the Tabla also has an onomatopoetic syllable to represent it. So the Tabla player must learn to speak a new language in addition to playing. These syllables are, in fact, the main mode of teaching and communicating Tabla material. They help the student understand the sound to be produced and aid the memorization of compositions.

Diagram of Tabla-Bayan

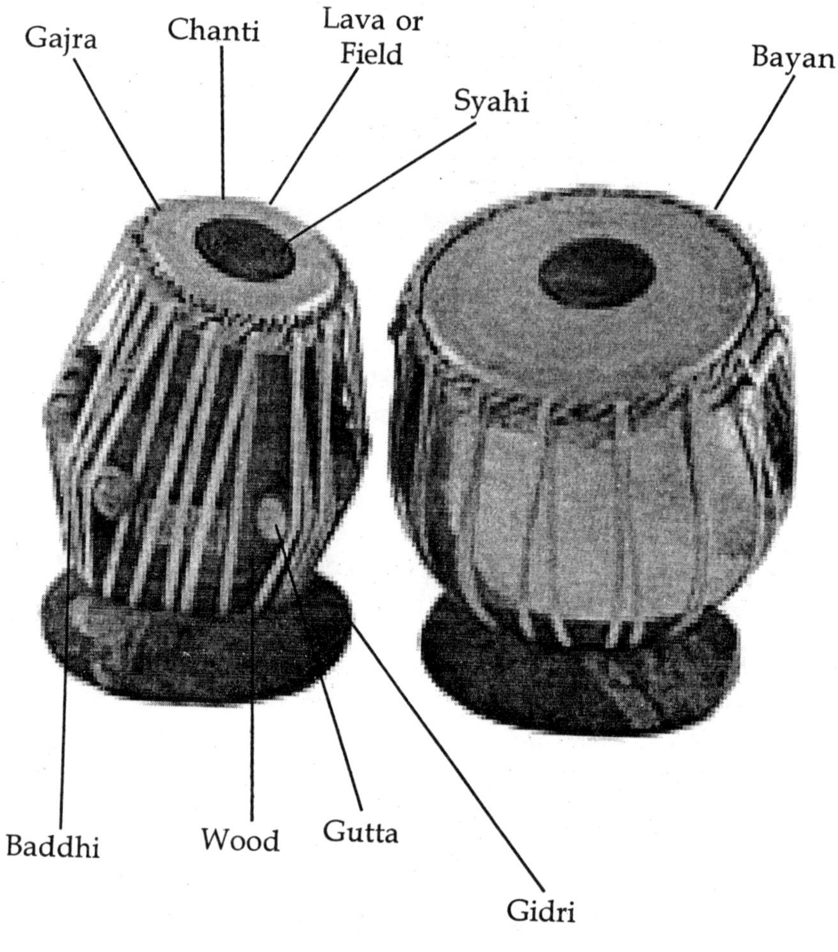

1. Syahi
2. Chanti
3. Lava or Field
4. Gajra
5. Baddhi
6. Wood
7. Gutta
8. Gidri

Tabla

It is made of wood. Different types of wood are used for making Tabla viz. Vijay Sar, Catechu, Teak (Timber), Sandal, Margosa, Mango, Acacia and Jack-tree etc. Mainly the dry wood of Vijay Sar, Catechu and Teak are used for making Tabla. ¾ part of Tabla is hollow from inside and ¼ part is solid. The solid part of wood which is weighty, gives more effective echo. The solid part of Tabla helps in keeping it still.

Bayan or Dagga

Normally it is made of either brass, copper, wood or clay, though copper and brass are the most common for performance. It is called 'Kudi'. As the clay Kudi is easily breakable, it is made of brass and copper sheet. Although, in Punjab, wooden Kudi is used, yet the sound of Bayan made of clay, is the best.

Pudi

The leather or skin used for covering Tabla and Bayan is called 'Pudi'. Normally, it is goat skin. Chanti, Lav and Syahi are parts of Pudi. The Pudi of Tabla is thin in comparision to Bayan. It is tuned at high tone. Bayan's Pudi is little thick and it is tuned at sober tone. The sound of Bayan is defined as male sound and sound of Tabla as female sound.

Chanti

At the edge of Pudi, there is an additional leather stripe, called 'Chanti'. 'Varnas' (letters viz. a,b,c....) of Tabla are played on Tabla's Chanti and there is no Varna in Bayan's Chanti.

Lav

The place in between Chanti & Syahi (i.e. original Pudi), is called 'Lav'. 'Ta' and 'Tin' is played on right Tabla's Lav and 'Ge' is played on Bayan's Lav. Lav is called 'Maidan' also.

Syahi

There is a black round shape on Pudi called 'Syahi'. It is a paste of iron powder (ash). The Syahi of right instrument i.e. Tabla is exactly in the centre of Pudi whereas left Dugga's Syahi is at the edge of Chanti at ½ inch distance only.

Gajra

Pudi is surrounded and tied by a leather belt called 'Gajra'. There are 16 holes in Gajra called 'Ghar'. Gajra is known as 'Singar' and 'Dwal' also.

Gudri or Gidri

There is a small Gajra or wheel made of leather at the bottom of Tabla and Bayan, called 'Gudri'.

Gutta

'Gutta' is made of wooden pieces, also called 'Gulli'. By placing at up & down, the 'Swara' becomes high & low. Gutta is used in right Tabla only and not in Bayan.

Baddhi

A leather thread (strip) tightens the Pudi through the holes of Gajra and keeps a pressure on Gutta, is called 'Baddhi'.

Baddhi and cotton thread, both are used in Dugga. Brass rings are used in cotton thread to tighten the Dugga.

Indri

'Indri' is a thick ring made of cloth which is used for placing Tabla and Bayan during recital. It improves the echo of Tabla.

VARNAS OF TABLA

Different words (Varnas) are created by striking the Tabla with different fingers. There are three kinds of Varnas:

1. Varnas created by right hand
2. Varnas created by left hand
3. Varnas created by both the hands

There are so many dissensions for Varnas. As per different opinions 7 Varnas, 8 Varnas and 10 Varnas are in practice. At present, 10 Varnas are prevalent as under:

(a) Varnas created (to be struck) by right hand only:

1. Ta or Na
2. Tin or Tee
3. Din or Thun
4. Tu
5. Ti
6. Te, Ta or Ra

(b) Varnas created by left hand only:

1. Ge, Gi, or Ghe, Ghi, Gha
2. Ke, Ki, Ka or Kat

(c) Varnas created by both the hands:

1. Dha
2. Dhin

As per the opinion of the scholars of Banaras Gharana, there are some more (additional) Varnas of Tabla.

Fingers are used in various style for different Varanas and these fingers are named as under:

1. Right finger
2. Middle finger
3. Ring finger
4. Little finger
5. Thumb

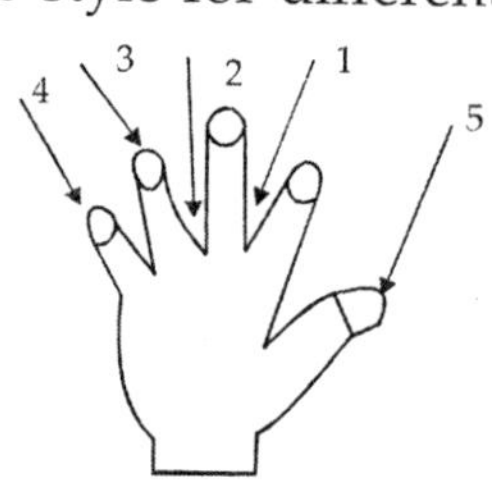

The use of fingers for different Varnas is apparent from the following table:

Use of Right Hand

	Varna	*Place*	*Finger*
1.	Taa, Naa, Ti	Lav	Ring finger (curved) and the edge of Syahi to be struck.
2.	Ta, Na, Da or Ra	Chanti	Right finger
3.	Tin	Syahi	Right finger (open Swara)
4.	Din or Tu or Thun	Syahi	Combined four fingers (open Swara)
5.	Te, Ta, T	Syahi	To be struck by combined ring finger and middle finger.
6.	Ta, Da or Ra, T, Tet, Na	Syahi	Combined four fingers and (combined ring finger and middle finger)
7.	Te, Ra, Re	Syahi	By right finger
8.	Taan	Syahi	By little finger
9.	Tra, Tri	Chanti	By ring finger, middle finger, right finger

Use of Left Hand

	Varna	*Place*	*Finger*
1.	Ka, Kat, Ki, Ke	Syahi	Making an open strike bycombined four fingers like a pat.
2.	Ga, Gi, Ge, Gha, Ghi, Ghe	Beyond the other side of Syahi	To make a solid little strike by ring finger, middle finger and right finger by placing the wrist on the bottom edge of Syahi.

Use of Both the Hand Simultaneously

	Varna	*Place*	*Finger*
1.	Dha	Lav and Chanti	Right finger
2.	Dhin	Lav	Right finger
3.	Dhet	Syahi	Right finger and middle finger + ring finger and, combined four fingers.
4.	Dhinn	Syahi	Right finger and combined four fingers.

Method of Creating (playing) Varnas on Tabla

Note: Numbered fingers will be convenient viz.

1. Right finger
2. Middle finger
3. Ring finger
4. Little finger

5. Thumb

Method of Playing Varnas on Tabla by Right Hand Only

1. Ta or Ṅa

Keep No.3 finger (curved) constant at the bottom edge of Syahi and strike on Lav by No.1 finger. It should be noted that No.1 finger is up immediately after strike, and it should not stick with the Lav. Another method to sound 'Ta' or 'Na' is to strike on Chanti with No.1 finger and No.2 finger should be upward (lifted).

In Banaras Gharana, 'Ta' and 'Na' are played on Lav as well as on Chanti. But, in other Gharanas, 'Ta' and 'Na' are played on Chanti only.

2. Tin or Ti

The method of striking on Lav by No.1 finger, likewise 'Ta'.

3. Din or Thun

Joining four fingers, strike lightly (without pressure) on the edge of Syahi and immediately lift up. Other part of the wrist i.e. below fingers should remain on Chanti.

4. Tun or Tu

The edge of Syahi (right direction) to be struck lightly (without any pressure) by No.1 finger and No.3 finger to be lifted a bit simultaneously.

5. Te or Ti

There are two types to sound 'Te' or 'Ti':

(*a*) The centre of Syahi to be struck by No.2 finger with pressure.
(*b*) The centre of Syahi to be struck by No.2 & 3 fingers jointly with pressure.

6. Tey, Ta or Ra

This is used immediately after 'Te', viz. TeTey (Tite), Ter (Tir). So, strike by No.1 finger right on that particular place.

Method of Playing Varnas by Left Hand Only

1. Ga, Ge, Gi or Gha, Ghe, Ghi

Placing the wrist with little pressure on the bottom edge of Syahi on Bayan (Dugga) and striking on Lav i.e. on other side of Syahi by finger No.1 or 2 or 3 of left hand.

2. Ka, Ke, Ki, Kat

Placing the wrist of left hand on the bottom edge of Syahi (without pressure) and striking by all fingers jointly like a pat.

3. Dha

Striking right hand's 'Ta' and left hand's 'Ge' simultaneously will sound 'Dha'. Though, 'Dha' can be created by joining Bayan's (left) 'Ge' with any of Varnas of Tabla (right).

4. Dhin

Striking right hand's 'Tin' and left hand's 'Ge' simultaneously will sound 'Dhin'.

Method of Playing (sound) Joint Bols

1. TiTe or Tir

The centre of Syahi of (right) Tabla to be truck by middle finger and ring finger jointly, then removing a little both the fingers in right direction, the same place to be struck by right finger, will sound 'Tir' or 'TiTe'.

2. Tirakita

After playing 'Tir' by the aforesaid method on right Tabla, play 'Ka' on left Dugga like a pat, then 'Te' on Syahi of right Tabla by middle and ring fingers, will sound 'Tirakita'.

Therefore, Tira+Ka+Te = Tirakita

3. Kitataka

There are two methods to sound 'Kitataka'. In the first method, 'Ta' of Kitataka will be played on Lav as 'Taa' and in second method 'Ta' will be played as 'Te' on Syahi.

Therefore,

First method

Ka+Te+Taa+Ka = Kitataka

Second method

Ka+Ti+Te+Ka = Kitataka

4. Ghedanaga or Gheranage

This will be played in three types.

1st type

Play Varna 'Ge' on left Dugga, after that Varna 'Ti' on Syahi of right Tabla, then Varna 'Taa' on right Tabla and again 'Ge' on left Dugga. This will sound 'Ghedanaga'.

Therefore, Ge+Ti+Taa+Ge = Ghedanaga

2nd type

Ge+Ti+Te+Ge = Ghedanaga

3rd type

Ge+Ti+Naa+Ge = Ghedanaga

Naa: Chanti right Tabla to be struck by right finger.
Ti: Syahi of right Tabla to be struck by middle finger.

5. Dinataka

Play 'Tin' i.e. 'Tu' by right finger at the bottom edge of Syahi on right Tabla and varna 'Ge' on left Dugga, both simultaneously, after that varna 'Ti' on the Syahi and varna 'Taa' on the Lav of Tabla, and then Varna 'Ka' on the left Dugga. This will sound 'Dinataka'.

That is to say Tin + Ge = Dhin or Din
Therefore, Din + Ti + Taa + Ka = Dinataka

6. Kradhan or Kdadhan

Play Varna 'Ka' on left Dugga and Varna 'Ti' on the Syahi of right Tabla in such a manner that Varna 'Ka' sounds first followed by Varna 'Ti' immediately i.e. like 'Kti', after that Varna 'Dha' (on Lav) and Varna 'Ti' lightly on Tabla. This will sound 'Kradhan' or 'Kdadhan'.

Therefore, Kti + Dha + Ti = Kradhan or Kdadhan

7. Dhadagin or Dharagin

Strike on Chanti of right Tabla by the tip of right finger and Varna 'Ge' on left Dugga simultaneously, after that the same place of Chanti of Tabla to be struck by the fore part of middle and right fingers jointly like Varna 'Ti', then play Varna 'Ge' on Dugga and the Chanti of right Tabla to be struck like 'Ti' as aforesaid. This will sound 'Dhadagin' or 'Dharagin'

Therefore, Dha + Ti + Ge + Ti = Dhadagin (only on Chanti)

8. Katan and Kdan or Kran

Play Varna 'Ka' on the left Dugga and Varna 'Taa' on the Lav of right Tabla, after that Varna 'Ti' on the Syahi of Tabla, this will sound 'Katan'. And, play Varna 'Ka' & 'Taa' keeping very little gap like 'Kta' and after that Varna 'Ti', this will sound 'Kdan'. Therefore,

Ka + Taa + Ti = Katan
Kta + Ti = Kdan or Kran

9. Dhir or Dher

Keep the right hand joining all the fingers on right Tabla in such a manner that the Syahi of Tabla is completely covered by the palm of the hand, and, strike right portion (half) of the wrist on Tabla and play Varna 'Ge' on Bayan Dugga simultaneously to sound 'Dhi' or 'Dhe', then strike left portion (half) of the palm (wrist) on Tabla to sound 'Ra'. Therefore, right half portion of the palm will play 'Dhi' or 'Dhe' and left half portion will play 'Ra' i.e. 'Dhir' or 'Dher'.

As the Varna 'TiTe' is played on the Syahi of Tabla, like that, covering whole 'Pudi' of Tabla by the palm and Varna 'Ge' on Bayan Dugga simultaneously will sound 'Dhir' or 'Dher'. Some people play 'Dher' by the fingers only and lift the palm a little, in this way the sound will be 'Dher' but there will be no gravity in the Bol (sound).

10. Tan

It is called 'Ta' of 'Thap' (pat) also. This is played on right Tabla only. To sound 'Tan', the bottom portion of the Syahi of Tabla is to be struck by all the four fingers of right hand particularly by little finger with pressure, but it is ensured that the hand is immediately lifted up.

Different methods for playing a particular 'Joint Bol' in different Gharanas by applying different fingers have been given below:

Joint Bol—Tirakita

Gharana	*Ti*	*ra*	*ki*	*ta*
Delhi	**On Tabla**	**On Tabla**	**On Bayan**	**On Tabla**
	Middle finger	Right finger	"	Ring finger
Ajrada	Middle finger	Right finger	"	Ring finger
Lucknow	Middle finger	Right finger	"	Middle and Ring finger jointly
Farrukh-abad	Middle finger	Right finger	"	Middle and Ring finger jointly
Banaras	Middle, Ring and Little finger jointly	Right finger	"	Middle, Ring and Little finger jointly
Panjab	Middle and Ring finger jointly	Right finger	"	Middle and Ring finger jointly

Joint Bol—Gheranage

Gharana	*Ghe*	*Ra(da)*	*Na*	*ge*
Delhi	On Bayan	On Tabla	On Tabla	On Bayan
	"	Middle finger	Right finger	"
Ajrada	"	Middle finger	Right finger	"

(Contd.)

Gharana	*Ghe*	*Ra(da)*	*Na*	*ge*
Lucknow	"	Middle finger or Right finger	Ring finger	"
Farrukhabad	"	Middle finger or Right finger	Ring finger	"
Banaras	"	Middle, Ring and Little finger jointly	Right finger	"
Panjab	"	Middle finger and Ring finger jointly	Right finger	"

4

Method of Tuning Tabla

It is very important to tune the Tabla before playing, because the Tabla which is not tuned is not proper for music. Therefore, it is very necessary to know the art of tuning Tabla. The method of tuning is as under:

There are two methods of tuning:

First

Some people tune it by making first hole (Ghar) equal to its opposite hole, viz. 9th hole after first, 13th hole after 5th and so on all 16 holes.

Second

In this method, all 16 holes are tuned in a sequence. Generally, Tabla is tuned in the 'Shadaj' (musical first note) of 'Madhya' (middle) and 'Tar Saptak', because the male sound (voice) tunes with first 'Kala' (C sharp) and second 'Kala' (D sharp) or fourth 'white' in Harmonium, whereas female sound tunes with third (F sharp), fourth (G sharp) and fifth (A sharp) 'Kala'. Therefore, both the different sounds (tone) require separate Tabla for tuning. High tone requires small faced Tabla and low tone requires large faced Tabla.

Gajra and Gutta of Tabla are used for tuning the Tabla in high or low tone. When these are struck by a small hammer from up towards down, the Pudi tightens resulting Tabla is tuned at high tone. Similarly, strike by hammer from down towards up, it is tuned at low tone.

The Tabla accompanist should watch attentively the 'Swara' (tone) of the vocalist or instrument player before tuning the Tabla. Then striking by finger on the Lav of Tabla, he should compare its echo with the high or low tone of the vocalist or instrument artist. If there is a little difference, it should be tuned by striking the Gajra only. Gutta should be struck for tuning the Tabla at high or low level if there is a remarkable difference. It is advisable not to strike on Gajra again and again because it shortens the life of Pudi, so it is better tune Tabla by Gutta. Apart from this, sometimes there may be a difference between Lav and Chanti. Such type of Pudi should be changed immediately.

5

Tal or Taal

Song i.e. vocal music, instrumental music and dance are based on 'Tal'. Tal can be defined as plinth or base also. In 'Amarkosh' of Pt. Amar Singh, it is described that the means used for measuring the time in music is called 'Tal'. In other words, the means for measuring the length of vocal-instrumental music, is known as Tal. Tal is created by many 'Vibhagas' and 'Matras' (cells & units). Tal binds the music in a stipulated time frame.

Matra (Beat)

In the field of music, 'Matra' is very important for rhythm. Matra is the unit for measuring the time in music. Measurement of Tals used in music is 'Matra'. To show the Laya (rhythm) Tali (clap) is used and the duration between two Talis is known as Matra (Beat).

Laya (Rhythm)

Normally Laya means 'Gati' (speed). The constant speed of time in music is called Laya. There are three kinds of Laya-'Drut' (fast), 'Madhya' (middle) and 'Vilambit' (delayed).

Vilambit Laya: When there is a big gap between two Matras in vocal-instrumental music and dance, it is called 'Thah' or Vilambit Laya.

Example: Teental in Vilambit Laya:

1	2	3	4
DhaS S S	Dhin S S S	Dhin S S S	Dha S S S
5	6	7	8
Dha S S S	Dhin S S S	Dhin S S S	Dha S S S
9	10	11	12
Dha S S S	Tin S S S	Tin S S S	Ta S S S
13	14	15	16
Ta S S S	Dhin S S S	Dhin S S S	Dha S S S

Madhya Laya: When the speed of Laya is in between fast and slow, it is called Madhya Laya.

Example: Teental in Madhya Laya:

1	2	3	4
Dha S	Dhin S	Dhin S	Dha S
5	6	7	8
Dha S	Dhin S	Dhin S	Dha S
9	10	11	12
Dha S	Tin S	Tin S	Ta S
13	14	15	16
Ta S	Dhin S	Dhin S	Dha S

Drut Laya: When the speed of Laya is very fast, it is called Drut Laya.

Example: Teental in Drut Laya:

1	2	3	4	5	6	7	8
Dha	Dhin	Dhin	Dha	Dha	Dhin	Dhin	Dha
9	10	11	12	13	14	15	16
Dha	Tin	Tin	Ta	Ta	Dhin	Dhin	Dha

Therefore, Drut Laya is double of Madhya Laya and Madhya Laya is double of Vilambit.

Vibhag

The whole 'Theka' of Tal is devided into several small cells called 'Vibhag'. Normally Vibhagas are of 2, 3, 4 and 5 matras.

e.g. there are 16 matras in Teen Tal and it has 4 Vibhagas having 4 matras in each Vibhag. Tal Jhaptal has 10 matras and 4 Vibhagas, but every Vibhag is different by matras because its Vibhagas are of 2, 3, 2, 3 matras.

Sum

Tal is started by first matra, so first matra of the Tal is defined as 'Sum'. Although, there are several rotation in different 'Bandish' (composition) of vocal and instrumental music and their original 'Sum' is also different, but the Tabla player starts his recital with first matra of Tal and concludes also on first matra. Therefore, the 'Sum' of Tal-Vadya (Percussion instrument) is first matra of Tal. So, the first matra of each and every Tal is called 'Sum'.

Taali

First matra of Vibhag of any Tal is indicated by 'Taali' (clap), is called 'Bhari' also. First matra of each and every Tal is indicated by 'Taali'. Tal Rupak is exception, because first matra of Tal Rupak is 'Khali' (without clap i.e. showing open hand). Apart from this, first matra of different Vibhagas of Tal, is also shown by Tali.

Khaali

First matra of any Vibhag of Tal on which the right hand is bent a little instead of Tali, is called 'Khali'. Khali comes in between or so, in the Tal.

6

Technical Words of Tabla

Bol

In the science of Tabla the most prevalent word is 'Bol'. The groups of words created by Varnas, played on Tabla, are called 'Bol'. In the group of Bols, small, large, strong or soft or any type of Laya, is applicable. Kayada, Bant, Rela, Gat, Paran, Tukda, Chakradar etc. are also different forms of Bol.

Theka

The main Bols created by Varnas, played on Tabla for presenting the Tal, are called 'Theka'. When a presentable group of Bols is played on Tabla, according to the weight of a Tal in its different Matras, is called 'Theka' of that Tal. e.g. 16 Matras are there in Teen Tal and Theka is created by Varnas of Tabla:

Theka (Bol)

1	2	3	4	5	6	7	8
Dha	Dhin	Dhin	Dha	Dha	Dhin	Dhin	Dha
×				2			
9	10	11	12	13	14	15	16
Dha	Tin	Tin	Ta	Ta	Dhin	Dhin	Dha
0				3			

12 Matras are there in Ek Tal and Theka is created by Varnas of Tabla:

Theka (Bol)

1	2	3	4	5	6	7	8	9	10	11	12
Dhin	Dhin	Dhage	Tirkit	Tu	Na	Kat	Ta	Dhage	Tirkit	Dhin	Na
×		0		2		0		3		4	

Avritti or Avartan (Rotation)

The area from first Matra to last Matra of a Tal is known as 'Avritti' or 'Avartan'. e.g. there will be 16 Matras in one Avritti of Teen Tal and 10 Matras in one Avritti of Jhaptal. Its next Avritti will start again from first Matra. As many times the Tal is repeated, the number of Avritti will increase. e.g. In Tal Jhaptal, 10 Matras are in one Avritti, 20 Matras are in two Avritti and 30 Matras in three Avritti, but counting will be made from first to 10th Matra in each Avritti every time. Therefore, first Matra to last Matra in each and every Tal will be called Avritti or Avartan.

Kism (Kind)

According to weight of Bols used in Tal, new shape is given by adorning each Matra, this is called 'Kism'. For example, some 'Kism' in Teen Tal are given below:

Main Theka

Dha Dhin Dhin Dha	Dha Dhin Dhin Dha	Dha Tin Tin Ta	Ta Dhin Dhin Dha
×	2	0	3

Kism (1)

Dha ×	Dhin	DhinDhin	Dhati	Dha 2	Dhin	DhinDhin	Dhati
Dha 0	Tin	TinTin	Tati	TaTa 3	Dhin	DhinDhin	Dhati

Kism (2)

DhaSTrak ×	Dhinna	DhinDhin	Dhati |
DhaSTrak 2	DhinSSKra	DhinDhin	Dhati |
DhaSTrak 0	Tinna	TinTin	Tati |
TaSTrak 3	DhinSSKra	DhinDhin	Dhati |

In the same way, some 'Kism' are given below in Tal Dadra:

Main Theka

	Dha ×	Dhin	Na |	Dha 0	Tu	Na |
Kism (1)	Dha ×	Dhin	NaNa |	Dha 0	Tu	NaNa |
Kism (2)	DhaSTete ×	DhinDhin	NaNa |	DhaSTete 0	TinTin	NaNa |
Kism (3)	DhaSgina ×	DhageTrak	Dhinagina |			
	DhaSgina 0	DhageTrak	Tinakina |			

Tihai

When a group of Bols, adding 'Dha' Varna, is played thrice and the last (third) 'Dha' is ended on 'Sum', this is called 'Tiya' or 'Tihai'. Dha Varna is much potential in Varnas of Tabla, so, it is eminent to add Dha Varna with any group of Bols to make Tihai effective. Although, other Varnas are also used, but 'Dha' Varna is used in general.

There are two kinds of Tihai-'Dumdar' and 'Bedum'.

1. Dumdar Tihai

In Dumdar Tihai, there is a pause of one Matra or more after adding one Dha in each group of Bols. But the third (last) Dha ends on 'Sum' and there is no need of any pause. e.g. Tihai in Tal Jhaptal is given below:

Titekata Gadigana	DhaS Titekata	Gadigana Dha	STitekata Gadigana
×	2	0	3
Dha			
×			

2. Bedum Tihai

In 'Bedum' Tihai, there is no pause or halt after adding 'Dha' in each group of Bols. e.g. ,

(Bedum Tihai of Tal Teen Tal)

Dhage	Tite	Kata	Gadi	Gana	Dha,Dha	GeTi	teKa	
×				2				
TaGa	DiGa	naDha	Dhage	Tite	Kata	Gadi	Gana	Dha
0				3				×

There are two opinions for Bedum Tihai. According to first opinion there is no existence of Bedum Tihai as 'Dha' itself is strong. As per second opinion the shape of 'Dha' is already plump and the time taken for 'Dha' cannot be defined as 'Dum'.

According to second opinion an example of Bedum Tihai in 'Ada Chartal' is given below:

Tite Dhagi	naDha Tite	Dha Tite	Dhagi naDha	Tite Dha	Tite Dhagi
×	2	0	3	0	4
naDha Tite	Dha				
0	×				

Gi Na	Ti Te	Dha Gi	Na Ti	Te Dha	Gi Na	Ti Te	Dha
×	2	0	3	0	4	0	×

Nauhakka

When a Tihai is played thrice and the last i.e. nineth 'Dha' ends on 'Sum', it is called 'Nauhakka'. As per another definition, when a Bedum Tihai is played thrice without any pause and the last 'Dha' ends on 'Sum', it is called 'Nauhakka' Tihai. For example,—in Teen Tal, from sixth Matra, a Nauhakka Tihai will be as under:

Dha	Dhin	Dhin	Dha
×			
Dha	Krdhatite	DhaKradhati	teDhaKradha
2			
TiteDha,Kra	dhatiteDha	Kradhatite	Dha,Kradhati
0			
teDha,Kradha	titeDhaKra	dhatiteDha	Kradhatite
3			
Dha			
×			

Nauhakka is likewise Dumdar and Bedum Tihai. According to the first definition aforesaid, a Nauhakka in Tal Dhamar is given below:

KradhaTite	DhaऽKradha	TiteDhaऽ	KradhaTite	Dhaऽऽऽ
×				
KradhaTite	DhaऽKradha	TiteDhaऽ	KradhaTite	Dhaऽऽऽ
2		0		
KradhaTite	DhaऽKradha	TiteDhaऽ	KradhaTite	Dha
3				×

Kayada

'Kayada' means method, regulation, law etc. It is defined as under:

Kayada is an arranged creation of original Varnas used in Tabla which is based on Matra, Tali, Khali and Vibhag. More and more expansion of Kayada is possible and both the hands can be made speedy in correct manner by its practice and Tabla can also be played correctly.

In literary words, vowel-consonants and Varnas are introduced by different words, in the same way, original Varnas of Tabla are introduced by Kayadas. As to enrich the language knowledge, letter 'a' is introduced by several words like apple, air, ant, aeroplane etc., likewise Varnas are introduced by expanding Kayadas and its 'Paltas'.

In creation of Kayada the following points are to be noted:

1. The creation of Kayada is based on Matra, Tali, Khali of Tal.
2. Kayadas are created by the original Varnas used in Tabla.
3. A vigilant attention is paid to its Varnas as it can be expanded more and more.
4. Kayada consists of one Avartan or more.
5. As in Theka, there are two parts in the construction of Kayada, 'Bhari' and 'Khali'.

6. Its first part is made of 'Bhari' (open) Varnas and the second part is made of 'Khali' (closed) Varnas.

In Banaras the training of Tabla starts from Kayada. For example:

Dha Dha Ti Te	Dha Dha Tu Na	Ta Ta Ti Te	Dha Dha Dhin Na
×	2	0	3

Prastar (Expanse)

The creations, as a result of expansion of Bols used in Kayada, are called 'Prastar', 'Vistar', 'Palta', 'Pench', Variation etc.

The 'Prastar' of Kayada is based on the following rules:

1. Prastar must consist the Bols used in Kayada only.
2. 'Bhari' or 'Khali' Bols are composed according to Tali-Khali.
3. Prastar should be in a regular manner to make it convenient to expand.
4. In Prastar, it is very important to note that the form of joint Bols of Kayada is not spoiled. For example:

Kayada (original)

Dha Dha Ti Te	Dha Dha Tu Na	Ta Ta Ti Te	Dha Dha Dhin Na
×	2	0	3

In the above Kayada, 'Dha' and 'Ta' are individual Varna, and TiTe, TiNa and Dhina are joint Bols. 'Dha' and 'Ta' can be used several times and in different types, but TiTe, TiNa or Dhina cannot be divided. If these joint Bols are divided, the form and sense of Kayada will be spoiled, because 'Bandish' (Composition) of every Kayada has an identity and it consists a meaningful sense. The example of proper and improper Prastar of the above Kayada is given below:

Proper

Dha Dha Ti Te	Dha Dha Ti Te	Dha Dha Ti Te	Dha Dha Tu Na
×	2	0	3
Ta Ta Ti Te	Ta Ta Ti Te	Dha Dha Ti Te	Dha Dha Dhin Na
×	2	0	3

Improper

Dha Ti Ti Te | Dha Ti Tin Na

OR

Dha Te Ti Dha | Te Ti Na Dhin

Some Prastar in the fundamental Kayada are given below successively:

In this way, many Prastars can be made. Apart from this, Prastar with Layakari can also be made.

(Prastar of the Bols of first Vibhag of Kayada)

Fan. Ka.	Dha Dha Ti Te ×	Dha Dha Tin Na 2	Ta Ta Ti Te 0	Dha Dha Dhin Na 3
Prastar	Dha Dha Ti Te	Dha Dha Ti Te	Dha Dha Ti Te	Dha Dha Tin Na
	Ta Ta Ti Te	Ta Ta Ti Te	Dha Dha Ti Te	Dha Dha Dhin Na
"	Dha Dha Ti Te	Ti Te Ti Te	Dha Dha Ti Te	Dha Dha Tin Na
	Ta Ta Ti Te	Ti Te Ti Te	Dha Dha Ti Te	Dha Dha Dhin Na
"	Dha Dha Ti Te	Ti Te Dha Dha	Ti Te Ti Te	Dha Dha Tin Na
	Ta Ta Ti Te	Ti Te Dha Dha	Ti Te Ti Te	Dha Dha Dhin Na
"	Dha Ti Te Dha	Dha Ti Te Dha	Dha Dha Ti Te	Dha Dha Tin Na
	Ta Ti Te Ta	Ta Ti Te Ta	Dha Dha Ti Te	Dha Dha Dhin Na
"	Dha Ti Te Dha	Ti Te Ti Te	Dha Dha Ti Te	Dha Dha Tin Na
	Ta Ti Te Ta	Ti Te Ti Te	Dha Dha Ti Te	Dha Dha Dhin Na
"	Dha Ti Te Ti	Te Dha Ti Te	Dha Dha Ti Te	Dha Dha Tin Na
	Ta Ti Te Ti	Te Ta Ti Te	Dha Dha Ti Te	Dha Dha Dhin Na
"	Dha Dha Dha Dha	Ti Te Ti Te	Dha Dha Ti Te	Dha Dha Tin Na
	Ta Ta Ta Ta	Ti Te Ti Te	Dha Dha Ti Te	Dha Dha Dhin Na
"	Dha Dha Dha Dha	Dha Dha Ti Te	Dha Dha Ti Te	Dha Dha Tin Na
	Ta Ta Ta Ta	Ta Ta Ti Te	Dha Dha Ti Te	Dha Dha Dhin Na
"	Dha Dha Dha Dha	Ti Te Dha Dha	Dha Dha Ti Te	Dha Dha Tin Na
	Ta Ta Ta Ta	Ti Te Ta Ta	Dha Dha Ti Te	Dha Dha Dhin Na
"	Ti Te Dha Ti	Te Dha Ti Te	Dha Dha Ti Te	Dha Dha Tin Na
	Ti Te Ta Ti	Te Ta Ti Te	Dha Dha Ti Te	Dha Dha Dhin Na
"	Ti Te Dha Dha	Ti Te Ti Te	Dha Dha Ti Te	Dha Dha Tin Na
	Ti Te Ta Ta	Ti Te Ti Te	Dha Dha Ti Te	Dha Dha Dhin Na

(Prastar by applying the Bols of second Vibhag of Kayada)

Prastar	Dha Dha Ti Te	Dha Dha Tin Na	Dha Dha Tin Na	Dha Dha Tin Na
	Ta Ta Ti Te	Dha Dha Din Na	Dha Dha Dhin Na	Dha Dha Dhin Na
"	Dha Ti Te, Dha	DhinNa, Dha Ti	Te, Dha Dhin Na	Dha Dha Tin Na
	Ta Ti Te, Ta	Tin Na, Dha Ti	Te, Dha Dhin Na	Dha Dha Dhin Na
"	Dha Ti Te, Dha	DhinNa, Dha Dhin	Na, Dha Dhin Na	Dha Dha Tin Na
	Ta Ti Te, Ta	Tin Na, Dha Dhin	Na, Dha Dhin Na	Dha Dha Dhin Na
"	Dha Ti Te, Dha	DhinNa, Ti Te	Dha Dhin Na, Ti	Te Dha Tin Na
	Ta Ti Te, Ta	Tin Na, Ti Te	Dha Dhin Na, Ti	Te Dha Dhin Na
"	Dha Dha Ti Te	Dha Dha Din Na	Dhin Na Dhi n Na	Dha Dha Tin Na
	Ta Ta Ti Te	Ta Ta Tin Na	Dhin Na Dhin Na	Dha Dha Dhin Na
"	Dhin Na DhinNa	Dha Dha Dhin Na	Dha Dha Ti Te	Dha Dha Tin Na
	Tin Na Tin Na	Ta Ta Tin Na	Dha Dha Ti Te	Dha Dha Dhin Na

(Contd.)

"	Dhin	Na	Dha	Dhin	Na	Dha	Dhin	Na	Dha	Dha	Ti	Te	Dha	Dha	Tin	Na
	Tin	Na	Ta	Tin	Na	Ta	Tin	Na	Dha	Dha	Ti	Te	Dha	Dha	Dhin	Na
"	Dhin	Na	Dha	Dha	Dhin	Na	Dhin	Na	Dha	Dha	Ti	Te	Dha	Dha	Tin	Na
	Tin	Na	Ta	Ta	Tin	Na	Tin	Na	Dha	Dha	Ti	Te	Dha	Dha	Dhin	Na
"	Dhin	Na	Dha	Dha	Ti	Te	Dha	Dha	Ti	Te	Ti	Te	Dha	Dha	Tin	Na
	Tin	Na	Ta	Ta	Ti	Te	Ta	Ta	Ti	Te	Ti	Te	Dha	Dha	Dhin	Na
"	Dhin	Na,	Dha	Ti	Te	Dha	Dhin	Na	Dha	Dha	Ti	Te	Dha	Dha	Tin	Na
	Tin	Na	Ta	Ti	Te	Ta	Tin	Na	Dha	Dha	Ti	Te	Dha	Dha	Dhin	Na
"	Dhin	Na	Dha	Dha	Ti	Te	Ti	Te	Dha	Dha	Ti	Te	Dha	Dha	Tin	Na
	Tin	Na	Ta	Ta	Ti	Te	Ti	Te	Dha	Dha	Ti	Te	Dha	Dha	Dhin	Na

(Applying 'Dum' Repose Prastar)

Prastar	Dha	S	Ti	Te	S	Dha	Ti	Te	Dha	S	Ti	Te	Dha	Dha	Tin	Na
	Ta	S	Ti	Te	S	Ta	Ti	Te	Dha	S	Ti	Te	Dha	Dha	Dhin	Na
Prastar	Dha	S	Ti	Te	S	Dha	Ti	Te	S	Dha	Ti	Te	S	Dha	Tin	Na
	Ta	S	Ti	Te	S	Ta	Ti	Te	S	Dha	Ti	Te	S	Dha	Dhin	Na
Prastar	S	Dha	Ti	Te	Dha	S	Ti	Te	S	Dha	Ti	Te	S	Dha	Tin	Na
	S	Ta	Ti	Te	Ta	S	Ti	Te	S	Dha	Ti	Te	S	Dha	Dhin	Na
Prastar	S	Dha	Ti	Te	S	Dha	S	Dha	S	Dha	Ti	Te	S	Dha	Tin	Na
	S	Ta	Ti	Te	S	Ta	S	Ta	S	Dha	Ti	Te	S	Dha	Dhin	Na
Prastar	S	Dha	S	Dha	S	Dha	Ti	Te	S	Dha	Ti	Te	S	Dha	Tin	Na
	S	Ta	S	Ta	S	Ta	Ti	Te	S	Dha	Ti	Te	S	Dha	Dhin	Na
Prastar	S	Dha	S	Dha	Ti	Te	S	Dha	S	Dha	Ti	Te	S	Dha	Tin	Na
	S	Ta	S	Ta	Ti	Te	S	Dha	S	Dha	Ti	Te	S	Dha	Dhin	Na
Prastar	S	Dha	Ti	Te	Dha	S	S	Dha	S	Dha	Ti	Te	S	Dha	Tin	Na
	S	Ta	Ti	Te	Ta	S	S	Dha	S	Dha	Ti	Te	S	Dha	Dhin	Na
Prastar	S	Dha	Ti	Te	Ti	Te	S	Dha	S	Dha	Ti	Te	S	Dha	Tin	Na
	S	Ta	Ti	Te	Ti	Te	S	Ta	S	Dha	Ti	Te	S	Dha	Dhin	Na
Prastar	Ti	Te	S	Dha	S	Dha	Ti	Te	Dha	S	S	Dha	S	Dha	Tin	Na
	Ti	Te	S	Ta	S	Ta	Ti	Te	Dha	S	S	Dha	S	Dha	Dhin	Na

Mukhda or Mohra

There are different opinions about 'Mukhda' or 'Mohra'. According to one of the opinions, Mukhda and Mohra are different terms, but another opinion says that both are one and the same. In fact, the literal meaning of both the words is same.

According to those who are having different opinions about the both, the word Mohra is applied in two different sense. When the Tabla player, after playing small groups on Tabla, meets on the 'Sum' of the vocalist or instrument player, it is called Mohra. For example:

13	14	15	16	1
Kitataka	Tirakita	TakataS	Tirakita	Dha
3				×

In another sense, the Bols of Mohra come on the 'Sum' after completing the rotation of Tihai. For example:

1	2	3	4	5	6	7	8	
Dha	Tuna	Kitataka	TaStira	Kitataka	Tirakita	TakataS	Tirakita	
×				2				
9	10	11	12	13	14	15	16	
Dha	Tirakita	TakataS	Tirakita	Dha	Tirakita	TakataS	Tirakita	Dha
0				3				×

As per the scholars who are of the view that Mukhda or Mohra is one and the same, Mukhda is a form of Tukda having one Avartan or two which is applied for meeting attractively on the 'Sum' of the Tal in vocal-instrumental music. It can be with Tihai or without Tihai. Therefore, the large Mohra, normally known as Mukhda, it would be proper to say Tukda.

Normally, Mukhda or Mohra is applied in accom-panying vocal-instrumental music, because when vocal-instrumental musician, after completing the Avritti (Avartan) of the sound, adopts the Mukhda of the song for the 'Sum', then the Bols of small or large Tihai or Bols without Tihai, applied by the Tabla accompanist to meet on the 'Sum', is called Mukhda or Mohra. It is not proper to say that Mohra has small Bols and Mukhda has large & strong Bols. In fact, in vocal-instrumental music, large 'Chakradar' (spiral) 'Paran' or 'Gat' etc. are not played. Mohra or Mukhda is applied to make the vocal-instrumental music charming and effective.

Tukda (Tukra)

The literal meaning of 'Tukda' is small or large group of Bols played on Tabla. Actually, the practical form of Tukda is different. e.g. the inherent difference between Tihai and Nauhakka and Tukda and Chakradar is the same. When a group of Bols with any Tihai is applied thrice, it becomes 'Nauhakka', likewise group of Bols with any Tihai is played thrice, it is called simple Chakradar. A group of Bols with Tihai (which is a 'Tukda' of eleven Matras in Tal Teen Tal), if played once, will be called 'Tukda' only. Therefore, the group of Bols with Tihai, from one Avritti to three or four Avritti, is called 'Tukda'. There are different types of Tukda:

1. Tukda without Tihai (though, it is applied like Mukhda).
2. Tukda with one Tihai.
3. Tukda with three Tihais.

Example for the above three is given below:

1. *Tukda without Tihai:*

1	2	3	4	
DhirDhir	Kitataka	Dha	Kitataka	
×				
5	6	7	8	
Dhara	Sn	TaS	DhaS	
2				
9	10	11	12	
DhirDhir	Kitataka	DhaStira	Kitataka	
0				
13	14	15	16	
Tirakita	TakataS	Titekata	Gadigana	Dha
3				×

2. *Tukda with one Tihai (the group of Bols consiting eight Matras and Tihai of eight Matras):*

1	2	3	4	
DhageTite	TageTite	TakadinS	Nagetite	
×				
5	6	7	8	
Titetagi	SnaDhete	Taginna	DheSTaS	
2				
9	10	11	12	
TrakaDheS	Taginna	Dha	TrakaDheS	
0				
13	14	15	16	
Taginna	Dha	TrakaDheS	Taginna	Dha
3				×

3. *Tukda with three Tihais:*

1	2	3	4
Dhati	SDha	tiS	Dhati
×			
5	6	7	8
DhaStira	kitataka	TaStira	kitataka
2			
9	10	11	12
Tirakita	TakataS	Tirakita	Dhati
0			

13	14	15	16	
Dha	Dhati	Dha	Dhati	
3				
1	2	3	4	
DhaS	STa	Tirakita	Dhati	
×				
5	6	7	8	
Dha	Dhati	Dha	Dhati	
2				
9	10	11	12	
DhaS	STa	Tirakita	Dhati	
0				
13	14	15	16	
Dha	Dhati	Dha	Dhati	Dha
3				×

Other forms (variety):

1	2	3	4	
DhetS	DhirDhir	Kitataka	DhaStira	
×				
5	6	7	8	
Kitataka	Tirakita	Taka,Taka	Tirakita	
2				
9	10	11	12	
DhaS	STaka	Tirakita	DhaSSS	
0				
13	14	15	16	
Takatira	kitaDhaS	SSTaka	Tirakita	
3				
1	2	3	4	
DhaS	STaka	Tirakita	DhaSSS	
×				
5	6	7	8	
Takatira	kitaDhaS	SSTaka	Tirakita	
2				
9	10	11	12	
DhaS	STaka	Tirakita	DhaSSS	
0				
13	14	15	16	
Takatira	kitaDhaS	SSTaka	Tirakita	Dha
3				×

Bant

According to some scholars, 'Bant' is defined as expansion of 'Laggi'. But literally it can be defined as distribution. Although, it is notable that expansion of a 'Bandish' (composition) is called 'Palta', 'Pench' etc., but the expansion of 'Laggi' only is defined as a different name (Bant), whereas there is no independent composition named 'Palta', 'Pench' etc., and 'Bant' is addressed as an idependent name. Therefore, it would be proper to accept 'Bant' as an independent compositon.

There has been a tradition of playing 'Bant' specifically in Banaras Gharana. There are two kinds of 'Bant': (1) Independent Bant (2) Arranged Bant. Like other composition, Bant is also played in 'Thah' (slow), 'Dugun' (double), 'Chaugun' (fourfold) etc.

Independent Bant has a simple movement. For example:

DhinS	Dhina	Tirakita	Dhina	Dhage	naTi	ke,ti	Nara
×				2			
TinS	Tina	Tirakita	Dhina	Dhage	naDhi	Ge,Dhi	Nara
0				3			

The aforesaid Bant can also be played by applying 'Ge' instead of 'Dum' S (pause), e.g.

Dhige	Dhina	Tirakita	Dhina	Dhage	naTi	ke,ti	Nara
×				2			
Tike	Tina	Tirakita	Dhina	Dhage	naDhi	ge,Dhi	Nara
0				3			

The above composition is called 'Kayada' also by some people, but in Banaras it is called Bant.

Another kind of Bant has certain conditions because 'Rela' is played after this Bant. Certain rules are given as under:

1. After expansion of this Bant, 'Rela' of the same method is played.
2. Arranged Bant is based on any of the 'Chhandas' (metres).
3. In Banaras, likewise 'Chhand Bant', 'Rela' of the same 'Chhand' is played in double 'Laya'.
4. Independent Rela and Independent Bant can be played in different laya, but no such liberty prevails in arranged Bant or Rela.

Example for arranged Bant and its Rela:

Bant

Dha	ra	Dha	ti	na	ti	na	ra
×				2			
Ta	ra	Dha	Dhi	na	Dhi	na	ra
0				3			

Rela

Dha-	Tirakita	Taka	Dhin	Taka	Tin	Ta-	Tirakita
×				2			
Ta-	Tirakita	Taka	Dhin	Taka	Dhin	Dha-	Tirakita
0				3			

Rela

Rela' is created as per construction of 'Kayada'. The difference is only in the selection of 'Bols'. The 'Bols' selected for Rela, can be played easily in a fast 'Laya' (rhythm). Although, Rela in slow speed, appears to be a type of Kayada, but when it is played in the Laya of fourfold or eightfold, it is listened in a fluent way. Rela is a group of such Bols which can be played in a very fast Laya without trouble and this is its great speciality.

Some of the Bols in Tabla are of the nature of being played in fast Laya viz. Tirkit, DherDher, Dhinagin, Dhadagin etc. Thus, these Bols are placed in Rela necessarily. Apart from the aforesaid, in the Bols of Kayada and Rela, expansion is made with 'Bhari' (stuff) and 'Khali' (blank).

There are several types of Rela-e.g., Independent Rela, Kayada Rela, Theka's Rela, Angushtana's Rela and Bant Rela. In this part of the Book, Independent Rela, Kayada Rela and Bant Rela are being introduced. e.g.:

Independent Rela:

DhaSStira	Gheranage	Dinataka	DhaSStira
×			
Gheranage	Dinataka	TaSStira	kitataka
2			
TaSStira	Keranake	Tinataka	TaSStira
0			
Gheranage	Dinataka	DhaSStira	kitataka
3			

Rela-created by Kayada:

DhaSStir	Kitataka	Tinna	Kitataka
TaSStira	Kitataka	Dhinna	Kitataka

Rela of Bant:

Dha ×	Tirakita	Taka	Din	Taka 2	Tin	Ta	Tirakita
Ta 0	Tirakita	Taka	Din	Taka 3	Dhin	Dha	Tirakita

Rau

If a portion of Rela, without expanding, is played fluently, a constant sound is listened and it is called 'Rau'. Sometimes complete Rela is played without expanding and it creates the 'Rau'. But Rela is used like 'Rau' in Solo recital and 'Rau' is used in both i.e. accompaniment and Solo recital.

There is Independent 'Rau' too like Independent Rela, e.g.-

(Rau created by a part of Rela):

DhaSḻtir	KitaDhaSḻ	Gheranage	Tinataka
TaSḻtira	KitaDhaSḻ	Gheranage	Dinataka

(Independent Rau):

DhaSḻtir	KitatinSḻ	NaSḻtira	Kitataka
TaSḻtira	KitadhinSḻ	NaSḻtira	Kitataka

Gat

'Gat' is very important in Tabla Solo recital. It is a special 'Bandish' (composition) of different joint Bols which is played as from 'Dha' (solid) first and from 'Ta' (blank or Khali) second time. Since 'Prastar' (expansion) is not possible for the reasons of being a composition of different Bols, 'Gat' is presented as a special composition in Solo recital. It concludes by playing in 'Thaah' (slow), double and fourfold. There are several types of 'Gat', viz. Dupalli-Gat, Tipalli-Gat, Chaupalli-Gat, Chakradar-Gat, Punjabi-Gat, Lahori-Gat etc. e.g.

Gat: 1

3 Fold – (Tigun)

KaSḻta ×	DheTite	Kataga	digana
DhaSḻtirakita 2	DheTite	Kataga	digana
Narana 0	ranara	Tinati	natina
DhaSḻtirakita 3	DheTite	Kataga	digana
KaSḻta ×	TeTite	Kataka	tikana

TaSstirakita	TeTite	Kataka	tikana
2			
Narana	ranara	Tinati	natina
0			
DhaSstirakita	DheTite	Kataga	digana
3			

4 Fold – (Chaugun)

KaStaDhe	TiteKata	KaStaga	diSganaa
×			
DhaStirakitaDhe	TiteKata	KaStaga	diSgana
2			
Naranara	SnaNara	NaraNara	Tinatina
0			
DhaStirakitaDhe	TiteKata	KaStaga	diSgana
3			
KaStaTe	TiteKata	KaStaka	tiSkanaa
×			
TaStirakitaTe	TiteKata	KaStaka	tiSkana
2			
Naranara	SnaNara	NaraNara	Tinatina
0			
DhaStirakitaDhe	TiteKata	KaStaga	diSgana
3			

6 Fold – (Chhaigun)

KaStaDheTite	Katagadigana	DhaStirakitaDheTiTe	Katagadigana
Naranaranara	Tinatinatina	DhaStirakitaDheTite	Katagadigana
KaStaTeTite	Katakatikana	TaStirakitaTeTite	Katakatikana
Naranaranara	Tinatinatina	DhaStirakitaDheTite	Katagadigana

Gat: 2

DhaSS	Ghinage	Takita	Ghinage
DhaSTirakita	Dhetite	kataga	digana
Nagina	Nagina	Takita	Ghinage
DhaSTirakita	Dhetite	kataga	digana
TaSS	Kinake	Takita	Kinake
TaSTirakita	Tetite	kataka	tikana
Nagina	Nagina	Takita	Ghinage
DhaSTirakita	Dhetite	kataga	digana

Dupalli-Gat: 3

Dugun:	Taki	taDha	Sra	Dhina
	×			
	gina	Taka	Dhina	gina
	2			
Chaugun:	Dinataka	Takitadha	SradhaS	Gheranage
	0			
	Dhinagina	takadhina	ginataka	dhinagina
	3			
Dugun:	Taki	taTa	Sra	Tina
	×			
	kina	Taka	Tina	kina
	2			
Chaugun:	Dinataka	Takitadha	SradhaS	Gheranage
	0			
	Dhinagina	takadhina	ginataka	dhinagina
	3			

Tipalli or Tripalli—Gat: 4

Tigun:	DhageS	Takita	Dhageti	rakita
	×			
	DhaStirakita	Dhetete	kataga	digana
	2			
Chugun:	Tirakita	DhaStirakitadhe	Tetekata	gadigana
	0			
Chhaigun:	DhageSTakita	Dhagetirakita	DhStirakitaDheTete	katagadigana
	3			

Chaupalli Gat: 5

Ekgun:	Dha	S	Ghe	ra	Na	ge	Te	te
	×				2			
Dugun:	Ghera	naga	Tete	Ghera	Sna	Taka	Dina	Taka
	0				3			
Tigun:	Takata	kataka	TinaTu	nakita	Takadi	nataka	Teteghe	raSna
	×				2			

Chaugun:	DhirDhirkitataka	DhaStirakitataka	DhaSSSkitataka	DhirDhirkitataka
	0			
	DhaStirakitataka	DhaSSSkitataka	DhirDhirkitataka	DhaStirakitataka
	3			

Ekgun:	Ta	S	Ke	ra	Na	ke	Te	te
	×				2			
Dugun:	Kera	naka	Tete	Kera	Sna	Taka	Tina	Taka
	0				3			
Tigun:	Takata	kataka	TinaTu	nakita	Takadi	nataka	Teteghe	raSna
	×				2			

Chaugu:	DhirDhirkitataka	DhaStirakitataka	DhaSSSkitataka	DhirDhirkitataka
	0			
	DhaStirakitataka	DhaSSSkitataka	DhirDhirkitataka	DhaStirakitataka
	3			
	Dha			
	×			

Chakradar-Gat: 6

DhaSS	Ghinage	Dinata	katite
×			
Gherana	gedina	takaTa	kataka
2			
Tinatu	nakita	DhaSDha	Sgina
0			
DhaSTirakita	Dhetite	kataga	digana
3			
DhaSS	DhaSTirakita	Dhetite	kataga
×			
Digana	DhaSS	DhaSTirakita	Dhetite
2			
kataga	digana	DhaSS,	DhaSS
0			
Ghinage	Dinata	katite	Gherana
3			
gedina	taka,Ta	kataka	Tinatu
×			
nakita	DhaSDha	Sgina	DhaSTirakita
2			
Dhetite	kataga	digana	DhaSS
0			
DhaSTirakita	Dhetite	kataga	digana
3			
DhaSS	DhaSTirakita	Dhetite	kataga
×			

Digana	DhaSS	DhaSS	Ghinage
2			
Dinata	katite	Gherana	gedina
0			
takaTa	kataka	Tinatu	nakita
3			
DhaSDha	Sgina	DhaSTirakita	Dhetite
×			
kataga	digana	DhaSS	DhaSTirakita
2			
Dhetite	kataga	digana	DhaSS
0			
DhaSTirakita	Dhetite	kataga	digana
3			
Dha			
×			

Panjabi-Gat (Tidhari-Gat): 7

DhinaDhi	naDhina	Dhagina	Dhagina
×			
Dhagina	Takita	Takita	Takita
2			
Dharagi	naDhara	ginaDha	ragina
0			
Takadi	naTaka	dinaTa	kadin
3			
TakaTa	kaTaka	TinaTi	naTina
×			
Tagina	Tagina	Tagina	DhaStirakita
2			
Dhagina	DhaStirakita	Dhagina	DhaStirakita
0			
Dhagina	Ghinage	Ghinage	Ghinage
3			
TinaTi	naTina	Takina	Takina
×			
Takina	Takita	Takita	Takita
2			
Taraki	naTara	kinaTa	rakina
0			
Takati	naTaka	tinaTa	katina
3			
TakaTa	kaTaka	TinaTi	naTina
×			
Tagina	Tagina	Tagina	DhaStirakita
2			

Dhagina	DhaStirakita	Dhagina	DhaStirakita
0			
Dhagina	Ghinage	Ghinage	Ghinage
3			

Lahori-Gat (Dodhari-Gat): 8

GhinaS	dhaSra	GhinaS	dhaSra
×			
Dhagena	gedhina	Dhagena	gedhina
2			
Takita	dhaSra	Takita	dhaSra
0			
Takadi	nataka	Takadi	nataka
3			
TakaTa	kaTina	TinaTa	kaTaka
×			
TiteTi	teKata	KataGi	dinGidin
2			
Gheghedin	SdinS	Gheghedin	SdinS
0			
Ghetirakita	takaTetS	Ghetirakita	takaTetS
3			
KinaS	taSra	KinaS	taSra
×			
Takena	ketina	Takena	ketina
2			
Takita	taSra	Takita	taSra
0			
Takati	nataka	Takati	nataka
3			
TakaTa	kaTina	TinaTa	kaTaka
×			
TiteTi	teKata	KataGi	dinGidin
2			
Gheghedin	SdinS	Gheghedin	SdinS
0			
Ghetirakita	takaTetS	Ghetirakita	takaTetS
3			

Fard

'Fard', 'Farad' and 'Ekkad' all three are synonyms. These mean one piece, peerless etc. But it does not mean that there is no existence of another similar 'Farad'. The words 'peerless' & 'one piece' have been used in the reference of extra-ordinary composition having special effects. The word 'Farad' is applied in general conversation. The senior scholars of Banaras have composed 'Fard' or 'Farad' with open and emphatic Bols. 'Fard' is performed by the Tabla players of Banaras compulsorily in their Solo presentation. 'Fard' is very important in Solo performance of Banaras Gharana in comparision to other Gharanas. 'Fard' of Banaras Gharana has gained special popularity.

Therefore, the Tabla players of Banaras Gharana perform 'Fard' or 'Farad' in the form of pairs also. Fard is played with 'Dha' only as 'Khaali' & 'Bhari' both are found applied in its composition. Fard's sound appears to be as of 'Paran' but generally it is concluded with the following group of Bols:

TirakitatakaTa KatDhirakitataka

or

TirakitatakaTa GeDhirakitataka

or

Tirakita takaDhira kitataka

or

'Dhirakitataka' only

It is not played in the sequence of open (Dha) and close (Ta) as in 'Gat' or 'Kayada'. It is played in 'Thah' or 'Dugun' (double) only.

Examples:

(1)

DhaSTite ×	TiteDhage	TiteGhara	SnaDhage
TiteTite 2	KradhaTite	GhinaTite	GhinaTuna
TaTite,Ta 0	titeKrata	TiteTite	DhaTite,Dha
TiteDhagi 3	naDhagina	Tirakitatakata	geDhirakitataka
Dha ×			

(2)

DhaSTite ×	KradhaTite	DhaTitedha	GhegheTite
GhegheTite 2	TiteGheghe	TiteGheghe	DinSSS
NanaTite 0	NaTiteNa	TinnaTite	NanaTite
DheteDhaS 3	Gheranagatet	Tirakitatakata	geDhirakitataka
Dha ×			

(3)

DheteKradha	ऽna Dhage	Titekradha	TiteDhage
×			
DinऽऽNa	TiteTite	GhinaTite	GhinaTinna
2			
TakitaTa	ऽna Taka	dinऽऽऽ	Katऽऽऽ
0			
DhiraDhirakitataka	DhaऽTirakitataka	Tirakitatakata	geDhirakitataka
3			
Dha			
×			

(4)

DhaऽTite	DhageTite	KradhaTite	DhageTite
×			
DhaginaTa	kitaDhage	Titekradha	TiteTite
2			
TaTiteTa	TiteTake	TinऽTinऽ	TiteTite
0			
KaऽteDha	ऽnDha	Katऽ,Tirakita	takaDhirakitataka
3			
Dha			
×			

Gat-Kayada

The creation of 'Gat' that differs from the aforesaid Gats, contains a little use of different joint Bols and can be expanded to a valid extent, is called 'Gat Kayada'. A 'Gat Kayada' of Banaras Gharana is given below for example:

Dinataka	Dinataka	Takadina	Takadina
×			
TakaTaka	Dinataka	Dhaऽtira	Kitataka
2			
Takatira	KitaDhaऽ	Gheranage	Dinataka
0			
DhiraDhira	Kitataka	Taऽtira	Kitataka
3			
Tinataka	Tinataka	Takatina	Takatina
×			
TakaTaka	Tinataka	Taऽtira	Kitataka
2			
Takatira	KitaDhaऽ	Gheranage	Dinataka
0			
DhiraDhira	Kitataka	Dhaऽtira	Kitataka
3			

Uthan

The word 'Uthan' pertains to Banaras Gharana. In other five Gharanas, Tabla recital starts from 'Peshkar'. But, in Banaras Gharana, Tabla recital starts from 'Uthan'. In the ancient period, there were several 'Uthan' for accom-panying vocal-instrumental music and dance as well as for Solo recital. But, presently, the Uthan used in dance, is very popular, therefore, the Bols of Uthan contain all the characteristic features of 'Paran'. In Uthan, the composition is played first in equal Laya, then double and 'Aad Laya' and double of 'Aad' or double's double i.e. 'Chaugun' (fourfold) in the end, and thereafter, other compositions are played.

Example: Uthan in Teen Tal is given below:

Dhaऽ Traka	DheTiteDha	GinaDhaऽ	Kradhatuna
×			
KaTiteDin	ऽNaTite	TiteKraDha	ऽnaKatऽ
2			
TiteKradha na	DhageTiteGhina	Dhageऽ Digina	Ghinऽ Taraऽ na
0			
KaTiteTaginaDhete	DhageTitekatagadi	GanaDhaऽ kradhaऽ n	Dhaऽ gadiganadhaऽ
3			
Kradhaऽ naDhaऽ Gadi	GanaDhaऽ kradhaऽ na	Dhaऽ ghinऽ Taraऽ na	KaTiteTaginaDhete
×			
DhageTitekatagadi	GanaDhaऽ kradhaऽ na	Dhaऽ gadiganadhaऽ	Kradhaऽ naDhaऽ Gadi
2			
GanaDhaऽ kradhaऽ na	Dhaऽ ghinऽ Taraऽ na	KaTiteTaginaDhete	DhageTitekatagadi
0			
GanaDhaऽ kradhaऽ na	Dhaऽ gadiganadhaऽ	Kradhaऽ naDhaऽ Gadi	GanaDhaऽ kradhaऽ na
3			
Dha			
×			

Paran

'Paran' relates to Pakhawaj mainly, but has been connected with Tabla since a long. The composition made of strong and open Bols is called 'Paran'. Its main characteristics are as under:

1. It is essential that 'Paran' should contain at least two rotations (Avartan).
2. 'Paran' may also contain a good number of rotations.
3. The group of 'Bols' in Paran repeats itself.
4. Paran(s) are with Tihai as well as without Tihai.
5. Several Bols are repeated in 'Paran' containing a number of rotations.
6. There are mainly four kinds of 'Paran'- *(a)* Saath-Paran *(b)* Gat-Paran *(c)* Tal-Paran *(d)* Bol-Paran.

7. Bols applied in 'Paran', viz. Dhagetite, Tagetite, Kradhatite, Kradhe dhetite, Kradhan, Dhetta, Ghednag, Taginna etc.

A very popular 'Paran' in Teen Tal is given below for example:

DhageTite ×	DhageTite	TageTite	TageTite	
KradhaTite 2	DhageTite	Gadigana	NageTite	
KaTiteTa 0	GinaTaka	Titekata	Gadigana	
DhaSDhaS 3	DhaSTite	kataGadi	gana DhaS	
DhaSDhaS ×	Titekata	Gadigana	DhaSDhaS	
DhaS 2	SS	DhageTite	DhageTite	
TageTite 0	TageTite	KradhaTite	DhageTite	
Gadigana 3	NageTite	KaTiteTa	GinaTaka	
Titekata ×	Gadigana	DhaSDhaS	DhaSTite	
kataGadi 2	ganaDhaS	DhaSDhaS	Titekata	
Gadigana 0	DhaSDhaS	DhaS	SS	
DhageTite 3	DhageTite	TageTite	TageTite	
KradhaTite ×	DhageTite	Gadigana	NageTite	
KaTiteTa 2	GinaTaka	Titekata	Gadigana	
DhaSDhaS 0	DhaSTite	kataGadi	gana DhaS	
DhaSDhaS 3	Titekata	Gadigana	DhaSDhaS	Dha ×

Chakradar

When a group of 'Bols' with Tihai, is played thrice and the last 'Dha' ends on 'Sum', it is called 'Chakradar'. It is also named a 'Chakradar Tukda' and 'Chakradar Paran'.

'Chakra' means revolving, therefore, the group of Bols with Tihai revolving thrice, completes at least two 'Avritti' of the Tal, and the last 'Dha' reaches at 'Sum', it will be called 'Chakradar'. Mainly, there are three types of Chakradar:

1. Simple Chakradar
2. Farmaishi Chakradar
3. Kamali Chakradar

Simple Chakradar

Simple Chakradar contains at least two to five 'Avritti' (rotations) or more. For example, (Chakradar of two Avritti in Tin Tal)-11 Matras in its one rotation:

TrakaDhetS	TrakaDhetS	DhiraDhiraKitataka	DhiraDhirakatS
×			
DhiraDhiraKitataka	DhaSTirakitataka	Takkran	DhaSTak
2			
KranDha	Takkran	Dha-	TrakaDhetS
0			
TrakaDhetS	DhiraDhiraKitataka	DhiraDhirakatS	DhiraDhiraKitataka
3			
DhaSTirakitataka	Takkran	DhaSTak	KranSDha
×			
Takkran	Dha-	TrakaDhetS	TrakaDhetS
2			
DhiraDhiraKitataka	DhiraDhirakatS	DhiraDhiraKitataka	DhaSTirakitataka
0			
Takkran	DhaSTak	KranSDha	Takkran
3			
Dha			
×			

(Chakradar of five Avritti in Teen Tal)

There are total 81 Matras in this Chakradar. Its one 'Chakra' (rotation) contains 27 Matras. There are three Laya i.e. equal, 'Adi', equal in this Chakradar. This Chakradar starts with 'Sum' and after playing all three 'Chakra' the final 'Dha' will come on 'Sum'. The peculiarity of this Chakradar is that any 'Dha' of Tihais in the Chakradar does not touch the 'Sum' except final 'Dha'. For example:

DhageTite	TiteTage	TiteTite	TakaDinS
×			
DinSNage	TiteTite	TiteTagi	SnaDhetS
2			
Taginna	Dha-,	DhaSKradhetite	DhaTrakadhetite
0			
DheteDheteDhete	KradheSDhetite	Katagadigana	NagetirakitaGhin
3			
TaraSnaGadigana	Dha&DhiraDhirakitataka	DhaStirakitatakaTakkran	DhaSSSGadigan
×			

Dha&DhiraDhirakitataka DhaSirakitatakaTakkran DhaSSSGadigana Dha&DhiraDhirakitataka
2
DhaStirakitatakaTakkran DhaSSSGadigana Dha-, DhageTite
0
TiteTage TiteTite TakaDinS DinSNage
3
TiteTite TiteTagi SnaDhetS Taginna
×
Dha- , Dha ·Kradhetite DhaTrakadhetite DheteDheteDhete
2
KradheSDhetite Katagadigana NagetirakitaGhin Tara ·naGadigana
0
Dha&DhiraDhirakitataka DhaStirakitatakaTakkran DhaSSSGadigana
Dha&DhiraDhirakitataka
3
DhaStirakitatakaTakkran DhaSSSGadigan Dha&DhiraDhirakitataka
DhaStirakitatakaTakkran
×

DhaSSSGadigana Dha- , DhageTite TiteTage
2
TiteTite TakaDinS DinSNage TiteTite
0
TiteTagi SnaDhetS Taginna Dha-,
3
DhaSKradhetite DhaTrakadhetite KradheSDhetite DheteDheteDhete
×
Katagadigana, NagetirakitaGhin TaraSnaGadigana Dha&DhiraDhirakitataka
2
DhaStirakitatakaTakkran DhaSSSGadigan Dha&DhiraDhirakitataka
DhaStirakitatakaTakkran
0
DhaSSSGadigan Dha&DhiraDhirakitataka DhaStirakitatakaTakkran
DhaSSSGadigan
3
Dha
×

Farmaishi-Chakradar (Adalaya)

Farmaishi Chakradar contains at least five 'Avritti'. Its one chakra (rotation) contains 27 Matras. There is one Tihai in one Chakra of Farmaishi Chakradar. First 'Dha' of Tihai comes at 'Sum', second 'Dha' of second Tihai in the second round comes at 'Sum' and last i.e. final 'Dha' of Tihai in the third round concludes at 'Sum'.

e.g.

Ka-Tirakita	DheTite	Ka-Tirakita	DheTite	
×				
KataKa	taKata	Ka-Tirakita	DheTite	
2				
Ka-Tirakita	DheTite	Kataga	digana	
0				
Dha-Tirakita	DheTite	Kataga	digana	
3				
Dha	Dha-Tirakita	DheTite	Kataga	
×				
digana	Dha	Dha-Tirakita	DheTite	
2				
Kataga	digana	Dha,	Ka-Tirakita	
0				
DheTite	Ka-Tirakita	DheTite	KataKa	
3				
taKata	Ka-Tirakita	DheTite	Ka-Tirakita	
×				
DheTite	Kataga	digana	Dha-Tirakita	
2				
DheTite	Kataga	digana	Dha	
0				
Dha-Tirakita	DheTite	Kataga	digana	
3				
Dha	Dha-Tirakita	DheTite	Kataga	
×				
digana	Dha,	Ka-Tirakita	DheTite	
2				
Ka-Tirakita	DheTite	KataKa	taKata	
0				
Ka-Tirakita	DheTite	Ka-Tirakita	DheTite	
3 ·				
Kataga	digana	Dha-Tirakita	DheTite	
×				
Kataga	digana	Dha	Dha-Tirakita	
2				
DheTite	Kataga	digana	Dha	
0				
Dha-Tirakita	DheTite	Kataga	digana	Dha
3				×

Kamali-Chakradar

Kamali Chakradar also contains at least 5 or 7 'Avritti'. There are 9 (nine) Dha in one Chakra of Kamali Chakradar. First 'Dha' of first chakra comes at 'Sum', 5th 'Dha' of second chakra comes at 'Sum' and the last i.e. 9th 'Dha' of the third Chakra concludes at 'Sum'.

e.g. (containing 7 Avritti)

Dhete	Dhete	Kradhe	Tete	DhaTe	teDha	Kradhe	Tete	
×				2				
Kata	Kata	Kate	teDhe	Tete	Kata	Gadi	gana	
0				3				
Dha	Dha	Dha	Kate	teDhe	Tete	Kata	Gadi	
×				2				
gana	Dha	Dha	Dha	Kate	teDhe	Tete	Kata	
0				3				
Gadi	gana	Dha	Dha	Dha	S	Dhete	Dhete	
×				2				
Kradhe	Tete	DhaTe	teDha	Kradhe	Tete	Kata	Kata	
0				3				
Kate	teDhe	Tete	Kata	Gadi	gana	Dha	Dha	
×				2				
Dha	Kate	teDhe	Tete	Kata	Gadi	gana	Dha	
0				3				
Dha	Dha	Kate	teDhe	Tete	Kata	Gadi	gana	
×				2				
Dha	Dha	Dha	S	Dhete	Dhete	Kradhe	Tete	
0				3				
DhaTe	teDha	Kradhe	Tete	Kata	Kata	Kate	teDhe	
×				2				
Tete	Kata	Gadi	gana	Dha	Dha	Dha	Kate	
0				3				
teDhe	Tete	Kata	Gadi	gana	Dha	Dha	Dha	
×				2				
Kate	teDhe	Tete	Kata	Gadi	gana	Dha	Dha	Dha
0				3				×

Kamali-Chakradar (5 Avritti):

Katrakadhe	TiteKatra	kadheTite	Katakata
×			
KataKatra	kadheTite	Katrakadhe	TiteKata
2			
KataKata	Katrakadhe	TiteKata	gadigan
0			
Katrakadhe	Titedhage	TiteKata	gadigan
3			
Dha	Dha	Dha	gadigan
×			
Dha	Dha	Dha	gadigan
2			
Dha	Dha	Dha,	Ktrakadhe
0			

TiteKatra	kadheTite	Katakata	KataKatra	
3				
kadheTite	Katrakadhe	TiteKata	KataKata	
×				
Katrakadhe	TiteKata	gadigan	Katrakadhe	
2				
Titedhage	TiteKata	gadigan	Dha	
0				
Dha	Dha	gadigan	Dha	
3				
Dha	Dha	gadigan	Dha	
×				
Dha	Dha ,	Ktrakadhe	TiteKatra	
2				
kadheTite	Katakata	KataKatra	kadheTite	
0				
Katrakadhe	TiteKata	KataKata	Katrakadhe	
3				
TiteKata	gadigan	Katrakadhe	Titedhage	
×				
TiteKata	gadigan	Dha	Dha	
2				
Dha	gadigan	Dha	Dha	
0				
Dha	gadigan	Dha	Dha	Dha
3				×

7

Layakari

Writing of Layakari

When two, three or four Bols are played or likewise 'Swar' (notes) are sung in the single Matra's period, the action is known as 'Layakari'. Although, the words 'Laya' and 'Layakari' are used for the similar meaning, but there are mainly three types of Laya viz. 'Vilambit' (slow), 'Madhya' (in between slow & fast) and 'Drut' (fast), whereas Layakari is having several types, e.g. when more or less than one Bol is played in the timing of one Matra, it will be called 'Layakari'. Therefore, the rules for writing and speaking of Layakaris are as under:

THAH (i.e. writing & speaking one Matra in one Matra)

In this Layakari, every 'Bol' or 'Swar' is counted by giving 'Tali' (clap) on each and every Matra and this is called 'Thah' or Layakari of 'Ekgun'. For this, writing of separate numbers only, is sufficient. viz. 1, 2, 3, 4 (every number denotes one Matra).

ADHAGUN (writing & speaking of 1 Matra in 2 Matras)

In this Layakari, every 'Bol' or 'Swar' is increased by one Matra. In this way, the Layakari is halved and it is called 'Adhagun'. As in 'Swar-Lipi' (script or notation), if any 'Swar' is supposed to be increased or paused ahead by one Matra, the sign (-) or (·) is applied, in the same manner the Layakari of 'Adhagun' is written, viz. 1- 2- 3- 4- or 1 · 2 · 3 · 4 ·

DUGUN (writing or speaking 2 Matras in 1 Matra)

Speaking or singing of 2 Matras in the timing of 1 Matra, is called the Layakari of 'Dugun' or 'Doon' (double). In this Layakari of 'Dugun', every Matra is not shown by 'Tali' (clap) and 2 Matras are counted in 1 Matra. These couples of Matras are kept in a bracket and every couple is supposed to be one Matra, as given below: <u>1,2</u> <u>3,4</u> <u>5,6</u> <u>7,8</u>

TIGUN (writing & speaking 3 Matras in 1 Matra)

When 3 Matras are spoken in the period or timing of 1 Matra, the Layakari of 'Tigun' (triple) is formed. The method of writing the Layakari of 'Tigun' will be same as aforesaid method of 'Dugun'. The difference is that, in brackets, three numbers will be written:

1,2,3 4,5,6 7,8,9 10,11,12

In the same way aforesaid, the Layakaris of fourfold, 5-fold, 6-fold, 7-fold and eight-fold etc. will be written.

Apart from above plain Layakaris, there are some tough Layakaris, viz. 3 Matras in 2 Matras, 2 Matras in 3 Matras, 4 in 3 Matras, 5 in 4 Matras, 6 in 5 Matras, 7 in 4 Matras etc. These Layakaris are written or shown orally as under (first by counting and then as per Bols of Tal).

First, we should determine that how many Matras are to be written in a particular number of Matras. To make it easy to understand, we should form two parts of Matras named 'A' & 'B'. First of all, numbers equal to Matras of 'B' will be written. For this, 'Avagrah' (·) will be applied before each number to make it equal to number of 'A'. Finally, 'Avagrahas' will also be counted as separate 'Vibhagas' and 'Vibhagas' of 'B' numbers will be placed in brackets of 1 Matra. e.g.- writing of 3 Matras in 2 Matras - 1 ·2, ·3 · This Layakari will be called 'Aad' (one and a half), i.e. speaking of 1½ Matras in 1 Matra will be 'Aad' Laya and it will be half of 'Tigun' (triple).

In the same way, other Layakaris are given below:

2 Matras in 3 Matras– 1S S2 SS

4 Matras in 3 Matras– 1SS2 SS3S S4SS

3 Matras in 4 Matras– 1SS S2S SS3 SSS

5 Matras in 4 Matras– 1SSS2 SSS3S SS4SS S5SSS

4 Matras in 5 Matras– 1SSS S2SS SS3S SSS4 SSS

7 Matras in 4 Matras– 1SSS2SS S3SSS4S SS5SSS6 SSS7SSS

4 Matras in 7 Matras– 1SSS SSS2 SSSS SS3S SSSS S4SS SSSS

Kuaad

There are two opinions about this Layakari. According to first opinion, 'Savagun' (a quarter more i.e. 5 in 4) is the 'Kuaad' and that will be written as under:

1 S S S 2 S S S 3 S S S 4 S S S 5 S S S S

As per second opinion, 'Aad' to 'Aad' is known as 'Kuaad'. Since 'Aad' is 3/2 Matras in 1 Matra, therefore, 'Kuaad' will be $3/2 \times 3/2 = 9/4$ in one Matra i.e. 9 Matras in 4 Matras, and it will be written as under:

1 S S S 2 S S S 3 S S S 4 S S S 5 S

S S 6 S S S 7 S S S 8 S S S 9 S S S

Beaad

There are also two opinions about 'Beaad'. According to first opinion, quarter to double (7 Matras in 4 Matras) is 'Beaad' i.e. 1¾ Matras in one Matra and it will be written as under:

1 S S S 2 S S	S 3 S S S 4 S
S S 5 S S S 6	S S S 7 S S S

As per second opinion, 'Aad' to 'Kuaad' is known as 'Beaad', therefore, 9/4 × 3/2 = 27/8 i.e. 27 Matras in 8 Matras and it will be written as under:

1 S S S S S S S **2** S S S S S S S **3** S S S S S S S **4** S S

S S S S S **5** S S S S S S S **6** S S S S S S S **7** S S S S S

S S **8** S S S S S S S **9** S S S S S S S **10** S S S S S S S **11**

S S S S S S S **12** S S S S S S S **13** S S S S S S S **14** S S S

S S S S **15** S S S S S S S **16** S S S S S S S **17** S S S S S S

S **18** S S S S S S S **19** S S S S S S S **20** S S S S S S S **21** S

S S S S S S **22** S S S S S S S **23** S S S S S S S **24** S S S S

S S S **25** S S S S S S S **26** S S S S S S S **27** S S S S S S S

As per aforesaid rules for Layakari, any Layakari can easily be written and can be applied in practical music by practice.

Writing in Notation the Different Layakaris of Talas

All Layakaris described earlier, are shown in numbers. Since music is a performing and experimental subject, every student of music is supposed to be well conver sant with Talas. So, it is compulsory to speak and write in notation the different Talas in different Layakaris.

There are two methods of speaking and writing Layakaris in Talas by its Bols. (1) The multiple of Layakari of the Tal to be shown, we should write the Bols (Theka) of that Tal for such multiple times and by keeping the exact multiples of Matras in single separate brackets, we should put the sign of 'Tali-Khali' Vibhagas.

In terms of first method, Layakaris are given below:

(Tal-Teental—in the Layakari of 'Dugun')

DhaDhin	DhinDha	DhaDhin	DhinDha
×			
Dhatin	TinTa	TaDhin	DhinDha
2			
DhaDhin	DhinDha	DhaDhin	DhinDha
0			
Dhatin	TinTa	TaDhin	DhinDha
3			

(Tal-Jhaptal—in the Layakari of 'Tigun')

DhiNaDhi	DhiNaTi	NaDhiDhi	Na,DhiNa	DhiDhiNa
×		2		
TiNaDhi	DhiNa,Dhi	NaDhiDhi	NaTiNa	DhiDhiNa
0		3		

(Tal Ektal—in the Layakari of 'Chaugun')

DhinDhin DhageTirakita	TuNa KatTa
×	
DhageTirakitaDheena	DhinDhin DhageTirakita
0	
TuNa KatTa	DhageTirakitaDheena
2	
DhinDhin DhageTirakita	TuNa KatTa
0	
DhageTirakitaDhina	DhinDhin DhageTirakita
3	
TuNa KatTa	DhageTirakitaDhina
4	

Method of writing the Layakari in 'Aad', 'Kuaad' and 'Biaad', means the Tal containing Bols of half Matra and one fourth Matra, viz. Ek Tal, Aada Chartal etc. 'Avagrahas' are applied very carefully in writing 'Aad' etc. of these Talas.

Writing in 'Aad'

Single 'Avagrah' is applied to divide each one Matra's Bol of the Tal into two parts. But, if one Matra is read as 'Dhage', then 'Dha' and 'ge' are written separately instead of applying 'Avagrah'. And, if one Matra is read as 'Tirkit', then 'Tir' and 'kit' are written with separate small brackets for dividing that Matra into two parts. Examples:

(Tal-Teental—in 'Aad' Layakari)

DhaऽDhin	ऽDhinऽ	DhaऽDha	ऽDhinऽ
×			
DhinऽDha	ऽDhaऽ	TinऽTin	ऽTaऽ
2			
Ta Dhin	ऽDhinऽ	DhaऽDha	ऽDhinऽ
0			
DhinऽDha	ऽDhaऽ	DhinऽDhin	ऽDhaऽ
3			
DhaऽTin	ऽTinऽ	TaऽTa	ऽDhinऽ
×			
DhinऽDha	ऽDhaऽ	DhinऽDhin	ऽDhaऽ
2			
DhaऽDhin	ऽDhinऽ	DhaऽDha	ऽTinऽ
0			
TinऽTa	ऽTaऽ	DhinऽDhin	ऽDhaऽ
3			

(Tal-Ektal—in 'Aad' Layakari)

DhinऽDhin	ऽDhage	TirakitaTu	ऽNaऽ	KatऽTa	ऽDhage
×		0			2
TirakitaDhi	ऽNaऽ	DhinऽDhin	ऽDhage	TirakitaTu	ऽNaऽ
0		3			4
KatऽTa	ऽDhage	TirakitaDhi	ऽNaऽ	DhinऽDhin	ऽDhage
×		0			2
TirakitaTu	ऽNaऽ	KatऽTa	ऽDhage	TirakitaDhi	ऽNaऽ
0		3			4

(Tal-Jhoomra—in 'Aad' Layakari)

DhinऽDha	ऽTirakita	DhinऽDhin	
×			
ऽDhage	TirakitaTin	ऽTaऽ	TirakitaDhin
2			
ऽDhinऽ	DhageTir	kitaDhinऽ	
0			
DhaऽTira	kitaDhinऽ	DhinऽDha	ge,Tirakita
3			
TinऽTa	ऽTirakita	DhinऽDhin	
×			

SDhage 2	TirakitaDhin	SDhaS	TirakitaDhin
SDhinS 0	DhageTira	kitaTinS	
TaSTira 3	kitaDhinS	DhinSDha	ge,Tirakita

Writing in 'Kuaad'

Three 'Avagrahas' are applied to make four parts of each one Matra's Bol of the Tal. But, if one Matra is read as 'Dhage', then one 'Avagrah' before 'Dha' and one 'Avagrah' before 'ge' will be applied to make it four. And, if one Matra is read as 'Tirkit', then it will be written as such instead of applying 'Avagrah'.

Examples:

(Tal-Ektal—in 'Kuaad' Layakari)

DhinSSSDhin ×	SSSDhaSSS	geSTiraki 0	taTuSSS	NaSSSKat 2	SSSTaS
SSDhaSSge 0	STirakit	DhinSSSNa 3	SSSDhinS	SSDhinSS 4	SDhaSge
TirakitaTu ×	SSSNaS	SSKatSS 0	STaSSS	DhaSgeS 2	TirakitaDhinS
SSNaSS 0	SDhinSSS	DhinSSSDha 3	SgeSTira	kitaTuSS 4	SNaSSS
KatSSSTa ×	SSSDhaS	geSTiraki 0	taDhinSSS	NaSSSDhin 2	SSSDhinS
SSDhaSge 0	STirakita	TuSSSNa 3	SSSKatS	SSTaSS 4	SDhaSgeS
TirakitaDhin ×	SSSNaS	SSDhinSS 0	SDhinSSS	DhaSgeSTi 2	rakitaTuS
SSNaSS 0	SKatSSS	TaSSSDha 3	SgeSTira	kitaDhinSS 4	SNaSSS

(Tal-Aada Chartal—in 'Kuaad' Layakari)

DhinSSSTi ×	rakitaDheeS	SSNaSS 2	STuSSS
NaSSSKat 0	SSSTaS	SSTiraki 3	taDheeSSS
NaSSSDhee 0	SSSDheeS	SSNaSS 4	SDhinSSS

TirakitaDhee	SSSNaS	0	SSTuSS	SNaSSS	×
KatSSSTa	SSSTira	2	kitaDheeSS	SNaSSS	0
DheeSSSDhee	SSSNaS	3	SSDhinSS	STirakita	0
DheeSSSNa	SSSTuS	4	SSNaSS	SKatSSS	0
TaSSSTi	rakitaDheeS	×	SSNaSS	SDheeSSS	2
DheeSSSNa	SSSDhinS	0	SSTiraki	taDheeSSS	3
NaSSSTu	SSSNaS	0	SSKatSS	STaSSS	4
TirakitaDhee	SSSNaS	0	SSDheeSSS	SDheeSSS	×
NaSSSDhin	SSSTira	2	kitaDheeSS	SNaSSS	0
TuSSSNa	SSSKatS	3	SSTaSS	STirakita	0
DheeSSSNa	SSSDheeS	4	SSDheeSS	SNaSSS	0

Writing in 'Biaad'

Three 'Avagrahas' will be applied for making four of each one Matra's Bol as in 'Kuaad' and 'Dhage' & 'Tirkit' will be written in the same manner.

Example:

(Tal-Ektal—in 'Biaad' Layakari)

DhinSSSDhinSS	SDhaSgeSTira	×	KitaTuSSSNa	SSSKatSSS	0
TaSSSDhaSge	STirakitaDhinS	2	SSNaSSSDhin	SSSDhinSSS	0
DhaSgeSTiraki	taTuSSSNaS	3	SSKatSSSTa	SSSDhaSgeS	4
TirakitaDhinSS	SNaSSSDhinS	×	SSDhinSSSDha	SgeSTirakita	0

TuSSSNaSS	SKatSSSTaS	SSDhaSgeSTi	rakitaDhinSSS
2		0	
NaSSSDhinSS	SDhinSSSDhaS	SSgeSTirakitaTu	SSSNaSSS
3		4	
KatSSSTaSS	SDhaSgeSTira	kitaDhinSSSNa	SSSDhinSSS
×		0	
DhinSSSDhaSge	STirakitaTuS	SSSNaSSSKat	SSSTaSSS
2		0	
DhaSgeSTiraki	taDhinSSSNaS	SSDhinSSSDhin	SSSDhaSgeS
3		4	
TirakitaTuSS	SNaSSSKatS	SSTaSSSDha	SgeSTirakita
×		0	
DhinSSSNaSS	SDhinSSSDhinS	SSDhaSgeSTi	rakitaTuSSS
2		0	
NaSSSKatSS	STaSSSDhaS	geSTirakitaDhin	SSSNaSSS
3		4	

Part–II

PRACTICAL

8

Traditional Composition in Teen Tal

Kayada of Banaras Gharana

Ekgun

Dha	Dha	Ti	Te	Dha	Dha	Tin	na
×				2			
Ta	Ta	Ti	Te	Dha	Dha	Dhin	na
0				3			

Dugun

Dhadha	Tite	Dhadha	Tinna	Tata	Tite	Dhadha	Dhinna
×				2			
Dhadha	Tite	Dhadha	Tinna	Tata	Tite	Dhadha	Dhinna
0				3			

Chaugun

Dhadhatite	Dhadhatinna	Tatatite	Dhadhadhinna
×			
Dhadhatite	Dhadhatinna	Tatatite	Dhadhadhinna
2			
Dhadhatite	Dhadhatinna	Tatatite	Dhadhadhinna
0			
Dhadhatite	Dhadhatinna	Tatatite	Dhadhadhinna
3			

Prstar-1

Dhadhatite	Dhadhatite	Dhadhatite	Dhadhatina
×			
Tatatite	Tatatite	Dhadhatite	Dhadhadhinna
2			
Dhadhatite	Dhadhatite	Dhadhatite	Dhadhatina
0			
Tatatite	Tatatite	Dhadhatite	Dhadhadhinna
3			

Prstar-2

Dhadhatite	Titetite	Dhadhatite	Dhadhatinna
×			
Tatatite	Titetite	Dhadhatite	Dhadhadhinna
2			
Dhadhatite	Titetite	Dhadhatite	Dhadhatinna
0			
Tatatite	Titetite	Dhadhatite	Dhadhadhinna
3			

Prstar-3

DhadhaTite	titeDhadha	Titetite	Dhadhatinna
×			
TataTite	titeDhadha	Titetite	Dhadhadhinna
2			
DhadhaTite	titeDhadha	Titetite	Dhadhatinna
0			
TataTite	titeDhadha	Titetite	Dhadhadhinna
3			

Prstar-4

Dhadhadhadha	Titetite	Dhadhatite	Dhadhatinna
×			
Tatatata	Titetite	Dhadhatite	Dhadhadhinna
2			
Dhadhadhadha	Titetite	Dhadhatite	Dhadhatinna
0			
Tatatata	Titetite	Dhadhatite	Dhadhadhinna
3			

Prstar-5

Dhadhadhadha	TiteDhadha	DhadhaTite	Dhadhatinna
×			
Tatatata	TiteDhadha	DhadhaTite	Dhadhadhinna
2			
Dhadhadhadha	TiteDhadha	DhadhaTite	Dhadhatinna
0			
Tatatata	TiteDhadha	DhadhaTite	Dhadhadhinna
3			

Prstar-6

Dhadhadhadha	Titetite	Dhadhadhadha	Tinnatinna
×			
Tatatata	Titetite	Dhadhadhadha	Dhinnadhinna
2			
Dhadhadhadha	Titetite	Dhadhadhadha	Tinnatinna
0			
Tatatata	Titetite	Dhadhadhadha	Dhinnadhinna
3			

Tihai–from 9th Beats

Dhadhatite	Dhadhatinna	Tatatite	Dhadhadhinna
×			
Dhadhatite	Dhadhatinna	Tatatite	Dhadhadhinna
2			
Dhadhatite	Dhadhadhinna	DhaSSS	Dhadhatite
0			
Dhadhadhinna	DhaSSS	Dhadhatite	Dhadhadhinna
3			
Dha			
×			

KAYADA-2

Ekgun

Dha	Dha	Tite	Tite	Dha	Dha	Tin	na
×				2			
Ta	Ta	Tite	Tite	Dha	Dha	Dhin	na
0				3			

Dugun

Dhadha	TiteTite	Dhadha	Tinna	Tata	TiteTite	Dhadha	Dhinna
×				2			
Dhadha	TiteTite	Dhadha	Tinna	Tata	TiteTite	Dhadha	Dhinna
0				3			

Chugun

Dhadha Tite Tite	DhadhaTinna	Tata Tite Tite	DhadhaDhinna
×			
Dhadha Tite Tite	DhadhaTinna	Tata Tite Tite	DhadhaDhinna
2			

Dhadha Tite Tite	DhadhaTinna	Tata Tite Tite	DhadhaDhinna
0			
Dhadha Tite Tite	DhadhaTinna	Tata Tite Tite	DhadhaDhinna
3			

Prstar-1

Dhadha Tite Tite, ×	Dhadha Tite Tite,	Dhadha Tite Tite,	DhadhaTinna
Tata Tite Tite, 2	Tata Tite Tite,	Dhadha Tite Tite,	DhadhaDhinna
Dhadha Tite Tite, 0	Dhadha Tite Tite,	Dhadha Tite Tite,	DhadhaTinna
Tata Tite Tite, 3	Tata Tite Tite,	Dhadha Tite Tite,	DhadhaDhinna

Prstar-2

Dhadha Tite Tite, ×	Tite Tite Tite Tite,	Dhadha Tite Tite,	DhadhaTinna
Tata Tite Tite, 2	Tite Tite Tite Tite,	Dhadha Tite Tite,	DhadhaDhinna
Dhadha Tite Tite, 0	Tite Tite Tite Tite,	Dhadha Tite Tite,	DhadhaTinna
Tata Tite Tite, 3	Tite Tite Tite Tite,	Dhadha Tite Tite,	DhadhaDhinna

Prastar-3

Dhadha Tite Tite, ×	Dha- Tite Tite Tite,	Dhadha Tite Tite,	DhadhaTinna
Tata Tite Tite , 2	Ta- Tite Tite Tite,	Dhadha Tite Tite,	DhadhaDhinna
Dhadha Tite Tite, 0	Dha- Tite Tite Tite,	Dhadha Tite Tite,	DhadhaTinna
Tata Tite Tite, 3	Ta- Tite Tite Tite,	Dhadha Tite Tite,	DhadhaDhinna

Prastar-4

Dhadha Tite Tite, ×	DhaS Tite Tite DhaS,	Dhadha Tite Tite,	DhadhaTinna
Tata Tite Tite , 2	TaS Tite Tite DhaS,	Dhadha Tite Tite,	DhadhaDhinna
Dhadha Tite Tite, 0	DhaS Tite Tite DhaS,	Dhadha Tite Tite,	DhadhaTinna
Tata Tite Tite, 3	TaS Tite Tite DhaS,	Dhadha Tite Tite,	DhadhaDhinna

Prastar-5

DhaSTite Tite DhaS, ×	DhaSTite Tite DhaS,	Dhadha Tite Tite ,	DhadhaTinna
TaSTite TiteTaS, 2	TaSTite Tite DhaS,	Dhadha Tite Tite ,	DhadhaDhinna
DhaSTite Tite DhaS, 0	DhaSTite Tite DhaS,	Dhadha Tite Tite ,	DhadhaTinna
TaSTite TiteTaS, 3	TaSTite Tite DhaS,	Dhadha Tite Tite ,	DhadhaDhinna

Prastar-6

DhaSTite Tite Tite, ×	DhaSTite Tite Tite,	Dhadha Tite Tite,	DhadhaTinna
TaSTite Tite Tite, 2	TaSTite Tite Tite,	Dhadha Tite Tite,	DhadhaDhinna
DhaS Tite Tite Tite, 0	DhaSTite Tite Tite,	Dhadha Tite Tite,	DhadhaTinna
TaSTite Tite Tite, 3	TaSTite Tite Tite,	Dhadha Tite Tite,	DhadhaDhinna

Tihai-from 9th Beats

Dhadha Tite Tite, ×	Dhadha Tinna,	Tata Tite Tite,	DhadhaDhinna
Dhadha Tite Tite, 2	Dhadha Tinna,	Tata Tite Tite,	DhadhaDhinna
Dhadha Tite Tite, ×	DhadhaDhinna,	DhaSSS,	Dhadha Tite Tite
DhadhaDhinna, 3	DhaSSS,	Dhadha Tite Tite,	DhadhaDhinna
Dha ×			

KAYADA-3

Ekgun

Dha ×	Dha	Tira	kita	Dha 2	Dha	Tin	na
Ta 0	Ta	Tira	kita	Dha 3	Dha	Dhin	na

Dugun

Dhadha ×	Tirakita	Dhadha	Tinna	Tata 2	Tirakita	Dhadha	Dhinna
Dhadha 0	Tirakita	Dhadha	Tinna	Tata 3	Tirakita	Dhadha	Dhinna

Chaugun

×	Dhadha Tira kita,	DhadhaTinna,	Tata Tira kita,	Dhadha Dhinna
2	Dhadha Tira kita,	DhadhaTinna,	Tata Tira kita,	Dhadha Dhinna
0	Dhadha Tira kita,	DhadhaTinna,	Tata Tira kita,	Dhadha Dhinna
3	Dhadha Tira kita,	DhadhaTinna,	Tata Tira kita,	Dhadha Dhinna

Prasta-1

×	Dhadha Tira kita,	Dhadha Tira kita,	Dhadha Tira kita,	Dhadha Tinna
2	Tata Tira kita,	Tata Tira kita,	Dhadha Tira kita,	Dhadha Dhinna
0	Dhadha Tira kita,	Dhadha Tira kita,	Dhadha Tira kita,	Dhadha Tinna
3	Tata Tira kita ,	Tata Tira kita,	Dhadha Tira kita,	Dhadha Dhinna

Prasta-2

×	Dhadha Dhadha,	Tira kita Dhadha,	Dhadha Tira kita,	Dhadha Tinna
2	Tata Tata,	Tira kita Dhadha,	Dhadha Tira kita,	Dhadha Dhinna
0	Dhadha Dhadha,	Tira kita Dhadha,	Dhadha Tira kita,	Dhadha Tinna
3	Tata Tata,	Tira kita Dhadha,	Dhadha Tira kita,	Dhadha Dhinna

Prasta-3

×	Dhadha Tira kita,	Dha Tira kita Dha,	Dhadha Tira kita,	Dhadha Tinna
2	Tata Tira kita,	Ta Tira kita Dha,	Dhadha Tira kita,	Dhadha Dhinna
0	Dhadha Tira kita,	Dha Tira kita Dha,	Dhadha Tira kita,	Dhadha Tinna
3	Tata Tira kita,	Ta Tira kita Dha,	Dhadha Tira kita,	Dhadha Dhinna

Prasta-4

Dha Tira kitaDha, ×	Dha Tira kita Dha,	Dhadha Tira kita,	Dhadha Tinna
Ta Tira kita Ta, 2	Ta Tira kita Dha,	Dhadha Tira kita,	Dhadha Dhinna
DhaTirakitaDha, 0	DhaTira kita Dha,	Dhadha Tira kita,	Dhadha Tinna
Ta Tira kita Ta, 3	Ta Tira kita Dha,	Dhadha Tira kita,	Dhadha Dhinna

Prasta-5

Dha DhaDhaTira, ×	kita Dha Tira kita,	Dhadha Tira kita,	Dhadha Tinna
Ta TaTa Tira, 2	Kita Ta Tira kita,	Dhadha Tira kita,	Dhadha Dhinna
Dha DhaDhaTira, 0	kita Dha Tira kita,	Dhadha Tira kita,	Dhadha Tinna
Ta TaTa Tira, 3	Kita Ta Tira kita,	Dhadha Tira kita,	Dhadha Dhinna

Prasta-6

Dha Tira kitaDha, ×	Tira kita Dha Tira,	kita Dha Tira kita,	Dhadha Tinna
Ta Tira kita Ta, 2	Tira kita Ta Tira,	kita Dha Tira kita,	Dhadha Dhinna
Dha Tira kitaDha, 0	Tira kita Dha Tira,	kita Dha Tira kita,	Dhadha Tinna
Ta Tira kita Ta, 3	Tira kita Ta Tira,	kita Dha Tira kita,	Dhadha Dhinna

Tihai-start from 9th Beats

Dhadha Tira kita, ×	DhadhaTinna,	Tata Tira kita,	Dhadha Dhinna
Dhadha Tira kita, 2	DhadhaTinna,	Tata Tira kita,	Dhadha Dhinna
Dhadha Tira kita, 0	Dhadha Dhinna	DhaSSS,	Dhadha Tira kita
Dhadha Dhinna 3	DhaSSS,	Dhadha Tira kita,	Dhadha Dhinna
Dha ×			

KAYAḌA-4

Ekgun

Dha	ge	Ti	te	Dha	ge	Ti	te
×				2			
Dha	ge	Na	ge	Tu	Na	Kat	Ta
0				3			
Ta	ke	Ti	te	Ta	ke	Ti	te
×				2			
Dha	ge	Na	ge	Dhin	Na	Kat	Ta
0				3			

Dugun

Dhage	Tite	Dhage	Tite	Dhage	Nage	Tuna	KatTa
×				2			
Take	Tite	Take	Tite	Dhage	Nage	Dhinna	KatTa
0				3			

Chaugun

DhageTite	DhageTite	Dhagenage	Tunakatta
×			
TakeTite	TakeTite	Dhagenage	Dhinnakatta
2			
DhageTite	DhageTite	Dhagenage	Tunakatta
0			
TakeTite	TakeTite	Dhagenage	Dhinnakatta
3			

Prastsar-1

DhageTite	TiteTite	Dhagenage	Dhinnakatta
×			
DhageTite	DhageTite	Dhagenage	Tunakatta
2			
TakeTite	TiteTite	Takenake	Tunakatta
0			
DhageTite	DhageTite	Dhagenage	Dhinnakatta
3			

Prastsar-2

DhageDhage	DhageTite	Dhagenage	Dhinnakatta
×			
DhageTite	DhageTite	Dhagenage	Tunakatta
2			

0	TakeTake	TakeTite	Takenake	Tunakatta
3	DhageTite	DhageTite	Dhagenage	Dhinnakatta

Prastsar-3

×	Dhagegege	DhageTite	Dhagenage	Dhinnakatta
2	DhageTite	DhageTite	Dhagenage	Tunakatta
0	Takekeke	TakeTite	Takenake	Tunakatta
3	DhageTite	DhageTite	Dhagenage	Dhinnakatta

Prastsar-4

×	DhagegeDha	gegeTite	Dhagenage	Dhinnakatta
2	DhageTite	DhageTite	Dhagenage	Tunakatta
0	TakekeTa	kekeTite	Takenake	Tunakatta
3	DhageTite	DhageTite	Dhagenage	Dhinnakatta

Prastsar-5

×	Dhagegege	gegeTite	Dhagenage	Dhinnakatta
2	DhageTite	DhageTite	Dhagenage	Tunakatta
0	Takekeke	kekeTite	Takenake	Tunakatta
3	DhageTite	DhageTite	Dhagenage	Dhinnakatta

Prastsar-6

×	Dhagnage	Dhinnakatta	Dhagenage	Dhinnakatta
2	DhageTite	DhageTite	Dhagenage	Tunakatta
0	Takenake	Tunakatta	Takenake	Tunakatta
3	DhageTite	DhageTite	Dhagenage	Dhinnakatta

Tihai-from Sum-

DhageTite ×	DhageTite	Dhagenage	Dhinnakatta
DhaSSS 2	SSSS	DhageTite	DhageTite
Dhagenage 0	Dhinnakatta	DhaSSS	SSSS
DhageTite 3	DhageTite	Dhagenage	Dhinnakatta
Dha ×			

KAYADA-5

Ekgun

DhaS ×	Tira	kita	taka	DhaS 2	Tira	kita	taka
DhaS 0	Tira	kita	taka	Tu 3	na	kita	taka
Ta S ×	Tira	kita	taka	TaS 2	Tira	kita	taka
DhaS 0	Tira	kita	taka	Dhin 3	na	kita	taka

Dugun

DhaSTira ×	kitataka	DhaSTira	kitataka	DhaSTira 2	kitataka	Tuna	kitataka
TaSTira 0	kitataka	TaSTira	kitataka	DhaSTira 3	kitataka	Dhinna	kitataka

Chaugun

DhaSTirakitataka ×	DhaSTirakitataka	DhaSTirakitataka	Tunakitataka
TaSTirakitataka 2	TaSTirakitataka	DhaSTirakitataka	Dhinnakitataka
DhaSTirakitataka 0	DhaSTirakitataka	DhaSTirakitataka	Tunakitataka
TaSTirakitataka 3	TaSTirakitataka	DhaSTirakitataka	Dhinnakitataka

Prastar-1

DhaऽTirakitataka	DhaऽDhaऽTirakita	DhaऽTirakitataka	Dhinnakitataka
×			
DhaऽTirakitataka	DhaऽTirakitataka	DhaऽTirakitataka	Tunakitataka
2			
TaऽTirakitataka	TaऽTaऽTirakita	TaऽTirakitataka	Tunakitataka
0			
DhaऽTirakitataka	DhaऽTirakitataka	DhaऽTirakitataka	Dhinnakitataka
3			

Prastar-2

DhaऽTirakitataka	Dhaऽऽऽkitataka	DhaऽTirakitataka	Dhinnakitataka
×			
DhaऽTirakitataka	DhaऽTirakitataka	DhaऽTirakitataka	Tunakitataka
2			
TaऽTirakitataka	Taऽऽऽkitataka	TaऽTirakitataka	Tunakitataka
0			
DhaऽTirakitataka	DhaऽTirakitataka	DhaऽTirakitataka	Dhinnakitataka
3			

Prastar-3

DhaऽTirakitaDhaऽ	TirakitaDhaऽDhaऽ	DhaऽTirakitataka	Dhinnakitataka
×			
DhaऽTirakitataka	DhaऽTirakitataka	DhaऽTirakitataka	Tunakitataka
2			
TaऽTirakitataka	TirakitaTaऽTaऽ	TaऽTirakitataka	Tunakitataka
0			
DhaऽTirakitataka	DhaऽTirakitataka	DhaऽTirakitataka	Dhinnakitataka
3			

Prastar-4

DhaऽTirakitaDhaऽ	TirakitaDhaऽTira	kitaDhaऽTirakita	Dhinnakitataka
×			
DhaऽTirakitataka	DhaऽTirakitataka	DhaऽTirakitataka	Tunakitataka
2			
TaऽTirakitaTaऽ	TirakitaTaऽTira	kitaTaऽTirakita	Tunakitataka
0			
DhaऽTirakitataka	DhaऽTirakitataka	DhaऽTirakitataka	Dhinnakitataka
3			

Prastar-5

DhaSTirakitataka	TirakitaDhaSSS	DhaSTirakitataka	Dhinnakitataka
×			
DhaSTirakitataka	DhaSTirakitataka	DhaSTirakitataka	Tunakitataka
2			
TaSTirakitataka	TirakitaTaSSS	TaSTirakitataka	Tunakitataka
0			
DhaSTirakitataka	DhaSTirakitataka	DhaSTirakitataka	Dhinnakitataka
3			

Prastar-6

DhaSTirakitataka	TirakitaDhaSSS	TirakitaDhaSSS	TirakitaDhaSSS
×			
DhaSTirakitataka	DhaSTirakitataka	DhaSTirakitataka	Tunakitataka
2			
TaSTirakitataka	TirakitaTaSSS	TirakitaTaSSS	TirakitaTaSSS
0			
DhaSTirakitataka	DhaSTirakitataka	DhaSTirakitataka	Dhinnakitataka
3			

Tihai-from 9th Beats

DhaSTirakitataka	DhaSTirakitataka	DhaSTirakitataka	Tunakitataka
×			
TaSTirakitataka	TaSTirakitataka	DhaSTirakitataka	Dhinnakitataka
2			
DhaSTirakitataka	Dhinnakitataka	DhaSSS	Dha-Tirakitataka
0			
Dhinnakitataka	DhaSSS	DhaSTirakitataka	Dhinnakitataka
3			
Dha			
×			

Only Tihai-from 9th Beats

9	10	11	12
DhaSTirakitataka	Dhinnakitataka	DhaSSS	DhaSTirakitataka
0			
13	14	15	16
Dhinnakitataka	DhaSSS	DhaSTirakitataka	Dhinnakitataka
3			
1			
Dha			
×			

KAYADA-6

Ekgun

DhaS	Tira	kita	taka	Taka	Tira	kita	taka
×				2			
DhaS	Tira	kita	taka	Tu	na	kita	taka
0				3			
TaS	Tira	kita	taka	Taka	Tira	kita	taka
×				2			
DhaS	Tira	kita	taka	Dhin	na	kita	taka
0				3			

Dugun

DhaSTira	kitataka	TakaTira	kitataka	DhaSTira	kitataka	Tuna	kitataka
×				2			
TaSTira	kitataka	TakaTira	kitataka	DhaSTira	kitataka	Dhinna	kitataka
0				3			

Chaugun

DhaSTirakitataka	TakaTirakitataka	DhaSTirakitataka	Tunakitataka
×			
TaSTirakitataka	TakaTirakitataka	DhaSTirakitataka	Dhinnakitataka
2			
DhaSTirakitataka	TakaTirakitataka	DhaSTirakitataka	Tunakitataka
0			
TaSTirakitataka	TakaTirakitataka	DhaSTirakitataka	Dhinnakitataka
3			

Prastar-1

DhaSTirakitataka	TakaTirakitataka	DhaSTirakitataka	TakaTirakitataka
×			
DhaSTirakitataka	TakaTirakitataka	DhaSTirakitataka	Tunakitataka
2			
TaSTirakitataka	TakaTirakitataka	TaSTirakitataka	TakaTirakitataka
0			
DhaSTirakitataka	TakaTirakitataka	DhaSTirakitataka	Dhinnakitataka
3			

Prastar-2

DhaSTirakitataka ×	TakaTirakitataka	TakaTirakitataka	TakaTirakitataka
DhaSTirakitataka 2	TakaTirakitataka	DhaSTirakitataka	Tunakitataka
TaSTirakitataka 0	TakaTirakitataka	TakaTirakitataka	TakaTirakitataka
DhaSTirakitataka 3	TakaSTirakitataka	DhaSTirakitataka	Dhinnakitataka

Prastar-3

DhaSTirakitaTaka ×	TakaTirakitataka	TakaTakaTakaTaka	TakaTirakitataka
DhaSTirakitataka 2	TakaTirakitataka	DhaSTirakitataka	Tunakitataka
TaSTirakitataka 0	TakaTirakitataka	TakaTakaTakaTaka	TakaTirakitataka
DhaSTirakitataka 3	TakaTirakitataka	DhaSTirakitataka	Dhinnakitataka

Prastar-4

TakaTakaTakaTaka ×	TakaTirakitataka	TakaTirakitataka	TakaTirakitataka
Dha-Tirakitataka 2	TakaTirakitataka	DhaSTirakitataka	Tunakitataka
TakaTakaTakaTaka 0	TakaTirakitataka	TakaTirakitataka	TakaTirakitataka
DhaSTirakitataka 3	TakaTirakitataka	DhaSTirakitataka	Dhinnakitataka

Prastar-5

TakaTakaTakaTira ×	kitatakaTakaTaka	TakaTirakitataka	TakaTirakitataka
DhaSTirakitataka 2	TakaSTirakitataka	TakaTirakitataka	Tunakitataka
TakaTakaTakaTira 0	kitatakaTakaTaka	TakaTirakitataka	TakaTirakitataka
DhaSTirakitataka 3	TakaTirakitataka	TakaTirakitataka	Dhinnakitataka

Prastar-6

TakaTakaTakaTaka	TakaTakaTakaTaka	TakaTirakitataka	TakaTirakitataka
×			
DhaSTirakitataka	TakaSTirakitataka	DhaSTirakitataka	Tunakitataka
2			
TakaTakaTakaTaka	TakaTakaTakaTaka	TakaTirakitataka	TakaTirakitataka
0			
DhaSTirakitataka	TakaTirakitataka	DhaSTirakitataka	Dhinnakitataka
3			

Tihai-from Sum

DhaSTirakitataka	TakaTirakitataka	DhaSTirakitataka	Dhinnakitataka
×			
Dha SSS	SSSS	Dha-Tirakitataka	TakaTirakitataka
2			
DhaSTirakitataka	Dhinnakitataka	Dha SSS	SSSS
0			
DhaSTirakitataka	TakaTirakitataka	DhaSTirakitataka	Dhinnakitataka
3			
Dha			
×			

KAYADA-7

Ekgun

Ghe	ra	na	ge	Ti	te	Ti	te	Ghe	ra	na	ge	Tu	S	na	S
×				2				0				3			
Ti	te	Ghe	ra	na	ge	Ti	te	Ghe	ra	na	ge	Tu	S	na	S
×				2				0				3			
Ke	ra	na	ke	Ti	te	Ti	te	Ke	ra	na	ke	Tu	S	na	S
×				2				0				3			
Ti	te	Ghe	ra	na	ge	Ti	te	Ghe	ra	na	ge	Dhin	S	na	S
×				2				0				3			

Dugun

Ghera	nage	Tite	Tite	Ghera	nage	Tu	naS
×				2			
Tite	Ghera	nage	Tite	Ghera	nage	TuS	naS
0				3			

Kera	nake	Tite	Tite	Kera	nake	Tuऽ	naऽ
×				2			
Tite	Ghera	nage	Tite	Ghera	nage	Dhinऽ	naऽ
0				3			

Chaugun

Gheranage	TiteTite	Gheranage	TuऽnaS
×			
TiteGhera	nageTite	Gheranage	Tuऽnaऽ
2			
Keranake	TiteTite	Keranake	Tuऽnaऽ
0			
TiteGhera	nageTite	Gheranage	Dhinऽnaऽ
3			

Athgun

GheranageTiteTite	GheranageTuऽnaऽ	TiteGheranageTite	GheranageTuऽnaऽ
×			
KeranakeTieTite	KeranakeTuऽnaऽ	TiteGheranageTite	GheranageDhinऽnaऽ
2			
GheranageTiteTite	GheranageTuऽnaऽ	TiteGheranageTite	GheranageTuऽnaऽ
0			
KeranakeTiteTite	KeranakeTuऽna	TiteGheranageTite	GheranageDhinऽnaऽ
3			

Prastar-1

GheranageTiteTite	GheranageTuऽnaऽ	GheranageTiteTite	GheranageTuऽnaऽ
×			
GheranageTiteTite	GheranageTuऽnaऽ	TiteGheranageTite	GheranageTuऽnaऽ
2			
KeranakeTiteTite	KeranakeTuऽnaऽ	KeranakeTiteTite	KeranakeTuऽnaऽ
0			
GheranageTiteTite	GheranageTuऽnaऽ	TiteGheranageTite	GheranageDhinऽnaऽ
3			

Prastar-2

GheranageTiteTite	GheranageTiteTite	GheranageTiteTite	GheranageTuऽnaऽ
×			
GheranageTiteTite	GheranageTuऽnaऽ	TiteGheranageTite	GheranageTuऽnaऽ
2			

KeranakeTiteTite | KeranakeTiteTite | KeranakeTiteTite | KeranakeTuऽnaऽ |
0
GheranageTiteTite | GheranageTuऽnaऽ | TiteGheranageTite | GheranageDhinऽnaऽ |
3

Prastar-3

GheranageTiteGhera | nageTiteGheranag | TiteGheranageTite | GheranageTuna |
×
GheranageTiteTite | GheranageTuऽnaऽ | TiteGheranageTite | GheranageTuऽnaऽ |
2
KeranakeTiteKera | nakeTiteKeranake | TiteKeranakeTite | KeranakeTuऽnaऽ |
0
GheranageTiteTite | GheranageTuऽnaऽ | TiteGheranageTite | GheranageDhinऽnaऽ |
3

Prastar-4

TiteTiteGheranage | TiteTiteGheranage | TiteGheranageTite | GheranageTuऽnaऽ |
×
GheranageTiteTite | GheranageTuऽnaऽ | TiteGheranageTite | GheranageTuऽnaऽ |
2
TiteTiteKeranake | TiteTiteKeranake | TiteKeranakeTite | KeranakeTuऽnaऽ |
0
GheranageTiteTite | GheranageTuऽnaऽ | TiteGheranageTite | GheranageDhinऽnaऽ |
3

Prastar-5

TiteGheranageTite | GheranageTuऽnaऽ | TiteGheranageTite | GheranageTuऽnaऽ |
×
GheranageTiteTite | GheranageTuऽnaऽ | TiteGheranageTite | GheranageTuऽnaऽ |
2
TiteKeranakeTite | KeranakeTuऽnaऽ | TiteKeranakeTite | KeranakeTuऽnaऽ |
0
GheranageTiteTite | GheranageTuऽnaऽ | TiteGheranageTite | GheranageDhinऽnaऽ |
3

Prastar-6

TiteGheranageTite | TiteGheranageTite | TiteGheranageTite | GheranageTuऽnaऽ |
×
GheranageTiteTite | GheranageTuऽnaऽ | TiteGheranageTite | GheranageTuऽnaऽ |
2

TiteKeranakeTite 0	TiteKeranakeTite	TiteKeranakeTite	KeranakeTuऽnaऽ
GheranageTiteTite 3	GheranageTuऽnaऽ	TiteGheranageTite	GheranageDhinऽnaऽ

Prastar-7

TiteGheranageTite ×	TiteTiteGheranage	TiteGheranageTite	GheranageTuऽnaऽ
GheranageTiteTite 2	GheranageTuऽnaऽ	TiteGheranageTite	GheranageTuऽnaऽ
TiteKeranakeTite 0	TiteTiteKeranake	TiteKeranakeTite	KeranakeTuऽnaऽ
GheranageTiteTite 3	GheranageTuऽnaऽ	TiteGheranageTite	GheranageDhinऽnaऽ

Prastar-8

TiteGheranageGhera ×	nageTiteGheranage	TiteGheranageTite	GheranageTuऽnaऽ
GheranageTiteTite 2	GheranageTuऽnaऽ	TiteGheranageTite	GheranageTuऽnaऽ
TiteKeranakeKera 0	nakaTiteKeranake	TiteKeranakeTite	KeranakeTuऽnaऽ
GheranageTiteTite 3	GheranageTuऽnaऽ	TiteGheranageTite	GheranageDhinऽnaऽ

Tihai

GheranageTiteTite ×	GheranageTuऽnaऽ	TiteGheranageTite	GheranageDhinऽnaऽ
Dha 2	ऽ	GheranageTiteTite	GheranageTu-na-
TiteGheranageTite 0	GheranageDhin-na-	Dha	ऽ
GheranageTiteTite 3	GheranageTuऽnaऽ	TiteGheranageTite	GheranageDhinऽnaऽ
Dha ×			

KAYADA-8

Ekgun

Dha	S	Ti	te	Dha	dha	Ti	te
×				2			
Dha	ge	din	S	Na	na	Ti	te
0				3			
Dha	Ti	te	Dha	Ti	te	Dha	dha
×				2			
Tu	na	Kita	taka	Ta-	Tira	kita	taka
0				3			
Ta	S	Ti	te	Ta	ta	Ti	te
×				2			
Ta	ke	tin	S	Na	na	Ti	te
0				3			
Dha	Ti	te	Dha	Ti	te	Dha	dha
×				2			
Dhin	na	kita	taka	Dha-	tira	kita	taka
0				3			

Dugun

DhaS	Tite	Dhadha	Tite	Dhage	dinS	Nana	Tite
×				2			
DhaTi	teDha	Tite	Dhadha	Tuna	Kitataka	Ta-Tira	kitataka
0				3			
TaS	Tite	Tata	Tite	Take	tinS	Nana	Tite
×				2			
DhaTi	teDha	Tite	Dhadha	Dhinna	kitataka	Dha-tira	kitataka
0				3			

Chaugun

DhaSTite	DhadhaTite	DhagedinS	NanaTite
×			
DhaTiteDha	TiteDhadha	TunaKitataka	Ta-Tirakitataka
2			
TaSTite	TataTite	TaketinS	NanaTite
0			
DhaTiteDha	TiteDhadha	Dhinnakitataka	Dha-tirakitataka
3			

DhaSTiteDhadhaTite
×
DhaTiteDhaTiteDhadha

TaSTiteTataTite
2
DhaTiteDhaTiteDhadha

DhaSTiteDhadhaTite
0
DhaTiteDhaTiteDhadha

TaSTiteTataTite
3
DhaTiteDhaTiteDhadha

DhaSTiteDhadhaTite
×
DhaSTiteDhadhaTite

DhaSTiteDhadhaTite
2
DhaTiteDhaTiteDhadha

TaSTiteTataTite
0
TaSTiteTataTite

DhaSTiteDhadhaTite
3
DhaTiteDhaTiteDhadha

DhaSTiteDhadhaTite
×
DhagedinSNanaTite

DhaSTiteDhadhaTite
2

Athgun

DhagedinSNanaTite

TunaKitatakaTa-Tirakitataka

TaketinSNanaTite

DhinnakitatakaDha-tirakitataka

DhagedinSNanaTite

TunaKitatakaTa-Tirakitataka

TaketinSNanaTite

DhinnakitatakaDha-tirakitataka

Prastar-1

DhagedinSNanaTite

DhagedinSNanaTite

DhagedinSNanaTite

TunaKitatakaTa-Tirakitataka

TaketinSNanaTite

TaketinSNanaTite

DhagedinSNanaTite

DhinnakitatakaDhaStirakitataka

Prastar-2

Dhagedin ·NanaTite

DhagedinSNanaTite

DhagedinSNanaTite

DhaTiteDhaTiteDhadha	TunaKitatakaTaSTirakitataka
TaSTiteTataTite	TaketinSNanaTite
0	
TaketinSNanaTite	TaketinSNanaTite
DhaSTiteDhadhaTite	DhagedinSNanaTite
3	
DhaTiteDhaTiteDhadha	DhinñakitatakaDhaStirakitataka

Prastar-3

DhaSTiteDhadhaTite	DhaSTiteDhadhaTite
×	
DhaSTiteDhadhaTite	DhagedinSNanaTite
DhaSTiteDhadhaTite	DhagedinSNanaTite
2	
DhaTiteDhaTiteDhadha	TunaKitatakaTaSTirakitataka
TaSTiteTataTite	TaSTiteTataTite
0	
TaSTiteTataTite	TaketinSNanaTite
DhaSTiteDhadhaTite	DhagedinSNanaTite
3	
DhaTiteDhaTiteDhadha	DhinnakitatakaDhaStirakitataka

Prastar-4

DhaTiteDhaTiteDhadha	TunaKitatakaTaSTirakitataka
×	
TaTiteTaTiteDhadha	DhinnakitatakaDhaStirakitataka
DhaTiteDhaTiteDhadha	TunaKitatakaTaSTirakitataka
2	
TaTiteTaTiteDhadha	DhinnakitatakaDhaStirakitataka
DhaTiteDhaTiteDhadha	TunaKitatakaTaSTirakitataka
0	
TaTiteTaTiteDhadha	DhinnakitatakaDhaStirakitataka
DhaTiteDhaTiteDhadha	TunaKitatakaTaSTirakitataka
3	
TaTiteTaTiteDhadha	DhinnakitatakaDhaStirakitataka

Prastar-5

DhaTiteDhaTiteDhadha	DhaTiteDhaTiteDhadh
×	
DhaTiteDhaTiteDhadha	TunaKitatakaTaऽTirakitataka
TaTiteTaTiteTata	TaTiteTaTiteTata
2	
DhaTiteDhaTiteDhadha	DhinnakitatakaDhaऽtirakitataka
DhaTiteDhaTiteDhadha	DhaTiteDhaTiteDhadha
0	
DhaTiteDhaTiteDhadha	TunaKitatakaTaऽTirakitataka
TaTiteTaTiteTata	TaTiteTaTiteTata
3	
DhaTiteDhaTiteDhadha	DhinnakitatakaDhaऽtirakitataka

Prastar-6

DhaTiteDhaTiteDhadha	TiteDhaDhaTiteDhadha
×	
DhaTiteDhaTiteDhadha	TunaKitatakaTaऽTirakitataka
TaTiteTaTiteTata	TiteTaTaTiteTata
2	
DhaTiteDhaTiteDhadha	DhinnakitatakaDhaऽtirakitataka
DhaTiteDhaTiteDhadha	TiteDhaDhaTiteDhadha
0	
DhaTiteDhaTiteDhadha	TunaKitatakaTaऽTirakitataka
TaTiteTaTiteTata	TiteTaTaTiteTata
3	
DhaTiteDhaTiteDhadha	DhinnakitatakaDhaऽtirakitataka

Prastar-7

DhaTiteDhaDhaTitedha	DhaTiteDhaTiteDhadha
×	
DhaTiteDhaTiteDhadha	TunaKitatakaTaऽTirakitataka
TaTiteTaTaTiteTa	TaTiteTaTiteTata
2	
DhaTiteDhaTiteDhadha	DhinnakitatakaDhaऽtirakitataka
DhaTiteDhaDhaTiteDha	DhaTiteDhaTiteDhadha
0	

DhaTiteDhaTiteDhadha TunaKitatakaTaSTirakitataka

TaTiteTaTaTiteTa TaTiteTaTiteTata

3

DhaTiteDhaTiteDhadha DhinnakitatakaDhaStirakitataka

Prastar-8

DhaTiteDhaTiteDhadha TunaKitatakaTaSTirakitataka

×

TunaKitatakaTaSTirakitataka TunaKitatakaTaSTirakitataka

TaTiteTaTiteDhadha DhinnakitatakaDha-tirakitataka

2

DhinnakitatakaDhaStirakitataka DhinnakitatakaDha tirakitataka

DhaTiteDhaTiteDhadha TunaKitatakaTaSTirakitataka

0

TunaKitatakaTaSTirakitataka TunaKitatakaTaSTirakitataka

TaTiteTaTiteDhadha DhinnakitatakaDhaStirakitataka

3

DhinnakitatakaDhaStirakitataka DhinnakitatakaDhaStirakitataka

Tihai-Chakradar

DhaTiteDhaTiteDhadha DhinnakitatakaDhaStirakitataka

×

DhaSSSDhinnakitataka Dha-tirakitataka DhaSSS

DhinnakitatakaDha-tirakitataka DhaSSS,DhaTiteDha

2

TiteDhadhaDhinnakitataka Dha tirakitataka DhaSSS

DhinnakitatakaDha-tirakitataka DhaSSSDhinnakitataka

0

Dha tirakitataka DhaSSS DhaTiteDhaTiteDhadha

DhinnakitatakaDha-tirakitataka DhaSSSDhinnakitataka

3

DhaStirakitataka DhaSSS DhinnakitatakaDhaStirakitataka

Dha

×

KAYADA-9

Ekgun

Dha ×	ge	Tira	kita	Dhee 2	na	gi	na
Dha 0	ge	na	ge	Tee 3	na	ki	na
Ta ×	ke	Tira	kita	Dhee 2	na	gi	na
Dha 0	ge	na	ge	Dhee 3	na	gi	na

Dugun

Dhage ×	Tirakita	Dheena	gina	Dhage 2	nage	Teena	kina
Take 0	Tirakita	Dheena	gina	Dhage 3	nage	Dheena	gina

Chaugun

DhageTirakita ×	Dheenagina	Dhagenage	Teenakina
TakeTirakita 2	Dheenagina	Dhagenage	Dheenagina
DhageTirakita 0	Dheenagina	Dhagenage	Teenakina
TakeTirakita 3	Dheenagina	Dhagenage	Dheenagina

Athgun

DhageTirakitaDheenagina ×	DhagenageTeenakina
TakeTirakitaDheenagina	DhagenageDheenagina
DhageTirakitaDheenagina 2	DhagenageTeenakina
TakeTirakitaDheenagina	DhagenageDheenagina
DhageTirakitaDheenagina 0	DhagenageTeenakina
TakeTirakitaDheenagina	DhagenageDheenagina
DhageTirakitaDheenagina 3	DhagenageTeenakina
TakeTirakitaDheenagina	DhagenageDheenagina

DhageTirakitaDheenagina
×
DhageTirakitaDheenagina
TakeTirakitaTeenakina
2
DhageTirakitaDheenagina
DhageTirakitaDheenagina
0
DhageTirakitaDheenagina
TakeTirakitaTeenakina
3
DhageTirakitaDheenagina

DhageTirakitaDheenagina
×
DhageTirakitaDheenagina
TakeTirakitaTeenakina
2
DhageTirakitaDheenagina
DhageTirakitaDheenagina
0
DhageTirakitaDheenagina
TakeTirakitaTeenakina
3
DhageTirakitaDheenagina

DhageTirakitaDheenagina
×
DhageTirakitaDheenagina
DhageTirakitaDheenagina
2
DhageTirakitaDheenagina
TakeTirakitaTeenakina
0

Prastar-1

DhageTirakitaDheenagina

DhagenageTeenakina
TakeTirakitaTeenakina

DhagenageDheenagina
DhageTirakitaDheenagina

DhagenageTeenakina
TakeTirakitaTeenakina

DhagenageDheenagina

Prastar-2

DhaSSSDheenagina

DhagenageTeenakina
TaSSSTeenakina

DhagenageDheenagina
DhaSSSDheenagina

DhagenageTeenakina
TaSSSTeenakina

DhagenageDheenagina

Prastar-3

DhaSSSDheenagina

DhaSSSDheenagina
DhaSSSDheenagina

DhagenageTeenakina

TaSSSTeenakina

TakeTirakitaTeenakina

DhageTirakitaDheenagina
3

DhageTirakitaDheenagina

DhageTirakitaDheenagina
×

DhaSSSDheenagina

DhageTirakitaDheenagina
2

DhageTirakitaDheenagina

TakeTirakitaTeenakina
0

TaSSSTeenakina

DhageTirakitaDheenagina
3

DhageTirakitaDheenagina

DhageTirakitaDhageTirakita
×

DhageTirakitaDheenagina

TakeTirakitaTakeTirakita
2

DhageTirakitaDheenagina

DhageTirakitaDhageTirakita
0

DhageTirakitaDheenagina

TakeTirakitaTakeTirakita
3

DhageTirakitaDheenagina

DhageTirakitaDhageTirakita
×

DhageTirakitaDheenagina

TaSSSTeenakina

DhaSSSDheenagina

DhagenageDheenagina

Prstar-4

DhaSSSDheenagina

DhaSSSDheenagina

DhaSSSDheenagina

DhagenageTeenakina

TaSSSTeenakina

TaSSSTeenakina

DhaSSSDheenagina

DhagenageDheenagina

Prastar-5

DhageTirakitaDheenagina

DhagenageTeenakina

TakeTirakitaTeenakina

DhagenageDheenagina

DhageTirakitaDheenagina

DhagenageTeenakina

TakeTirakitaTeenakina

DhagenageDheenagina

Prastar-6

DheenaginaDhageTirakita

DhagenageTeenakina

TakeTirakitaTakeTirakita TeenakinaTakeTirakita
2
DhageTirakitaDheenagina DhagenageDheenagina
DhageTirakitaDhageTirakita DheenaginaDhageTirakita
0
DhageTirakitaDheenagina DhagenageTeenakina
TakeTirakitaTakeTirakita TeenakinaTakeTirakita
3
DhageTirakitaDheenagina DhagenageDheenagina

Prastar-7

DhaSSSDheenagina DhagenageDheenagina
×
DhageTirakitaDheenagina DhagenageTeenakina
TaSSSTeenakina TakenakeTeenakina
2
DhageTirakitaDheenagina DhagenageDheenagina
DhaSSSDheenagina DhagenageDheenagina
0
DhageTirakitaDheenagina DhagenageTeenakina
TaSSSTeenakina TakenakeTeenakina
3
DhageTirakitaDheenagina DhagenageDheenagina

Prastar-8

DhageTirakitaDheenagina TirakitaDhageTirakitaDheena
×
GinaTirakitaDhageTirakita DhagenageTeenakina
TakeTirakitaTeenakina TirakitaTakeTirakitaTeena
2
kinaTirakitaDhageTirakita DhagenageDheenagina
DhageTirakitaDheenagina TirakitaDhageTirakitaDheena
0
GinaTirakitaDhageTirakita DhagenageTeenakina
TakeTirakitaTeenakina TirakitaTakeTirakitaTeena
3
kinaTirakitaDhageTirakita DhagenageDheenagina

Tihai-Chakradar

DhageTirakitaDheenagina ×	DhagenageDheenagina
DhaऽऽऽDhagenage	Dheenagina Dhaऽऽऽ
Dhagenage Dheenagina 2	DhaऽऽऽDhageTirakita
Dheenagina Dhagenage	Dheenagina Dhaऽऽऽ
DhagenageDheenagina 0	DhaऽऽऽDhagenage
Dheenagina Dhaऽऽऽ	DhageTirakitaDheenagina
DhagenageDheenagina 3	DhaऽऽऽDhagenage
Dheenagina Dhaऽऽऽ	Dhagenage Dheenagina
Dha ×	

KAYADA-10

Ekgun

Dha	ऽ	Ti	ra	Ki	ta	ta	ka	Ta	ka	ti	ra	ki	ta	ta	ka
×				2				0				3			
Dhi	ra	Dhi	ra	ki	ta	ta	ka	Tu	ऽ	na	ऽ	ki	ta	ta	ka
×				2				0				3			
Ta	ऽ	Ti	ra	ki	ta	ta	ka	Ta	Ka	ti	ra	ki	ta	ta	ka
×				2				0				3			
Dhi	ra	Dhi	ra	ki	ta	ta	ka	Dhin	ऽ	na	ऽ	ki	ta	ta	ka
×				2				0				3			

Dugun

Dhaऽ	Tira	kita	taka	Taka	tira	kita	taka
×				2			
Dhira	Dhira	kita	taka	Tuऽ	naऽ	kita	taka
0				3			
Taऽ	Tira	kita	taka	Taka	tira	kita	taka
×				2			
Dhira	Dhira	kita	taka	Dhinऽ	naऽ	kita	taka
0				3			

Chaugun

DhaSTira	kitataka	Takatira	kitataka	DhiraDhira	kitataka	TuSnaS	kitataka
×				2			
TaSTira	kitataka	Takatira	kitataka	DhiraDhira	kitataka	DhinSnaS	kitataka
0				3			
DhaSTira	kitataka	Takatira	kitataka	DhiraDhira	kitataka	TuSnaS	kitataka
×				2			
TaSTira	kitataka	Takatira	kitataka	DhiraDhira	kitataka	DhinaSnaS	kitataka
0				3			

Athgun

DhaSTirakitataka	Takatirakitataka	DhiraDhirakitataka	TuSnaSkitataka
×			
TaSTirakitataka	Takatirakitataka	DhiraDhirakitataka	DhinSnaSkitataka
2			
DhaSTirakitataka	Takatirakitataka	DhiraDhirakitataka	TuSnaSkitataka
0			
TaSTirakitataka	Takatirakitataka	DhiraDhirakitataka	DhinSnaSkitataka
3			

Prastar-1

DhaSTirakitataka	Takatirakitataka	DhaSTirakitataka	Takatirakitataka
×			
DhaSTirakitataka	Takatirakitataka	DhiraDhirakitataka	TuSnaSkitataka
2			
TaSTirakitataka	Takatirakitataka	TaSTirakitataka	Takatirakitataka
0			
DhaSTirakitataka	Takatirakitataka	DhiraDhirakitataka	DhinSnaSkitataka
3			

Prastar-2

DhaSTirakitataka	Takatirakitataka	DhiraDhirakitataka	DhaSTirakitataka
×			
DhaSTirakitataka	Takatirakitataka	DhiraDhirakitataka	TuSnaSkitataka
2			
TaSTirakitataka	Takatirakitataka	TiraTirakitataka	TaSTirakitataka
0			
DhaSTirakitataka	Takatirakitataka	DhiraDhirakitataka	DhinSnaSkitataka
3			

Prastar-3

DhaऽTirakitataka	Takatirakitataka	DhiraDhirakitataka	DhiraDhirakitataka
×			
DhaऽTirakitataka	Takatirakitataka	DhiraDhirakitataka	TuऽnaऽKitataka
2			
TaऽTirakitataka	Takatirakitataka	TiraTirakitataka	TiraTirakitataka
0			
DhaऽTirakitataka	Takatirakitataka	DhiraDhirakitataka	DhinऽnaऽKitataka
3			

Prastar-4

Takatirakitataka	DhiraDhirakitataka	Takatirakitataka	DhiraDhirakitataka
×			
DhaऽTirakitataka	Takatirakitataka	DhiraDhirakitataka	TuऽnaऽKitataka
2			
Takatirakitataka	TiraTirakitataka	Takatirakitataka	TiraTirakitataka
0			
DhaऽTirakitataka	Takatirakitataka	DhiraDhirakitataka	DhinऽnaऽKitataka
3			

Prastar-5

Takatirakitataka	DhiraDhirakitataka	DhiraDhirakitataka	DhiraDhirakitataka
×			
DhaऽTirakitataka	Takatirakitataka	DhiraDhirakitataka	TuऽnaऽKitataka
2			
Takatirakitataka	TiraTirakitataka	TiraTirakitataka	TiraTirakitataka
0			
DhaऽTirakitataka	Takatirakitataka	DhiraDhirakitataka	DhinऽnaऽKitataka
3			

Prastar-6

TakaTakaTakaTaka	Takatirakitataka	DhiraDhirakitataka	DhiraDhirakitataka
×			
DhaऽTirakitataka	Takatirakitataka	DhiraDhirakitataka	TuऽnaऽKitataka
2			
TakaTakaTakaTaka	Takatirakitataka	TiraTirakitataka	TiraTirakitataka
0			
DhaऽTirakitataka	Takatirakitataka	DhiraDhirakitataka	DhinऽnaऽKitataka
3			

Prastar-7

TakaTirakitataka	Takatirakitataka	DhiraDhirakitataka	Takatirakitataka
×			
DhaSTirakitataka	Takatirakitataka	DhiraDhirakitataka	TuSnaSkitataka
2			
Takatirakitataka	Takatirakitataka	TiraTirakitataka	Takatirakitataka
0			
DhaSTirakitataka	Takatirakitataka	DhiraDhirakitataka	DhinSnaSkitataka
3			

Prastar-8

DhaSTirakitataka	Takatirakitataka	DhiraDhirakitataka	DhiraDhirakitataka
×			
DhiraDhirakitataka	Takatirakitataka	DhiraDhirakitataka	TuSnaSkitataka
2			
TaSTirakitataka	Takatirakitataka	TiraTirakitataka	TiraTirakitataka
0			
DhiraDhirakitataka	Takatirakitataka	DhiraDhirakitataka	DhinSnaSkitataka
3			

Tihai

DhaSTirakitataka	Takatirakitataka	DhiraDhirakitataka	DhinSnaSkitataka
×			
Dha	S	DhaSTirakitataka	Takatirakitataka
2			
DhiraDhirakitataka	DhinSnaSkitataka	Dha	S
0			
DhaSTirakitataka	Takatirakitataka	DhiraDhirakitataka	DhinSnaSkitataka
3			
Dha			
×			

Tihai-Chakradar

DhaSTirakitataka	Takatirakitataka	DhiraDhirakitataka	DhinnaSkitataka
×			
Dha	DhiraDhirakitataka	DhinSnaSkitataka	Dha
2			
DhiraDhirakitatak	DhinSnaSkitataka	Dha,	DhaSTirakitataka
0			

Takatirakitataka 3	DhiraDhirakitataka	DhinSnaSkitataka	Dha
DhiraDhirakitataka ×	DhinSnaSkitataka	Dha	DhiraDhirakitataka
DhinSnaSkitataka 2	Dha,	DhaSTirakitataka	Takatirakitataka
DhiraDhirakitataka 0	DhinSnaSkitataka	Dha	DhiraDhirakitataka
DhinSnaSkitataka 3	Dha	DhiraDhirakitataka	DhinSnaSkitataka
Dha ×			

KAYADA-11

Ekgun

Dha ×	S	Ti	ra	ki 2	ta	ta	ka	Dhi 0	ra	Dhi	ra	ki 3	ta	ta	ka
Dha ×	S	Ti	ra	ki 2	ta	ta	ka	Tu 0	S	na	S	ki 3	ta	ta	ka
Ta ×	S	Ti	ra	ki 2	ta	ta	ka	Ti 0	ra	Ti	ra	ki 3	ta	ta	ka
Dha ×	S	Ti	ra	ki 2	ta	ta	ka	Dhin 0	S	na	S	ki 3	ta	ta	ka

Dugun

DhaS ×	Tira	kita	taka	Dhir 2	Dhir	kita	taka
DkaS 0	Tira	kita	taka	Tu 3	na	kita	taka
TaS ×	Tira	kita	taka	Tira **2**	Tira	kita	taka
DhaS 0	Tira	kita	taka	Dhin 3	na	kita	taka

Chaugun

DhaSTira ×	kitataka	DhirDhir	kitataka	DhaSTira 2	kitataka	Tuna	kitataka
TaSTira 0	kitataka	TiraTira	kitataka	DhaSTira 3	kitataka	Dhinna	kitataka

Athgun

DhaऽTirakitataka	DhiraDhirakitataka	DhaऽTirakitataka	Tunakitataka
×			
TaऽTirakitataka	TiraTirakitataka	DhaऽTirakitataka	Dhinnakitataka
2			
DhaऽTirakitataka	DhiraDhirakitataka	DhaऽTirakitataka	Tunakitataka
0			
TaऽTirakitataka	TiraTirakitataka	DhaऽTirakitataka	Dhinnakitataka
3			

Prastar-1

DhaऽTirakitataka	DhiraDhirakitataka	DhaऽTirakitataka	DhiraDhiraakitataka
×			
DhaऽTirakitataka	DhiraDhirakitataka	DhaऽTirakitataka	Tunakitataka
2			
TaऽTirakitataka	TiraTirakitataka	TaऽTirakitataka	TiraTirakitataka
0			
DhaऽTirakitataka	DhiraDhirakitataka	DhaऽTirakitataka	Dhinnakitataka
3			

Prastar-2

DhaऽTirakitataka	DhiraDhirakitataka	DhiraDhirakitataka	DhiraDhirakitataka
×			
DhaऽTirakitataka	DhiraDhirakitataka	DhaऽTirakitataka	Tunakitataka
2			
TaऽTirakitataka	TiraTirakitataka	TiraTirakitataka	TiraTirakitataka
0			
DhaऽTirakitataka	DhiraDhirakitataka	DhaऽTirakitataka	Dhinnakitataka
3			

Prastar-3

DhaऽTirakitataka	DhiraDhirakitataka	DhiraDhirakitataka	DhaऽTirakitataka
×			
DhiraDhirakitataka	DhiraDhirakitataka	DhaऽTirakitataka	Tunakitataka
2			
TaऽTirakitataka	TiraTirakitataka	TiraTirakitataka	DhaऽTirakitataka
0			
DhiraDhirakitataka	DhiraDhirakitataka	DhaऽTirakitataka	Dhinnakitataka
3			

Prastar-4

DhaSTirakitataka ×	DhiraDhirakitataka	DhiraDhirakitataka	DhaSTirakitataka
DhaSTirakitataka 2	DhiraDhirakitataka	DhaSTirakitataka	Tunakitataka
TaSTirakitataka 0	TiraTirakitataka	TiraTirakitataka	TaSTirakitataka
DhaSTirakitataka 3	DhiraDhirakitataka	DhaSTirakitataka	Dhinnakitataka

Prastar-5

DhiraDhirakitataka ×	DhiraDhirakitataka	DhiraDhirakitataka	DhaSTirakitataka
DhaSTirakitataka 2	DhiraDhirakitataka	DhaSTirakitataka	Tunakitataka
TiraTirakitataka 0	TiraTirakitataka	TiraTirakitataka	TaSTirakitataka
DhaSTirakitataka 3	DhiraDhirakitataka	DhaSTirakitataka	Dhinnakitataka

Prastar-6

DhiraDhirakitataka ×	DhiraDhirakitataka	DhaSTirakitataka	DhiraDhirakitataka
DhiraDhirakitataka 2	DhaSTirakitataka	DhaSTirakitataka	Tunakitataka
TiraTirakitataka 0	TiraTirakitataka	TaSTirakitataka	DhiraDhirakitataka
DhiraDhirakitataka 3	DhaSTirakitataka	DhaSTirakitataka	Dhinnakitataka

Prastar-7

Dha-Tirakitataka ×	DhiraDhirakitataka	DhaSSS	DhiraDhiraakitataka
DhaSTirakitataka 2	DhiraDhirakitataka	DhaSTirakitataka	Tunakitataka
TaSTirakitataka 0	TiraTirakitataka	TaSSS	TiraTirakitataka
DhaSTirakitataka 3	DhiraDhirakitataka	DhaSTirakitataka	Dhinnakitataka

Prastar-8

DhiraDhirakitataka ×	DhiraDhirakitataka	DhiraDhirakitataka	DhiraDhirakitataka
DhaSTirakitataka 2	DhiraDhirakitataka	DhaSTirakitataka	Tunakitataka
TiraTirakitataka 0	TiraTirakitataka	TiraTirakitataka	TiraTirakitataka
DhaSTirakitataka 3	DhiraDhirakitataka	DhaSTirakitataka	Dhinnakitataka

Tihai-

Dha-Tirakitataka ×	DhiraDhirakitataka	Dha-Tirakitataka	Dhinnakitataka
Dha 2	S	Dha-Tirakitataka	DhiraDhirakitataka
Dha-Tirakitataka 0	Dhinnakitataka	Dha	S
Dha-Tirakitataka 3	DhiraDhirakitataka	Dha-Tirakitataka	Dhinnakitataka
Dha ×			

Tihai-Chakradar

Dha-Tirakitataka ×	DhiraDhirakitataka	Dha-Tirakitataka	Dhinnakitataka
Dha 2	Dha-Tirakitataka	Dhinnakitataka	Dha
Dha-Tirakitataka 0	Dhinnakitataka	Dha,	Dha-Tirakitataka
DhiraDhirakitataka 3	Dha-Tirakitataka	Dhinnakitataka	Dha
Dha-Tirakitataka ×	Dhinnakitataka	Dha	Dha-Tirakitataka
Dhinnakitataka 2	Dha,	Dha-Tirakitataka	DhiraDhirakitataka
Dha-Tirakitataka 0	Dhinnakitataka	Dha	Dha-Tirakitataka
Dhinnakitataka 3	Dha	Dha-Tirakitataka	Dhinnakitataka
Dha ×			

KAYADA-12

Ekgun

Dhin	S	Dhi	na	Tira	kita	Dhi	na	Gi	na	Tin	S	Ti	na	ki	na
×				2				0				3			
Tin	S	Ti	na	Tira	kita	Dhi	na	Gi	na	Dhin	S	Dhi	na	Gi	na
×				2				0				3			

Dugun

DhinS	Dhina	Tirakita	Dhina	Gina	TinS	Tina	kina
×				2			
TinS	Tina	Tirakita	Dhina	Gina	DhinS	Dhina	Gina
0				3			

Chaugun

DhinSDhina	TirakitaDhina	GinaTinS	Tinakina
×			
TinSTina	TirakitaDhina	GinaDhinS	DhinaGina
2			
DhinSDhina	TirakitaDhina	GinaTinS	Tinakina
0			
TinSTina	TirakitaDhina	GinaDhinS	DhinaGina
3			

Athgun

DhinSDhinaTirakitaDhina	GinaTinSTinakina
×	
TinSTinaTirakitaDhina	GinaDhinSDhinaGina
DhinSDhinaTirakitaDhina	GinaTinSTinakina
2	
TinSTinaTirakitaDhina	GinaDhinSDhinaGina
DhinSDhinaTirakitaDhina	GinaTinSTinakina
0	
TinSTinaTirakitaDhina	GinaDhinSDhinaGina
DhinSDhinaTirakitaDhina	GinaTinSTinakina
3	
TinSTinaTirakitaDhina	GinaDhinSDhinaGina

Prastar-1

DhinऽDhinaTirakitaDhina DhinऽDhinaTirakitaDhina
×
DhinऽDhinaTirakitaDhina GinaTinऽTinakina |
TinऽTinaTirakitaTina TinऽTinaTirakitaTina
2
DhinऽDhinaTirakitaDhina GinaDhinऽDhinaGina |
DhinऽDhinaTirakitaDhina DhinऽDhinaTirakitaDhina
0
DhinऽDhinaTirakitaDhina GinaTinऽTinakina |
TinऽTinaTirakitaTina TinऽTinaTirakitaTina
3
DhinऽDhinaTirakitaDhina GinaDhinऽDhinaGina |

Prastar-2

DhinऽDhinaDhinऽDhina DhinऽDhinaTirakitaDhina
×
DhinऽDhinaTirakitaDhina GinaTinऽTinakina |
TinऽTina TinऽTina TinऽTinaTirakitaTina
2
DhinऽDhinaTirakitaDhina GinaDhinऽDhinaGina |
DhinऽDhina DhinऽDhina DhinऽDhinaTirakitaDhina
0
DhinऽDhinaTirakitaDhina GinaTinऽTinakina |
TinऽTina TinऽTina TinऽTinaTirakitaTina
3
DhinऽDhinaTirakitaDhina GinaDhinऽDhinaGina |

Prastar-3

DhinऽDhinaTirakitaDhinऽ DhinaTirakita DhinऽDhina
×
DhinऽDhinaTirakitaDhina GinaTinऽTinakina |
TinऽTina TirakitaTinऽ TinaTirakita TinऽTina
2
DhinऽDhinaTirakitaDhina GinaDhinऽDhinaGina |

DhinSDhinaTirakitaDhinS DhinaTirakita DhinSDhina
0
DhinSDhinaTirakitaDhina GinaTinSTinakina |
TinSTinaTirakitaTinS TinaTirakitaTinSTina
3
DhinSDhinaTirakitaDhina GinaDhinSDhinaGina |

Prastar-4

DhinSDhina DhinSDhinS DhinSDhina Tirakita Dhina
×
DhinSDhinaTirakitaDhina GinaTinSTinakina |
TinSTinaTinSTinS TinSTinaTirakita Tina
2
DhinSDhinaTirakitaDhina GinaDhinSDhinaGina |
DhinSDhina DhinSDhinS DhinSDhinaTirakita Dhina
0
DhinSDhinaTirakitaDhina GinaTinSTinakina |
TinSTina TinSTinS TinSTinaTirakitaTina
3
DhinSDhinaTirakitaDhina GinaDhinSDhinaGina |

Prastar-5

DhinSDhinSDhinaGina DhinSDhinSDhinaGina
×
DhinSDhinaTirakitaDhina GinaTinSTinakina |
TinSTinSTinakina TinSTinSTinakina
2
DhinSDhinaTirakitaDhina GinaDhinSDhinaGina |
DhinSDhinSDhinaGina DhinSDhinSDhinaGina
0
DhinSDhinaTirakitaDhina GinaTinSTinakina |
TinSTinSTinakina TinSTinSTinakina
3
DhinSDhinaTirakitaDhina GinaDhinSDhinaGina |

Prastar-6

DhinSDhinSDhinaTirakita DhinaDhinSDhinaGina
×

DhinSDhinaTirakitaDhina GinaTinSTinakina |
TinSTinSTina Tirakita TinaTin ·Tinakina
2
DhinSDhinaTirakitaDhina GinaDhinSDhinaGina |
DhinSDhinSDhinaTirakita DhinaDhinSDhinaGina
0
DhinSDhinaTirakitaDhina GinaTinSTinakina |
TinSTinSTinaTirakita TinaTinSTinakina
3
DhinSDhinaTirakitaDhina GinaDhinSDhinaGina |

Prastar-7

TirakitaDhinSDhinaGina TirakitaDhinSDhinaGina
×
DhinSDhinaTirakitaDhina GinaTinSTinakina |
TirakitaTinSTina kina TirakitaTinSTinakina
2
DhinSDhinaTirakitaDhina GinaDhinSDhinaGina |
TirakitaDhinSDhinaGina TirakitaDhinSDhinaGina
0
DhinSDhinaTirakitaDhina GinaTinSTinakina |
TirakitaTinSTinakina TirakitaTinSTinakina
3
DhinSDhinaTirakitaDhina GinaDhinSDhinaGina |

Prastar-8

TirakitaDhinSDhinaTirakita DhinSDhinaTirakitaDhina
×
DhinSDhinaTirakitaDhina GinaTinSTinakina |
TirakitaTinSTina Tirakita TinSTinaTirakitaTina
2
DhinSDhinaTirakitaDhina GinaDhinSDhinaGina |
TirakitaDhinSDhinaTirakita DhinSDhinaTirakitaDhina
0
DhinSDhinaTirakitaDhina GinaTinSTinakina |

TirakitaTinSTinaTirakita 3	TinSTinaTirakitaTina
DhinSDhinaTirakitaDhina	GinaDhinSDhinaGina |

Tihai-Chakradar

DhinSDhinaTirakitaDhina ×	GinaDhinSDhinaGina
DhaSSSGinaDhinS	DhinaGina DhaSSS |
GinaDhinSDhinaGina 2	DhaSSSDhinSDhina
TirakitaDhina GinaDhinS	DhinaGina DhaSSS |
GinaDhinSDhinaGina 0	DhaSSSGinaDhinS
DhinaGina DhaSSS	Dhin·DhinaTirakitaDhina |
GinaDhinSDhinaGina 3	DhaSSSGinaDhinS
DhinaGina DhaSSS	GinaDhinSDhinaGina |
Dha ×	

Kayada-13

Dugun

Dhagi ×	naDha	Tirakita	Dhagi	naDha 2	Tirakita	DhaDha	Tirakita
Dhagi 0	naDha	Tirakita	Tinna	kitataka 3	Tirakita	takTa-	Tirakita
Taki ×	naTa	Tirakita	Taki	naTa 2	Tirakita	TaTa	Tirakita
Dhagi 0	naDha	Tirakita	Dhinna	kitataka 3	Tirakita	takDha-	Tirakita

Chaugun

DhaginaDha ×	TirakitaDhagi	naDhaTirakita	DhaDhaTirakita
DhaginaDha 2	TirakitaTinna	kitatakaTirakita	takTa-Tirakita
TakinaTa 0	TirakitaTaki	naTaTirakita	TaTaTirakita
DhaginaDha 3	TirakitaDhinna	kitatakaTirakita	takDha-Tirakita

Prastar-1

DhaginaDha ×	TirakitaDhagi	naDhaTirakita	DhaDhaTirakita
DhaginaDha 2	TirakitaDhagi	naDhaTirakita	DhaDhaTirakita
DhaginaDha 0	TirakitaDhagi	naDhaTirakita	DhaDhaTirakita
DhaginaDha 3	TirakitaTinna	kitatakaTirakita	takTa-Tirakita
TakinaTa ×	TirakitaTaki	naTaTirakita	TaTaTirakita
TakinaTa 2	TirakitaTaki	naTaTirakita	TaTaTirakita
DhaginaDha 0	TirakitaDhagi	naDhaTirakita	DhaDhaTirakita
DhaginaDha 3	TirakitaDhinna	kitatakaTirakita	takDha-Tirakita

Prastar-2

DhaginaDha ×	Tirakita DhaDha	TirakitaDhagi	naDhaTirakita
DhaginaDha 2	TirakitaTinna	kitatakaTirakita	takTa-Tirakita
TakinaTa 0	Tirakita TaTa	TirakitaTaki	naTaTirakita
DhaginaDha 3	TirakitaDhinna	kitatakaTirakita	takDha-Tirakita

Prastar-3

DhaginaDha ×	Tirakita DhaDha	TirakitaDhagi	naDhaTirakita
DhaginaDha 2	Tirakita DhaDha	TirakitaDhagi	naDhaTirakita
DhaginaDha 0	Tirakita DhaDha	Tirakita Dhagi	naDhaTirakita
DhaginaDha 3	TirakitaTinna	kitatakaTirakita	takTa-Tirakita
TakinaTa ×	Tirakita TaTa	TirakitaTaki	naTaTirakita
TakinaTa 2	Tirakita TaTa	TirakitaTaki	naTaTirakita

DhaginaDha	Tirakita DhaDha	TirakitaDhagi	naDhaTirakita
0			
DhaginaDha	TirakitaDhinna	kitatakaTirakita	takDha-Tirakita
3			

Prastar-4

DhaDhaTirakita	DhaginaDha	Tirakita Dhagi	naDhaTirakita
×			
DhaginaDha	TirakitaTinna	kitatakaTirakita	takTa-Tirakita
2			
TaTaTirakita	TakinaTa	Tirakita Taki	naTaTirakita
0			
DhaginaDha	TirakitaDhinna	kitatakaTirakita	takDha-Tirakita
3			

Prastar-5

DhaDhaTirakita	DhaginaDha	Tirakita Dhagi	naDhaTirakita
×			
DhaDhaTirakita	DhaginaDha	Tirakita Dhagi	naDhaTirakita
2			
DhaDhaTirakita	DhaginaDha	Tirakita Dhagi	naDhaTirakita
0			
DhaginaDha	TirakitaTinna	kitatakaTirakita	takTa-Tirakita
3			
TaTaTirakita	TakinaTa	Tirakita Taki	naTaTirakita
×			
TaTaTirakita	TakinaTa	Tirakita Taki	naTaTirakita
2			
DhaDhaTirakita	DhaginaDha	Tirakita Dhagi	naDhaTirakita
0			
DhaginaDha	TirakitaDhinna	kitatakaTirakita	takDha-Tirakita
3			

Prastar-6

DhaginaDha	Tirakita DhaDha	DhaginaDha	Tirakita DhaDha
×			
DhaginaDha	TirakitaTinna	kitatakaTirakita	takTa-Tirakita
2			
TakinaTa	Tirakita TaTa	TakinaTa	Tirakita TaTa
0			
DhaginaDha	TirakitaDhinna	kitatakaTirakita	takDha-Tirakita
3			

Prastar-7

DhaginaDha	Tirakita DhaDha	Tirakita DhaDha	Tirakita DhaDha
×			
DhaginaDha	TirakitaTinna	kitatakaTirakita	takTa-Tirakita
2			
TakinaTa	Tirakita TaTa	Tirakita TaTa	Tirakita TaTa
0			
DhaginaDha	TirakitaDhinna	kitatakaTirakita	takDha-Tirakita
3			

Prastar-8

DhaginaDha	Tirakita Dha-Tira	kita Dha-Tirakita	DhaDha Tirakita
×			
DhaginaDha	TirakitaTinna	kitatakaTirakita	takTa-Tirakita
2			
TakinaTa	Tirakita Ta-Tira	kita Ta-Tirakita	TaTa Tirakita
0			
DhaginaDha	TirakitaDhinna	kitatakaTirakita	takDha-Tirakita
3			

Prastar-9

DhaginaDha	Tirakita Dha-Tira	kita Dha-Tirakita	DhaDha Tirakita
×			
DhaginaDha	Tirakita Dha-Tira	kita Dha-Tirakita	DhaDha Tirakita
2			
DhaginaDha	Tirakita Dha-Tira	kita Dha-Tirakita	DhaDha Tirakita
0			
DhaginaDha	TirakitaTinna	kitatakaTirakita	takTa-Tirakita
3			
TakinaTa	Tirakita Ta-Tira	kita Ta-Tirakita	TaTa Tirakita
×			
TakinaTa	Tirakita Ta-Tira	kita Ta-Tirakita	TaTa Tirakita
2			
DhaginaDha	Tirakita Dha-Tira	kita Dha-Tirakita	DhaDha Tirakita
0			
DhaginaDha	TirakitaDhinna	kitatakaTirakita	takDha-Tirakita
3			

Prastar-10

DhaginaDha ×	ginaDhagi	naDha-Tirakita	DhaDha Tirakita
DhaginaDha 2	TirakitaTinna	kitatakaTirakita	takTa-Tirakita
TakinaTa 0	kinaTaki	naTa-Tirakita	TaTaTirakita
DhaginaDha 3	TirakitaDhinna	kitatakaTirakita	takDha-Tirakita

Prastar-11

DhaginaDha ×	TirakitaTinna	kitatakaTirakita	takTa-Tirakita
TakinaTa 2	TirakitaDhinna	kitatakaTirakita	takDha-Tirakita
DhaginaDha 0	TirakitaTinna	kitatakaTirakita	takTa-Tirakita
TakinaTa 3	TirakitaDhinna	kitatakaTirakita	takDha-Tirakita

Prastar-12

kitatakaTirakita ×	takTa-Tirakita	kitatakaTirakita	takDha-Tirakita
kitatakaTirakita 2	takTa-Tirakita	kitatakaTirakita	takDha-Tirakita
kitatakaTirakita 0	takTa-Tirakita	kitatakaTirakita	takDha-Tirakita
kitatakaTirakita 3	takTa-Tirakita	kitatakaTirakita	takDha-Tirakita

Tihai

DhaginaDha ×	TirakitaDhinna	kitatakaTirakita	takDha-Tirakita
Dha 2	S	DhaginaDha	TirakitaDhinna
kitatakaTirakita 0	takDha-Tirakita	Dha	S
DhaginaDha 3	TirakitaDhinna	kitatakaTirakita	takDha-Tirakita
Dha ×			

Kayada-14 (Ada Laya)

×	DhaSTirakita	Dhagina	Dha	Dhagina
2	DhaSTirakita	Dhagina	Dhagetin	nakina
0	TaSTirakita	Takina	Ta	Takina
3	DhaSTirakita	Dhagina	Dhagedhin	nagina

Prastar-1

×	DhaSTirakita	Dhagina	Dha	Dhagina
2	DhaSTirakita	Dhagina	Dha	Dhagina
0	DhaSTirakita	Dhagina	Dha	Dhagina
3	DhaSTirakita	Dhagina	Dhagetin	nakina
×	TaSTirakita	Takina	Ta	Takina
2	TaSTirakita	Takina	Ta	Takina
0	DhaSTirakita	Dhagina	Dha	Dhagina
3	DhaSTirakita	Dhagina	Dhagedhin	nagina

Prastar-2

×	DhaSTirakita	Dhagina	Dha	Dhagina
2	Dha	Dhagina	Dha	Dhagina
0	DhaSTirakita	Dhagina	Dha	Dhagina
3	DhaSTirakita	Dhagina	Dhagetin	nakina

×	TaSTirakita	Takina	Ta	Takina
2	Ta	Takina	Ta	Takina
0	DhaSTirakita	Dhagina	Dha	Dhagina
3	DhaSTirakita	Dhagina	Dhagedhin	nagina

Prastar-3

×	DhaSTirakita	Dhagina	DhaSTirakita	Dhagina
2	DhaSTirakita	Dhagina	Dha	Dhagina
0	DhaSTirakita	Dhagina	Dha	Dhagina
3	DhaSTirakita	Dhagina	Dhagetin	nakina
×	TaSTirakita	Takina	TaSTirakita	Takina
2	TaSTirakita	Takina	Ta	Takina
0	DhaSTirakita	Dhagina	Dha	Dhagina
3	DhaSTirakita	Dhagina	Dhagedhin	nagina

Prastar-4

×	DhaSTirakita	Dhagina	Dhagina	Dhagina
2	DhaSTirakita	Dhagina	Dha	Dhagina
0	DhaSTirakita	Dhagina	Dha	Dhagina
3	DhaSTirakita	Dhagina	Dhagetin	nakina

TaSTirakita	Takina	Takina	Takina
×			
TaSTirakita	Takina	Ta	Takina
2			
DhaSTirakita	Dhagina	Dha	Dhagina
0			
DhaSTirakita	Dhagina	Dhagedhin	nagina
3			

Prastar-5

DhaSTirakita	Dhagina	Dhagetin	nakina
×			
TaSTirakita	Dhagina	DhageDhin	nagina
2			
DhaSTirakita	Dhagina	Dhagetin	nakina
0			
TaSTirakita	Dhagina	DhageDhin	nagina
3			

Prastar-6

DhaSTirakita	Dhagina	DhaSTirakita	Dhagina
×			
DhaSTirakita	Dhagina	DhageTin	nakina
2			
TaSTirakita	Takina	TaSTirakita	Takina
0			
DhaSTirakita	Dhagina	DhageDhin	nagina
3			

Prastar-7

DhaSTirakita	Dhagina	Dhagina	DhaSTirakita
×			
DhaSTirakita	Dhagina	DhageTin	nakina
2			
TaSTirakita	Takina	Takina	TasTirakita
0			
DhaSTirakita	Dhagina	DhageDhin	nagina
3			

Prastar-8

×	DhaSTirakita	DhaSTirakita	DhaSTirakita	Dhagina
2	DhaSTirakita	Dhagina	DhageTin	nakina
0	TaSTirakita	TaSTirakita	TaSTirakita	Takina
3	DhaSTirakita	Dhagina	DhageDhin	nagina

Prastar-9

×	DhaSTirakita	DhaSTirakita	Dhagina	DhaSTirakita
2	DhaSTirakita	Dhagina	DhageTin	nakina
0	TaSTirakita	TaSTirakita	Takina	DhaSTirakita
3	DhaSTirakita	Dhagina	DhageDhin	nagina

Prastar-10

×	Dhagedhin	naDhage	dhinnaDha	gedhinna
2	DhaSTirakita	Dhagina	DhageTin	nakina
0	Taketin	naTake	tinnaTa	ketinna
3	DhaSTirakita	Dhagina	DhageDhin	nagina

Prastar-11

×	DhageDha	geDhage	DhageDhin	nagina
2	DhaSTirakita	Dhagina	DhageTin	nakina
0	TakeTa	keTake	TakeTin	nakina
3	DhaSTirakita	Dhagina	DhageDhin	nagina

Chakradar-Tihai

DhaSTirakita ×	Dhagina	DhageDhin	nagina
Dha 2	DhageDhin	nagina	Dha
DhageDhin 0	nagina	Dha	DhaSTirakita
Dhagina 3	DhageDhin	nagina	Dha
DhageDhin ×	nagina	Dha	DhageDhin
Nagina 2	Dha	DhaSTirakita	Dhagina
DhageDhin 0	nagina	Dha	DhageDhin
nagina 3	Dha	DhageDhin	nagina
Dha ×			

Rela of Banaras Gharana

In Chaugun Laya

DhaऽTira	kitataka	Tuऽnaऽ	kitataka	TaऽTira	kitataka	Dhinऽnaऽ	kitataka
×				2			
DhaऽTira	kitataka	Tuऽnaऽ	kitataka	TaऽTira	kitataka	Dhinऽnaऽ	kitataka
0				3			
DhaऽTira	kitataka	Tuऽnaऽ	kitataka	TaऽTira	kitataka	Dhinऽnaऽ	kitataka
×				2			
DhaऽTira	kitataka	Tuऽnaऽ	kitataka	TaऽTira	kitataka	Dhinऽnaऽ	kitataka
0				3			

Athgun

DhaऽTirakitataka	Tuऽnaऽkitataka	TaऽTirakitataka	Dhinऽnaऽkitataka
×			
DhaऽTirakitataka	Tuऽnaऽkitataka	TaऽTirakitataka	Dhinऽnaऽkitataka
2			
DhaऽTirakitataka	Tuऽnaऽkitataka	TaऽTirakitataka	Dhinऽnaऽkitataka
0			
DhaऽTirakitataka	Tuऽnaऽkitataka	TaऽTirakitataka	Dhinऽnaऽkitataka
3			

Prastar-1

DhaऽTirakitataka	Dhaऽऽऽkitataka	DhaऽTirakitataka	Tuऽnaऽkitataka
×			
TaऽTirakitataka	Taऽऽऽkitataka	DhaऽTirakitataka	Dhinऽnaऽkitataka
2			
DhaऽTirakitataka	Dhaऽऽऽkitataka	DhaऽTirakitataka	Tuऽnaऽkitataka
0			
TaऽTirakitataka	Taऽऽऽkitataka	DhaऽTirakitataka	Dhinऽnaऽkitataka
3			

Prastar-2

DhaऽTirakitaDhaऽ	TirakitaDhaऽDhaऽ	DhaऽTirakitataka	Tuऽnaऽkitataka
×			
TaऽTirakitaTaऽ	TirakitaTaऽTaऽ	DhaऽTirakitataka	Dhinऽnaऽkitataka
2			
DhaऽTirakitaDhaऽ	TirakitaDhaऽDhaऽ	DhaऽTirakitataka	Tuऽnaऽkitataka
0			
TaऽTirakitaTaऽ	TirakitaTaऽTaऽ	DhaऽTirakitataka	Dhinऽnaऽkitataka
3			

Prastar-3

DhaSSSDhaSTira	kitakitaDhaSSS	DhaSTirakitataka	TuSnaSkitataka
×			
TaSSSTaSTira	kitatakaTaSSS	DhaSTirakitataka	DhinSnaSkitataka
2			
DhaSSSDhaSTira	kitakitaDhaSSS	DhaSTirakitataka	TuSnaSkitataka
0			
TaSSSTaSTira	kitatakaTaSSS	DhaSTirakitataka	DhinSnaSkitataka
3			

Prastar-4

DhaSTirakitaDhaS	SSSDhaSTirakita	DhaSTirakitataka	TuSnaSkitataka
×			
TaSTirakitaTaS	SSSTaSTirakita	DhaSTirakitataka	DhinSnaSkitataka
2			
DhaSTirakitaDhaS	SSSDhaSTirakita	DhaSTirakitataka	TuSnaSkitataka
0			
TaSTirakitaTaS	SSSTaSTirakita	DhaSTirakitataka	DhinSnaSkitataka
3			

Prastar-5

TirakitaDhaSTira	kitatakaTirakita	DhaSTirakitataka	TuSnaSkitataka
×			
TirakitaTaSTira	kitatakaTirakita	DhaSTirakitataka	DhinSnaSkitataka
2			
TirakitaDhaSTira	kitatakaTirakita	DhaSTirakitataka	TuSnaSkitataka
0			
TirakitaTaSTira	kitatakaTirakita	DhaSTirakitataka	DhinSnaSkitataka
3			

Prastar-6

TirakitaDhinSnaS	kitatakaTirakita	DhaSTirakitataka	TuSnaSkitataka
×			
TirakitaTinSnaS	kitatakaTirakita	DhaSTirakitataka	DhinSnaSkitataka
2			
TirakitaDhinSnaS	kitatakaTirakita	DhaSTirakitataka	TuSnaSkitataka
0			
TirakitaTinSnaS	kitatakaTirakita	DhaSTirakitataka	DhinSnaSkitataka
3			

Tihai

TirakitaDhinSnaS ×	kitatakaTirakita	DhaSTirakitataka	DhinSnaSkitataka
Dha 2	S	TirakitaDhinSnaS	kitatakaTirakita
Dha-Tirakitataka 0	Dhin-na-kitataka	Dha	S
TirakitaDhinSnaS 3	kitatakaTirakita	DhaSTirakitataka	DhinSnaSkitataka
Dha ×			

Rela-2

In Athgun Laya

Tira kitatakaTira	kitatakaTuSnaS	Tira kitatakaTira	kitatakaDhinSnaS
×			
Tira kitatakaTira	kitatakaTuSnaS	Tira kitatakaTira	kitatakaDhinSnaS
2			
Tira kitatakaTira	kitatakaTuSnaS	Tira kitatakaTira	kitatakaDhinSnaS
0			
Tira kitatakaTira	kitatakaTuSnaS	Tira kitatakaTira	kitatakaDhinSnaS
3			

Prastar-1

Tira kitatakaTira	kitatakaTakaTaka	Tira kitatakaTira	kitatakaTuSnaS
×			
Tira kitatakaTira	kitatakaTakaTaka	Tira kitatakaTira	kitatakaDhinSnaS
2			
Tira kitatakaTira	kitatakaTakaTaka	Tira kitatakaTira	kitatakaTuSnaS
0			
Tira kitatakaTira	kitatakaTakaTaka	Tira kitatakaTira	kitatakaDhinSnaS
3			

Prastar-2

Tira kitatakaTira	kitatakaTakaTaka	Tira kitatakaTira	kitatakaTakaTaka
×			
Tira kitatakaTira	kitatakaTakaTaka	Tira kitatakaTira	kitatakaTu-na-
2			
Tira kitatakaTira	kitatakaTakaTaka	Tira kitatakaTira	kitatakaTakaTaka
0			
Tira kitatakaTira	kitatakaTakaTaka	Tira kitatakaTira	kitatakaDhinSnaS
3			

Prastar-3

Tira kitatakaTira	kitatakaTirakita	takaTirakitataka	TirakitaTuSnaS
×			
Tira kitatakaTira	kitatakaTirakita	takaTirakitataka	TirakitaDhinSnaS
2			
Tira kitatakaTira	kitatakaTirakita	takaTirakitataka	TirakitaTuSnaS
0			
Tira kitatakaTira	kitatakaTirakita	takaTirakitataka	TirakitaDhinSnaS
3			

Prastar-4

KitatakaTirakita	takaTirakitataka	Tira kitatakaTira	kitatakaTuSnaS
×			
KitatakaTirakita	takaTirakitataka	Tira kitatakaTira	kitatakaDhinSnaS
2			
KitatakaTirakita	takaTirakitataka	Tira kitatakaTira	kitatakaTuSnaS
0			
KitatakaTirakita	takaTirakitataka	Tira kitatakaTira	kitatakaDhinSnaS
3			

Prastar-5

KitatakaTirakita	takaTirakitataka	KitatakaTirakita	takaTirakitataka
×			
KitatakaTirakita	takaTirakitataka	Tira kitatakaTira	kitatakaTuSnaS
2			
KitatakaTirakita	takaTirakitataka	KitatakaTirakita	takaTirakitataka
0			
KitatakaTirakita	takaTirakitataka	Tira kitatakaTira	kitatakaDhinSnaS
3			

Prastar-6

Tira kitatakakita	takaTira kitataka	Tira kitatakaTira	kitatakaTunaS
×			
Tira kitatakakita	takaTira kitataka	Tira kitatakaTira	kitatakaDhinSnaS
2			
Tira kitatakakita	takaTira kitataka	Tira kitatakaTira	kitatakaTuSnaS
0			
Tira kitatakakita	takaTira kitataka	Tira kitatakaTira	kitatakaDhinSnaS
3			

Tihai

Kitataka,Tirakita	taka,Tirakitataka	Tira kitataka,Tira	kitatakaDhinSnaS
×			
Dha	S	Kitataka,Tirakita	taka,Tirakitataka
2			
Tira kitataka,Tira	kitatakaDhinSnaS	Dha	S
0			
Kitataka,Tirakita	taka,Tirakitataka	Tira kitataka,Tira	kitatakaDhinSnaS
3			
Dha			
×			

Chakradar-Tihai

Kitataka,Tirakita ×	taka,Tirakitataka	Tira kitataka,Tira	kitatakaDhinSnaS
Dha 2	Tira kitataka,Tira	kitatakaDhinSnaS	Dha
Tira kitataka,Tira 0	kitatakaDhinSnaS	Dha	Kitataka,Tirakita
taka,Tirakitataka 3	Tira kitataka,Tira	kitatakaDhinSnaS	Dha
Tira kitataka,Tira ×	kitatakaDhinSnaS	Dha	Tira kitataka,Tira
kitatakaDhinSnaS 2	Dha,	Kitataka,Tirakita	taka,Tirakitataka
Tira kitataka,Tira 0	kitatakaDhinSnaS	Dha	Tira kitataka,Tira
kitatakaDhinSnaS 3	Dha	Tira kitataka,Tira	kitatakaDhinSnaS
Dha ×			

Rela-3

In Chaugun Laya

DhaSTira ×	Gheranage	Dinataka	DhaSTira
Gheranage 2	Dinataka	TaSTira	kitataka
TaSTira 0	Keranage	Tinataka	TaSTira
Gheranage 3	Dinataka	DhaSTira	kitataka

Prastar-1

DhaSTira ×	kitaDhaS	tirakita	DhaSTira
Gheranage 2	Dinataka	DhaSTira	kitataka
DhaSTira 0	Gheranage	Dinataka	DhaSTira
Gheranage 3	Dinataka	TaSTira	kitataka
TaSTira ×	kitaTaS	tirakita	TaSTira
Keranake 2	Tinataka	TaSTira	kitataka
DhaSTira 0	Gheranage	Dinataka	DhaSTira
Gheranage 3	Dinataka	DhaSTira	kitataka

Prastar-2

DhaSTira ×	kitaDhaS	tirakita	DhaSTira
kitaDhaS 2	tirakita	DhaSTira	Gheranage
DhaSTira 0	Gheranage	Dinataka	DhaSTira
Gheranage 3	Dinataka	TaSTira	kitataka

TaSTira	kitaTaS	tirakita	TaSTira
×			
kitaTaS	tirakita	TaSTira	keranake
2			
DhaSTira	Gheranage	Dinataka	DhaSTira
0			
Gheranage	Dinataka	DhaSTira	kitataka
3			

Prastar-3

DhaSSS	DhaSTira	kitataka	DhaSTira
×			
Gheranage	Dinataka	DhaSTira	kitataka
2			
DhaSTira	Gheranage	Dinataka	DhaSTira
0			
Gheranage	Dinataka	TaSTira	kitataka
3			
TaSSS	TaSTira	kitataka	TaSTira
×			
keranake	Tinataka	TaSTira	kitataka
2			
DhaSTira	Gheranage	Dinataka	DhaSTira
0			
Gheranage	Dinataka	DhaSTira	kitataka
3			

Prastar-4

DhaSTira	Gheranage	Dinataka	DhaSTira
×			
kitataka	Dha-Tira	Gheranage	Dinataka
2			
DhaSTira	Gheranage	Dinataka	DhaSTira
0			
Gheranage	Dinataka	TaSTira	kitataka
3			
TaSTira	keranake	Tinataka	TaSTira
×			

Kitataka	TaSTira	keranake	Tinataka
2			
DhaSTira	Gheranage	Dinataka	DhaSTira
0			
Gheranage	Dinataka	DhaSTira	kitataka
3			

Prastar-5

Dinataka	DhaSTira	kitataka	DhaSTira
×			
Gheranage	Dinataka	DhaSTira	kitataka
2			
DhaSTira	Gheranage	Dinataka	DhaSTira
0			
Gheranage	Dinataka	TaSTira	kitataka
3			
Tinataka	TaSTira	kitataka	TaSTira
×			
keranake	Tinataka	Ta-Tira	kitataka
2			
DhaSTira	Gheranage	Dinataka	DhaSTira
0			
Gheranage	Dinataka	DhaSTira	kitataka
3			

Prastar-6

Dinataka	DhaSTira	Gheranage	Dinataka
×			
DhaSTira	kitataka	DhaSTira	kitataka
2			
DhaSTira	Gheranage	Dinataka	DhaSTira
0			
Gheranage	Dinataka	TaSTira	kitataka
3			
Tinataka	TaSTira	keranake	Tinataka
×			

TaऽTira 2	kitataka	TaऽTira	kitataka
DhaऽTira 0	Gheranage	Dinataka	DhaऽTira
Gheranage 3	Dinataka	DhaऽTira	kitataka

Tihai

DhaऽTira ×	Gheranage	Dinataka	DhaऽTira
Gheranage 2	Dinataka	DhaऽTira	kitataka
Dha 0	ऽ	ऽ	ऽ
DhaऽTira 3	Gheranage	Dinataka	DhaऽTira
Gheranage ×	Dinataka	DhaऽTira	kitataka
Dha 2	ऽ	ऽ	ऽ
DhaऽTira 0	Gheranage	Dinataka	DhaऽTira
Gheranage 3	Dinataka	DhaऽTira	kitataka
Dha ×			

Rela-4

In Athgun laya

DhinnakitatakaS ×	DhaSTirakitataka	DhaSTirakitataka	Dhinnakitataka
DhaSTirakitataka 2	Dhinnakitataka	Tinnakitataka	TaSTirakitataka
Tinnakitataka 0	TaSTirakitataka	Ta Tirakitataka	Tinnakitataka
TaSTirakitataka 3	Dhinnakitataka	Dhinnakitataka	DhaSTirakitataka

Prastar-1

Dhinnakitataka ×	DhaSTirakitataka	DhaSTirakitataka	Dhinnakitataka
Dhinnakitataka 2	DhaSTirakitataka	DhaSTirakitataka	Dhinnakitataka
Dhinnakitataka 0	DhaSTirakitataka	DhaSTirakitataka	Dhinnakitataka
DhaSTirakitataka 3	Dhinnakitataka	Tinnakitataka	TaSTirakitataka
Tinnakitataka ×	TaSTirakitataka	TaSTirakitataka	Tinnakitataka
Tinnakitataka 2	TaSTirakitataka	TaSTirakitataka	Tinnakitataka
Dhinnakitataka 0	DhaSTirakitataka	DhaSTirakitataka	Dhinnakitataka
DhaSTirakitataka 3	Dhinnakitataka	Dhinnakitataka	DhaSTirakitataka

Prastar-2

Dhinnakitataka ×	DhaSTirakitataka	Dhinnakitataka	DhaSTirakitataka
Dhinnakitataka 2	DhaSTirakitataka	DhaSTirakitataka	Dhinnakitataka
Dhinnakitataka 0	DhaSTirakitataka	DhaSTirakitataka	Dhinnakitataka
DhaTirakitataka 3	Dhinnakitataka	Tinnakitataka	TaSTirakitataka

Tinnakitataka	TaऽTirakitataka	Tinnakitataka	TaऽTirakitataka
×			
Tinnakitataka	TaऽTirakitataka	TaऽTirakitataka	Tinnakitataka
2			
Dhinnakitataka	DhaऽTirakitataka	DhaऽTirakitataka	Dhinnakitataka
0			
DhaऽTirakitataka	Dhinnakitataka	Dhinnakitataka	DhaऽTirakitataka
3			

Prastar-3

Dhinnakitataka	DhaऽTirakitataka	DhaऽTirakitataka	Tinnakitataka
×			
Tinnakitataka	TaऽTirakitataka	DhaऽTirakitataka	Dhinnakitataka
2			
Dhinnakitataka	DhaऽTirakitataka	DhaऽTirakitataka	Tinnakitataka
0			
Tinnakitataka	TaऽTirakitataka	DhaऽTirakitataka	Dhinnakitataka
3			

Prastar-4

Dhinnakitataka	Dhinnakitataka	Dhinnakitataka	DhaऽTirakitataka
×			
Dhinnakitataka	DhaऽTirakitataka	DhaऽTirakitataka	Tinnakitataka
2			
Tinnakitataka	Tinnakitataka	Tinnakitataka	TaऽTirakitataka
0			
Dhinnakitataka	DhaऽTirakitataka	DhaऽTirakitataka	Dhinnakitataka
3			

Prastar-5

DhinnaDhinna	Dhinnakitataka	Dhinnakitataka	DhaऽTirakitataka
×			
DhaऽTirakitataka	Dhinnakitataka	Tinnakitataka	TaऽTirakitataka
2			
TinnaTinna	Tinnakitataka	Tinnakitataka	TaऽTirakitataka
0			
DhaऽTirakitataka	Dhinnakitataka	Dhinnakitataka	DhaऽTirakitataka
3			

Prastar-6

DhinnaDhinna ×	kitatakaDhinna	Dhinnakitataka	DhaSTirakitataka
DhaSTirakitataka 2	Dhinnakitataka	Tinnakitataka	TaSTirakitataka
TinnaTinna 0	kitatakaTinna	Tinnakitataka	TaSTirakitataka
DhaSTirakitataka 3	Dhinnakitataka	Dhinnakitataka	DhaSTirakitataka

Prastar-7

DhaSTirakitataka ×	Dhinnakitataka	Tinnakitataka	TaSTirakitataka
TaSTirakitataka 2	Tinnakitataka	Dhinnakitataka	DhaSTirakitataka
DhaSTirakitataka 0	Dhinnakitataka	Tinnakitataka	TaSTirakitataka
TaSTirakitataka 3	Tinnakitataka	Dhinnakitataka	DhaSTirakitataka

Tihai

DhaSTirakitataka ×	Dhinnakitataka	Dhinnakitataka	DhaSTirakitataka
Dha 2	S	DhaSTirakitataka	Dhinnakitataka
Dhinnakitataka 0	DhaSTirakitataka	Dha	S
DhaSTirakitataka 3	Dhinnakitataka	Dhinnakitataka	DhaSTirakitataka
Dha ×			

Gat-Kayada of Banaras Gharana

Dhinna	Kitataka	Dha	DhaऽStira	Gheranage	Tet	Dhinna	Kitataka
×				2			
Gheranage	Gheranage	Dhinna	Kitataka	DhiraDhira	Kitataka	TaऽStira	Kitataka
0				3			
Tinna	kitataka	Ta	TaऽTira	Keranake	Tet	Tinna	kitataka
×				2			
Gheranage	Gheranage	Dhinna	Kitataka	DhiraDhira	kitataka	DhaऽStira	kitataka
0				3			

Prastar-1

Dhinna	Kitataka	Dha	DhaऽStira	Gheranage	Tet	Dhinna	Kitataka
×				2			
Dhinna	Kitataka	Dha	DhaऽStira	Gheranage	Tet	Dhinna	Kitataka
0				3			
Dhinna	Kitataka	Dha	DhaऽStira	Gheranage	Tet	Dhinna	Kitataka
×				2			
Gheranage	Gheranage	Dhinna	Kitataka	DhiraDhira	kitataka	TaऽStira	Kitataka
0				3			
Tinna	kitataka	Ta	TaऽTira	Keranake	Tet	Tinna	kitataka
×				2			
Tinna	kitataka	Ta	TaऽTira	Keranake	Tet	Tinna	kitataka
0				3			
Dhinna	kitaaka	Dha	DhaऽStira	Gheranage	Tet	Dhinna	Kitataka
×				2			
Gheranage	Gheranage	Dhinna	kitaaka	DhiraDhira	kitataka	DhaऽStira	kitataka
0				3			

Prastar-2

Gheranake	Gheranake	Dhinna	Kitataka	DhiraDhira	kitataka	Ta-Tira	Kitataka
×				2			
Keranake	Keranake	Tinna	Kitataka	DhiraDhira	kitataka	DhaऽStira	Kitataka
0				3			
Gheranake	Gheranake	Dhinna	Kitataka	DhiraDhira	kitataka	TaऽStira	Kitataka
×				2			
Keranake	Keranake	Tinna	Kitataka	DhiraDhira	kitataka	DhaऽStira	Kitataka
0				3			

Prastar-3

Gheranake	Gheranake	Dhinna	Kitataka	Gheranake	Gheranake	Dhinna	Kitataka
×				2			
Gheranake	Gheranake	Dhinna	Kitataka	DhiraDhira	kitataka	Dhaऽtira	Kitataka
0				3			
Keranake	Keranae	Tinna	Kitataka	Keranake	Keranae	Tinna	Kitataka
×				2			
Gheranake	Gheranake	Dhinna	Kitataka	DhiraDhira	kitataka	Dhaऽtira	Kitataka
0				3			

Prastar-4

Gheranake	Dhinna	Kitataka	Gheranake	Dhinna	kitaaka	Dhinna	Kitataka
×				2			
Gheranake	Gheranake	Dhinna	Kitataka	DhiraDhira	kitataka	Ta-tira	Kitataka
0				3			
Keranake	Tinna	Kitataka	Keranake	Tinna	Kitataka	Tinna	Kitataka
×				2			
Gheranake	Gheranake	Dhinna	Kitataka	DhiraDhira	kitataka	Dhaऽtira	Kitataka
0				3			

Tihai

Gheranake	Gheranake	Dhinna	Kitatak	DhiraDhira	kitataka	Dhaऽtira	Kitatak
×				2			
Dha	ऽ	ऽ	ऽ	Gheranake	Gheranake	Dhinna	Kitatak
0				3			
DhiraDhira	kitataka	Dhaऽtira	Kitatak	Dha	ऽ	ऽ	ऽ
×				2			
Gheranake	Gheranake	Dhinna	Kitatak	DhiraDhira	kitataka	Dhaऽtira	Kitatak
0				3			
Dha							
×							

Gat-Kayada-2

Dintaka	Dintaka	TakaDin	TakaDin	TakaTaka	Dintaka	DhaSTira	kitataka
×				2			
TakaTira	kitaDha	Gheranage	Dintaka	DhirDhir	kitataka	TaSTira	kitataka
0				3			
Tintaka	Tintaka	TakaTin	TakaTin	TakaTaka	Tintaka	TaSTira	kitataka
×				2			
TakaTira	kitaDhaS	Gheranage	Dintaka	DhirDhir	kitataka	DhaSTira	kitataka
0				3			

Prastar-1

Dintaka	Dintaka	TakaDin	TakaDin	TakaTaka	Dintaka	DhaSTira	kitataka
×				2			
Dintaka	Dintaka	TakaDin	TakaDin	TakaTaka	Dintaka	DhaSTira	kitataka
0				3			
Dintaka	Dintaka	TakaDin	TakaDin	TakaTaka	Dintaka	DhaSTira	kitataka
×				2			
TakaTira	kitaDhaS	Gheranage	Dintaka	DhirDhir	kitataka	TaSTira	kitataka
0				3			
Tintaka	Tintaka	TakaTin	TakaTin	TakaTaka	Tintaka	TaSTira	kitataka
×				2			
Tintaka	Tintaka	TakaTin	TakaTin	TakaTaka	Tintaka	TaSTira	kitataka
0				3			
Dintaka	Dintaka	TakaDin	TakaDin	TakaTaka	Dintaka	DhaSTira	kitataka
×				2			
TakaTira	kitaDhaS	Gheranage	Dintaka	DhirDhir	kitataka	DhaSTira	kitataka
0				3			

Prastar-2

TakaTira	kitaDhaS	Gheranage	Dintaka	DhirDhir	kitataka	TaSTira	kitataka
×				2			
TakaTira	kitaTaS	Keranake	Tintaka	DhirDhir	kitataka	DhaSTira	kitataka
0				3			

Prastar-3

TakaTira	kitaDhaS	Gheranage	Dintaka	TakaTira	kitaDhaS	Gheranage	Dintaka
×				2			
TakaTira	kitaDhaS	Gheranage	Dintaka	DhirDhir	kitataka	TaSTira	kitataka
0				3			

TakaTira	kitaTaऽ	Keranake	Tintaka	TakaTira	kitaTaऽ	Keranake	Tintaka
×				2			
TakaTira	kitaDhaऽ	Gheranage	Dintaka	DhirDhir	kitataka	DhaऽTira	kitataka
0				3			

Prastar-4

TakaTira	kitaDhaऽ	Gheranage	Dintaka	DhaऽGhera	nageDhaऽ	Gheranage	Dintaka
×				2			
TakaTira	kitaDhaऽ	Gheranage	Dintaka	DhirDhir	kitataka	TaऽTira	kitataka
0				3			
TakaTira	kitaTaऽ	Keranake	Tintaka	Taऽkera	nakeTaऽ	Keranake	Tintaka
×				2			
TakaTira	kitaDhaऽ	Gheranage	Dintaka	DhirDhir	kitataka	DhaऽTira	kitataka
0				3			

Tihai

TakaTira	kitaDhaऽ	Gheranage	Dintaka	DhirDhir	kitataka	DhaऽTira	kitataka
×				2			
Dha	ऽ	ऽ	ऽ	TakaTira	kitaDhaऽ	Gheranage	Dintaka
0				3			
DhirDhir	kitataka	DhaऽTira	kitataka	Dha	ऽ	ऽ	ऽ
×				2			
TakaTira	kitaDhaऽ	Gheranage	Dintaka	DhirDhir	kitataka	DhaऽTira	kitataka
0				3			
Dha							
×							

Gat-Kayada-3 (Adalaya)

Dhagina	DhaSS	Tirakitataka	TetSS	DhaSTirakita	DheTite	Kataga	digana
×				2			
Takina	TaSS	Tirakitataka	TetSS	DhaSTirakita	DheTite	Kataga	digana
0				3			

Prastar-1

Dhagina	DhaSS	Tirakitataka	TetSS	Dhagina	DhaSS	Tirakitataka	TetSS
×				2			
Dhagina	DhaSS	Tirakitataka	TetSS	DhaSTirakita	DheTite	Kataga	digana
0				3			
Takina	TaSS	Tirakitataka	TeSS	Takina	TaSS	Tirakitataka	TetSS
×				2			
Dhagina	DhaSS	Tirakitataka	TetSS	DhaSTirakita	DheTite	Kataga	digana
0				3			

Prastar-2

Dhagina	DhaSS	Tirakitataka	TetSS	Tirakitataka	TetSS	Tirakitataka	TetSS
×				2			
Dhagina	DhaSS	Tirakitataka	TetSS	DhaSTirakita	DheTite	Kataga	digana
0				3			
Takina	TaSS	Tirakitataka	TetSS	Tirakitataka	TetSS	Tirakitataka	TetSS
×				2			
Dhagina	DhaSS	Tirakitataka	TetSS	DhaSTirakita	DheTite	Kataga	digana
0				3			

Prastar-3

Dhagina	DhaSS	Dhagina	DhaSS	Dhagina	DhaSS	Tirakitataka	TetSS
×				2			
Dhagina	DhaSS	Tirakitataka	TetSS	DhaSTirakita	DheTite	Kataga	digana
0				3			
Takina	TaSS	Takina	TaSS	Takina	TaSS	Tirakitataka	TetSS
×				2			
Dhagina	DhaSS	Tirakitataka	TetSS	DhaSTirakita	DheTite	Kataga	digana
0				3			

Prastar-4

Dhagina	DhaSS	SSS	Dhagina	DhaSS	SSS	Dhagina	DhaSS
×				2			
Dhagina	DhaSS	Tirakitataka	TetSS	DhaSTirakita	DheTite	Kataga	digana
0				3			
Takina	TaSS	SSS	Takina	TaSS	SSS	Takina	TaSS
×				2			
Dhagina	DhaSS	Tirakitataka	TetSS	DhaSTirakita	DheTite	Kataga	digana
0				3			

Prastar-5

Dhagina	DhaSS	Dhagina	Dhagina	DhaSS	Dhagina	Dhagina	DhaSS
×				2			
Dhagina	DhaSS	Tirakitataka	TetSS	DhaSTirakita	DheTite	Kataga	digana
0				3			
Takina	TaSS	Takina	Takina	TaSS	Takina	Takina	TaSS
×				2			
Dhagina	DhaSS	Tirakitataka	TetSS	DhaSTirakita	DheTite	Kataga	digana
0				3			

Prastar-6

Tiraki-tataka	Tiraki-tataka	Tirakitataka	TetSS	Tirakitataka	TetSS	Tirakitataka	TetSS
×				2			
Dhagina	DhaSS	Tirakitataka	TetSS	DhaSTirakita	DheTite	Kataga	digana
0				3			
Tiraki-tataka	Tiraki-tataka	Tirakitatka	TetSS	Tirakitataka	TetSS	Tirakitataka	TetSS
×				2			
Dhagina	DhaSS	Tirakitataka	TetSS	DhaSTirakita	DheTite	Kataga	digana
0				3			

Tihai

DhaSTirakita	DheTite	Kataga		digana Dha	S	DhaSTirakita	DheTite
×				2			
Kataga	digana	Dha	S	DhaSTirakita	DheTite	Kataga	digana
0				3			
Dha							
×							

Gat-Kayada-4

Taki	taDha	Tirakita	Dhite	Dhagi	naDhi	nage	Dhina
×				2			
NaTi	keDha	Tirakita	Dhet	DhiraDhira	kitataka	Ta-tira	kitataka
0				3			
Taki	taTa	Tirakita	Tite	Taki	naTi	nake	Tina
×				2			
NaTi	keDha	Tirakita	Dhet	DhiraDhira	kitataka	Dha-tira	kitataka
0				3			

Prastar-1

Taki	taDha	Tirakita	Dhite	Dhagi	naDhi	nage	Dhina
×				2			
Taki	taDha	Tirakita	Dhite	Dhagi	naDhi	nage	Dhina
0				3			
Taki	taDha	Tirakita	Dhite	Dhagi	naDhi	nage	Dhina
×				2			
NaTi	keDha	Tirakita	Dhet	DhiraDhira	kitataka	Ta-tira	kitataka
0				3			
Taki	taTa	Tirakita	Tite	Taki	naTi	nake	Tina
×				2			
Taki	taTa	Tirakita	Tite	Taki	naTi	nake	Tina
0				3			
Taki	taDha	Tirakita	Dhite	Dhagi	naDhi	nage	Dhina
×				2			
NaTi	keDha	Tirakita	Dhet	DhiraDhira	kitataka	Dha-tira	kitataka
0				3			

Prastar-2

Taki	taDha	Tirakita	Dhite	Taki	taDha	Tirakita	Dhite
×				2			
Taki	taDha	Tirakita	Dhite	Dhagi	naDhi	nage	Dhina
0				3			
Taki	taDha	Tirakita	Dhite	Dhagi	naDhi	nage	Dhina
×				2			
NaTi	keDha	Tirakita	Dhet	DhiraDhira	kitataka	Ta-tira	kitataka
0				3			
Taki	taTa	Tirakita	Tite	Taki	taTa	Tirakita	Tite
×				2			

Taki	taTa	Tirakita	Tite	Taki	naTi	nake	Tina
0				3			
Taki	taDha	Tirakita	Dhite	Dhagi	naDhi	nage	Dhina
×				2			
NaTi	keDha	Tirakita	Dhet	DhiraDhira	kitataka	Dha-tira	kitataka
0				3			

Prastar-3

Taki	taDha	Tirakita	Dhite	Dhagi	naDhi	nage	Dhina
×				2			
Dhagi	naDhi	nage	Dhina	Dhagi	naDhi	nage	Dhina
0				3			
Taki	taDha	Tirakita	Dhite	Dhagi	naDhi	nage	Dhina
×				2			
NaTi	keDha	Tirakita	Dhet	DhiraDhira	kitataka	Ta-tira	kitataka
0				3			
Taki	taTa	Tirakita	Tite	Taki	naTi	nake	Tina
×				2			
Taki	naTi	nake	Tina	Taki	naTi	nake	Tina
0				3			
Taki	taDha	Tirakita	Dhite	Dhagi	naDhi	nage	Dhina
×				2			
NaTi	keDha	Tirakita	Dhet	DhiraDhira	kitataka	Dha-tira	kitataka
0				3			

Prastar-4

NaTi	keDha	Tirakita	Dhet	DhiraDhira	kitataka	Ta-tira	kitataka
×				2			
NaTi	keTa	Tirakita	Dhet	DhiraDhira	kitataka	Dha-tira	kitataka
0				3			

Prastar-5

NaTi	keDha	Tirakita	Dhet	DhiraDhira	kitataka	Ta-tira	kitataka
×				2			
DhiraDhira	kitataka	Ta-tira	kitataka	DhiraDhira	kitataka	Ta-tira	kitataka
0				3			
NaTi	keTa	Tirakita	Dhet	DhiraDhira	kitataka	Dha-tira	kitataka
×				2			
DhiraDhira	kitataka	Dha-tira	kitataka	DhiraDhira	kitataka	Dha-tira	kitataka
0				3			

Tihai

NaTi	keDha	Tirakita	Dhet	DhiraDhira	kitataka	Dha-tira	kitataka
×				2			
Dha	S	S	S	NaTi	keDha	Tirakita	Dhet
0				3			
DhiraDhira	kitataka	Dha-tira	kitataka	Dha	S	S	S
×				2			
NaTi	keDha	Tirakita	Dhet	DhiraDhira	kitataka	Dha-tira	kitataka
0				3			
Dha							
×							

Bant of Banaras Gharana

Dhige	Dhina	Tirakita	Dhina	Dhage	naTi	keTi	Nara
×				2			
Tike	Tina	Tirakita	Dhina	Dhage	naDhi	geDhi	Nara
0				3			

Prastar-1

Dhige	Dhina	Tirakita	Dhina	Dhige	Dhina	Tirakita	Dhina
×				2			
Dhige	Dhina	Tirakita	Dhina	Dhage	naTi	keTi	Nara
0				3			
Tike	Tina	Tirakita	Tina	Tike	Tina	Tirakita	Tina
×				2			
Dhige	Dhina	Tirakita	Dhina	Dhage	naDhi	geDhi	Nara
0				3			

Prastar-2

Dhige	Dhina	Dhige	Dhina	Dhige	Dhina	Tirakita	Dhina
×				2			
Dhige	Dhina	Tirakita	Dhina	Dhage	naTi	keTi	Nara
0				3			
Tike	Tina	Tike	Tina	Tike	Tina	Tirakita	Tina
×				2			
Dhige	Dhina	Tirakita	Dhina	Dhage	naDhi	geDhi	Nara
0				3			

Prastar-3

Dhige	Dhige	Dhige	Dhina	Dhige	Dhina	Tirakita	Dhina
×				2			
Dhige	Dhina	Tirakita	Dhina	Dhage	naTi	keTi	Nara
0				3			
Tike	Tike	Tike	Tina	Tike	Tina	Tirakita	Tina
×				2			
Dhige	Dhina	Tirakita	Dhina	Dhage	naDhi	geDhi	Nara
0				3			

Prastar-4

Dhige	Dhina	Tirakita	Dhige	Dhina	Tirakita	Dhige	Dhina
×				2			
Dhige	Dhina	Tirakita	Dhina	Dhage	naTi	keTi	Nara
0				3			

Tike	Tina	Tirakita	Tike	Tina	Tirakita	Tike	Tina
×				2			
Dhige	Dhina	Tirakita	Dhina	Dhage	naDhi	geDhi	Nara
0				3			

Prastar-5

Dhige	Dhina	Tirakita	Dhina	Tirakita	Dhina	Tirakita	Dhina
×				2			
Dhige	Dhina	Tirakita	Dhina	Dhage	naTi	keTi	Nara
0				3			
Tike	Tina	Tirakita	Tina	Tirakita	Tina	Tirakita	Tina
×				2			
Dhige	Dhina	Tirakita	Dhina	Dhage	naDhi	geDhi	Nara
0				3			

Prastar-6

Dhage	naTi	keTi	Nara	Tage	naDhi	geDhi	Nara
×				2			
Dhage	naTi	keTi	Nara	Tage	naDhi	geDhi	Nara
0				3			
Dhage	naTi	keTi	Nara	Tage	naDhi	geDhi	Nara
×				2			
Dhage	naTi	keTi	Nara	Tage	naDhi	geDhi	Nara
0				3			

Tihai

Dhage	naDhi	geDhi	Nara	Dha	ऽ	Dhage	naDhi
×				2			
geDhi	Nara	Dha	ऽ	Dhage	naDhi	geDhi	Nara
0				3			
Dha							
×							

Chakradar-Tihai

Dhage	naDhi	geDhi	Nara	Dhage	naDhi	geDhi	Nara
×				2			
Dha	ऽ	Dhage	naDhi	geDhi	Nara	Dha	ऽ
0				3			
Dhage	naDhi	geDhi	Nara	Dha	ऽ	Dhage	naDhi
×				2			

geDhi	Nara	Dhage	naDhi	geDhi	Nara	Dha	ऽ
0				3			
Dhage	naDhi	geDhi	Nara	Dha	ऽ	Dhage	naDhi
×				2			
geDhi	Nara	Dha	ऽ	Dhage	naDhi	geDhi	Nara
0				3			
Dhage	naDhi	geDhi	Nara	Dha	ऽ	Dhage	naDhi
×				2			
geDhi	Nara	Dha	ऽ	Dhage	naDhi	geDhi	Nara
0				3			
Dha							
×							

Bant–2

DhaTrakaDhe	Titegina	Dharagina	Tunakatta
×			
Dharagina	Dharagina	Dharagina	Tunakatta
2			
TaTrakaTe	Titekina	Tarakina	Tunakatta
0			
Dharagina	Dharagina	Dharagina	Dhinnakatta
3			

Prastar-1

DhaTrakaDhe	Titegina	Dharagina	Tunakatta
×			
DhaTrakaDhe	Titegina	Dharagina	Tunakatta
2			
DhaTrakaDhe	Titegina	Dharagina	Tunakatta
0			
Dharagina	Dharagina	Dharagina	Tunakatta
3			
TaTrakaTe	Titekina	Tarakina	Tunakatta
×			
TaTrakaTe	Titekina	Tarakina	Tunakatta
2			
DhaTrakaDhe	Titegina	Dharagina	Tunakatta
0			
Dharagina	Dharagina	Dharagina	Dhinnakatta
3			

Prastar-2

DhaTrakaDhe	Titegina	DhaTrakaDhe	Titegina
×			
DhaTrakaDhe	Titegina	Dharagina	Tunakatta
2			
DhaTrakaDhe	Titegina	Dharagina	Tunakatta
0			
Dharagina	Dharagina	Dharagina	Tunakatta
3			
TaTrakaTe	Titekina	TaTrakaTe	Titekina
×			
TaTrakaTe	Titekina	Tarakina	Tunakatta
2			

DhaTrakaDhe 0	Titegina	Dharagina	Tunakatta
Dharagina 3	Dharagina	Dharagina	Dhinnakatta

Prastar-3

DhaTrakaDhe ×	Titegina	Dharagina,	DhaTrakaDhe
Titegina 2	Dharagina	Dharagina	Tunakatta
DhaTrakaDhe 0	Titegina	Dharagina	Tunakatta
Dharagina 3	Dharagina	Dharagina	Tunakatta
TaTrakaTe ×	Titekina	Tarakina ,	TaTrakaTe
Titekina 2	Tarakina	Tarakina	Tunakatta
DhaTrakaDhe 0	Titegina	Dharagina	Tunakatta
Dharagina 3	Dharagina	Dharagina	Dhinnakatta

Prastar-4

Dharagina ×	Dharagina	Dharagina	Tunakatta
Tarakina 2	Tarakina	Dharagina	Dhinnakatta
Dharagina 0	Dharagina	Dharagina	Tunakatta
Tarakina 3	Tarakina	Dharagina	Dhinnakatta

Prastar-5

Dharagina ×	Dharagina	Tunakatta	Dharagina
Dharagina 2	Tunakatta	Dharagina	Tunakatta
Tarakina 0	Tarakina	Tunakatta	Tarakina
Dharagina 3	Dhinnakatta	Dharagina	Dhinnakatta

Prastar-6

Dharagina ×	Dharagina	Dharagina	Dharagina
Dharagina 2	Dharagina	Dharagina	Tunakatta
Tarakina 0	Tarakina	Tarakina	Tarakina
Dharagina 3	Dharagina	Dharagina	Dhinnakatta

Tihai

Dharagina ×	Dharagina	Dharagina	Dhinnakatta
Dha 2	S	Dharagina	Dharagina
Dharagina 0	Dhinnakatta	Dha	S
Dharagina 3	Dharagina	Dharagina	Dhinnakatta
Dha ×			

Chakradar-Tihai

Dharagina ×	Dharagina	Dharagina	Dhinnakatta
Dha 2	Dharagina	Dhinnakatta	Dha
Dharagina 0	Dhinnakatta	Dha,	Dharagina
Dharagina 3	Dharagina	Dhinnakatta	Dha
Dharagina ×	Dhinnakatta	Dha	Dharagina
Dhinnakatta 2	Dha,	Dharagina	Dharagina
Dharagina 0	Dhinnakatta	Dha	Dharagina
Dhinnakatta 3	Dha	Dharagina	Dhinnakatta
Dha ×			

Bant–3

Dhara	DhaDhe	Tite	Dhara	Dhara	Dhatin	natin	Nara
×				2			
Tara	TaTe	Tite	Dhara	Dhara	DhaDhin	naDhin	Nara
0				3			

Prastar-1

Dhara	DhaDhe	Tite	Dhara	Dhara	DhaDhe	Tite	Dhara
×				2			
Dhara	DhaDhe	Tite	Dhara	Dhara	Dhatin	natin	Nara
0				3			
Tara	TaTe	Tite	Tara	Tara	TaTe	Tite	Tara
×				2			
Dhara	DhaDhe	Tite	Dhara	Dhara	DhaDhin	naDhin	Nara
0				3			

Prastar-2

Dhara	DhaDhe	Tite	Dhara	DhaDhe	Tite	Dhara	Dhara
×				2			
Dhara	DhaDhe	Tite	Dhara	Dhara	Dhatin	natin	Nara
0				3			
Tara	TaTe	Tite	Tara	TaTe	Tite	Tara	Tara
×				2			
Dhara	DhaDhe	Tite	Dhara	Dhara	DhaDhin	naDhin	Nara
0				3			

Prastar-3

Dhara	Dhara	Dhara	DhaDhe	Tite	Dhara	DhaDhe	Tite
×				2			
Dhara	DhaDhe	Tite	Dhara	Dhara	Dhatin	natin	Nara
0				3			
Tara	Tara	Tara	TaTe	Tite	Tara	TaTe	Tite
×				2			
Dhara	DhaDhe	Tite	Dhara	Dhara	DhaDhin	naDhin	Nara
0				3			

Prastar-4

DheTi	teDhe	Tite	Dhara	Dhara	DhaDhin	naDhin	Nara
×				2			
Dhara	DhaDhe	Tite	Dhara	Dhara	Dhatin	natin	Nara
0				3			

TeTi ×	teTe	Tite	Tara	Tara 2	natin	natin	Nara
Dhara 0	DhaDhe	Tite	Dhara	Dhara 3	DhaDhin	naDhin	Nara

Prastar-5

DheTi ×	teDhe	Tite	Dhara	Dhara 2	natin	natin	Nara
TeTi 0	teTe	Tite	Tara	Dhara 3	DhaDhin	naDhin	Nara

Prastar-6

Dhara ×	natin	natin	Nara	Tara 2	DhaDhin	naDhin	Nara
Dhara 0	natin	natin	Nara	Tara 3	DhaDhin	naDhin	Nara

Tihai

Dhara ×	DhaDhin	naDhin	Nara	Dha 2	S	Dhara	DhaDhin
naDhin 0	Nara	Dha	S	Dhara 3	DhaDhin	naDhin	Nara
Dha ×							

Bant–4

Dha- ×	Gheranage	Takedhin	Dhinnakita
Dha-Tira 2	kitaDhage	Taketin	Tinnakita
Ta- 0	Keranake	TakeTin	Tinnakita
Dha-Tira 3	kitaDhage	TakeDhin	Dhinnakita

Prastar-1

Dha- ×	Gheranage	Takedhin	Dhinnakita
Dha- 2	Gheranage	Takedhin	Dhinnakita
Dha- 0	Gheranage	Takedhin	Dhinnakita
Dha-Tira 3	kitaDhage	Taketin	Tinnakita
Ta- ×	Keranake	TakeTin	Tinnakita
Ta- 2	Keranake	TakeTin	Tinnakita
Dha- 0	Gheranage	Takedhin	Dhinnakita
Dha-Tira 3	kitaDhage	TakeDhin	Dhinnakita

Prastar-2

Dha- ×	Gheranage	Dha-	Gheranage
Dha- 2	Gheranage	Takedhin	Dhinnakita
Dha- 0	Gheranage	Takedhin	Dhinnakita
Dha-Tira 3	kitaDhage	Taketin	Tinnakita

Ta- ×	Keranake	Ta-	Keranake
Ta- 2	Keranake	TakeTin	Tinnakita
Dha- 0	Gheranage	Takedhin	Dhinnakita
Dha-Tira 3	kitaDhage	TakeDhin	Dhinnakita

Prastar-3

Dha- ×	Gheranage	Takedhin,	Dha-
Gheranage 2	Takedhin,	Takedhin	Dhinnakita
Dha- 0	Gheranage	Takedhin	Dhinnakita
Dha-Tira 3	kitaDhage	Taketin	Tinnakita
Ta- ×	Keranake	TakeTin	Ta-
Keranake 2	TakeTina	TakeTin	Tinnakita
Dha- 0	Gheranage	Takedhin	Dhinnakita
Dha-Tira 3	kitaDhage	TakeDhin	Dhinnakita

Prastar-4

Dha- ×	Gheranage	Takedhin	Dhinnakita
Takedhin 2	Dhinnakita	Takedhin	Dhinnakita
Dha- 0	Gheranage	Takedhin	Dhinnakita
Dha-Tira 3	kitaDhage	Taketin	Tinnakita

Ta- ×	Keranake	TakeTin	Tinnakita
TakeTin 2	Tinnakita	TakeTin	Tinnakita
Dha- 0	Gheranage	Takedhin	Dhinnakita
Dha-Tira 3	kitaDhage	TakeDhin	Dhinnakita

Prastar-5

Dha-Tira ×	kitaDhage	Taketin	Tinnakita
Ta-Tira 2	kitaDhage	TakeDhin	Dhinnakita
Dha-Tira 0	kitaDhage	Taketin	Tinnakita
Ta-Tira 3	kitaDhage	TakeDhin	Dhinnakita

Prastar-6

Dha-Tira ×	kitaDhage	Taketin	Tinnakita
Taketin 2	Tinnakita	Taketin	Tinnakita
Ta-Tira 0	kitaDhage	TakeDhin	Dhinnakita
TakeDhin 3	Dhinnakita	TakeDhin	Dhinnakita

Prastar-7

Taketin ×	Tinnakita	TakeDhin	Dhinnakita
Taketin 2	Tinnakita	TakeDhin	Dhinnakita
Taketin 0	Tinnakita	TakeDhin	Dhinnakita
Taketin 3	Tinnakita	TakeDhin	Dhinnakita

Tihai

Taketin ×	Tinnakita	TakeDhin	Dhinnakita
Dha 2	S	Taketin	Tinnakita
TakeDhin 0	Dhinnakita	Dha	S
Taketin 3	Tinnakita	TakeDhin	Dhinnakita
Dha ×			

Tukras of Banaras Gharana

DhaDha ×	DinDin	NaNa	TiteTite	
KaTite,ka 2	Tite,kata	DhaऽKata	DhaऽKata	
DhaऽTite 0	Tite,kata	DhaऽKata	DhaऽKata	
DhaऽTite 3	Tite,kata	DhaऽKata	DhaऽKata	Dha ×

Tukra-2

Dhaऽ ×	Tuna	kitataka	TaऽTira	
Kitataka 2	Tirakita	TakaTaऽ	Tirakita	
Dhaऽ 0	Tirakita	TakaTaऽ	Tirakita	
Dhaऽ 3	Tirakita	TakaTaऽ	Tirakita	Dha ×

Tukra-3

DhageTite ×	TageTite	Takadin	NageTite	
TiteTagi 2	ऽnaDhetऽ	Tagiऽna	DhetऽTaऽ	
TirakitaDhetऽ 0	Tagiऽna	Dhaऽऽऽ	TirakitaDhetऽ	
Taginऽa 3	Dhaऽऽऽ	TirakitaDhetऽ	Tagiऽna	Dha ×

Tukra-4

KatऽTite ×	GeGeTite	KataKata	GeGeTite
Katagege 2	TiteKata	GeGeTetऽ	DhaऽGeGe
TetऽDhaऽ 0	GegeTetऽ	Dhaऽऽऽ	KatऽTite

GeGeTite	KataKata	GeGeTite	Katagege	
3				
TiteKata	GegeTetS	DhaSGeGe	TetSDhaS	
×				
GeGeTetS	DhaSSS	KatSTite	GeGeTite	
2				
KataKata	GeGeTite	Katagege	TiteKata	
0				
GegeTetS	Dha·GeGe	TetSDhaS	GegeTetS	Dha
3				×

Tukra-5

DhageTite	TageTite	KradhaSKra	DhaSKitataka	
×				
DinSDinS	NaNaNaNa	KaTiteDha	SKaSTe	
2				
DhaSKaTe	DhaSKaTi	teDhaSKa	STeDhaS	
0				
KaTeDhaS	KaTiteDha	SKaSTe	DhaSKaTe	Dha
3				×

Tukra-Chakradar-1

DhageTite	TageTite	KradhaSKra	DhaS,Kitataka
×			
DinSDinS	NaNaNaNa	KitatakaDinS	DinSNaNa
2			
NaNa,Kitataka	DinSDinS	NaNaNaNa	KaTiteDha
0			
SKaSTe	DhaSKaTe	DhaSKaTi	teDhaSKa
3			
STeDhaS	KaTeDhaS	KaTiteDha	SKaSTe
×			
DhaSKaTe	DhaS,Dhage	TiteTage	TiteKraDha
2			
SKraDhaS	KitatakaDinS	DinSNaNa	NaNa,Kitataka
0			

DinSDinS 3	NaNaNaNa	KitatakaDinS	DinSNaNa	
NaNa, KaTi ×	teDhaSKa	STeDhaS	KaTeDhaS	
KaTiteDha 2	SKaSTe	DhaSKaTe	DhaSKaTi	
teDhaSKa 0	STeDhaS	KaTeDhaS	DhageTite	
TageTite 3	KradhaSKra	DhaS,Kitataka	DinSDinS	
NaNaNaNa ×	KitatakaDinS	DinSNaNa	NaNa, Kitataka	
DinSDinS 2	NaNaNaNa	KaTiteDha	SKaSTe	
DhaSKaTe 0	DhaSKaTi	teDhaSKa	STeDhaS	
KaTeDhaS 3	KaTiteDha	SKaSTe	DhaSKaTe	Dha ×

Tukra-Chakradar–2

Dha Dha Dha Dha ×	Din Din Din Din
NaNaNaNa	Tite Tite Tite Tite
KaTrakaDheTiteKaTe 2	DhaSKaTeDhaSKaTe
DhaSSDheTiteKaTe	DhaSKaTeDhaSKaTe
DhaSSDheTiteKaTe 0	DhaSKaTeDhaSKaTe
DhaSSS	Dha Dha Dha Dha
Din Din Din Din 3	NaNaNaNa
Tite Tite Tite Tite	KaTrakaDheTiteKaTe
DhaSKaTeDhaSKaTe ×	DhaSSDheTiteKaTe
DhaSKaTeDhaSKaTe	DhaSSDheTiteKaTe
DhaSKaTeDhaSKaTe 2	DhaSSS

Dha Dha Dha Dha	Din Din Din Din
NaNaNaNa 0	Tite Tite Tite Tite
KaTrakaDheTiteKaTe	DhaSKaTeDhaSKaTe
DhaSSDheTiteKaTe 3	DhaSKaTeDhaSKaTe
DhaSSDheTiteKaTe	DhaSKaTeDhaSKaTe
Dha ×	

Tukra-Chakradar-3

KaTitedhe ×	Titekradhe	Titekata	Gadigana
GhinTara 2	Snkata	Gadigana	DhaSGadi
ganaDhaS 0	Gadigana	DhaSkata	Gadigana
DhaSGadi 3	ganaDhaS	Gadigana	DhaSkata
Gadigana ×	DhaSGadi	ganaDhaS	Gadigana
Dha 2	S	KaTitedhe	Titekradhe
Titekata 0	Gadigana	GhinTara	Snkata
Gadigana 3	DhaSGadi	ganaDhaS	Gadigana
DhaSkata ×	Gadigana	DhaSGadi	ganaDhaS
Gadigana 2	DhaSkata	Gadigana	Dha·Gadi
ganaDhaS 0	Gadigana	Dha	S
KaTitedhe 3	Titekradhe	Titekata	Gadigana
GhinTara ×	Snkata	Gadigana	DhaSGadi

ganaDhaS 2	Gadigana	DhaSkata	Gadigana	
DhaSGadi 0	ganaDhaS	Gadigana	DhaSkata	
Gadigana 3	DhaSGadi	ganaDhaS	Gadigana	Dha ×

Tukra-Chakradar-4

KatSTite ×	TitekatS	TiteTite	KataKata
KaTiteDhe 2	TitekaTi	teDheTite	KradheTite
KaTiteTa 0	ginakatS	TiteDhaS	naDha·na
DhaSSTa 3	ginakatS	TiteDhaS	naDhaSna
DhaSSTa ×	ginakatS	TiteDhaS	naDhaSna
Dha 2	S	KatSTite	TitekatS
TiteTite 0	KataKata	KaTiteDhe	TitekaTi
teDheTite 3	KradheTite	KaTiteTa	ginakatS
TiteDhaS ×	naDhaSna	DhaSSTa	ginakatS
TiteDhaS 2	naDhaSna	DhaSSTa	ginakatS
TiteDhaS 0	naDhaSna	Dha	S
KatSTite 3	TitekatS	TiteTite	KataKata
KaTiteDhe ×	TitekaTi	teDheTite	KradheTite
KaTiteTa 2	ginakatS	TiteDhaS	naDhaSna

DhaSSTa 0	ginakatS	TiteDhaS	naDhaSna	
DhaSSTa 3	ginakatS	TiteDhaS	naDhaSna	Dha ×

Uthan of Banaras Gharana

DhaSKra ×	DheTite	Dha-Tirkita	DheTite	
KaSTe 2	DheTite	Kataga	digana	
Takita 0	TaSna	TaSS	SSKra	
DhaSna 3	DhaSna	DhaSKra	DhaSna	
DhaSna ×	DhaSKra	DhaSna	DhaSna	
Dha 2	S	DhaSKra	DheTite	
Dha-Tirkita 0	DheTite	KaSTe	DheTite	
Kataga 3	digana	Takita	TaSna	
TaSS ×	SSKra	DhaSna	DhaSna	
DhaSKra 2	DhaSna	DhaSna	DhaSKra	
DhaSna 0	DhaSna	Dha	S	
DhaSKra 3	DheTite	Dha-Tirkita	DheTite	
KaSTe ×	DheTite	Kataga	digana	
Takita 2	TaSna	TaSS	SSKra	
DhaSna 0	DhaSna	DhaSKra	DhaSna	
DhaSna 3	DhaSKra	DhaSna	DhaSna	Dha ×

Uthan–2

Dha ×	Tite	Kradha	Tite
Gheranage 2	Tirakita	NageTira	kitataka
DhaSGheranage 0	DhaSGheranage	Tirakitataka	Tirakitataka
DhiraDhirakitataka 3	Takkran	DhaSKata	DhaSkitataka
Takkran ×	DhaSKata	DhaSkitataka	Takkran
DhaSKata 2	DhaSSS	SSDhiraDhira	kitatakaTak-
KranDha 0	KataDhaS	kitatakaTak-	KranDha
KataDhaS 3	kitatakaTak-	KranDha	KataDhaS
SSSS ×	DhiraDhirakitataka	Takkran	DhaSKata
DhaSkitataka 2	Takkran	DhaSKata	DhaSkitataka
Takkran 0	DhaSKata	DhaSSS,	Dha
Tite 3	Kradha	Tite	Gheranage
Tirakita ×	NageTira	kitataka	DhaSGheranage
DhaSGheranage 2	Tirakitataka	Tirakitataka	DhiraDhirakitataka
Takkran 0	DhaSKata	DhaSkitataka	Takkran
DhaSKata 3	DhaSkitataka	Takkran	DhaSKata
DhaSSS ×	SSDhiraDhira	kitatakaTak-	KranDha
KataDhaS 2	kitatakaTak-	KranDha	KataDhaS

kitatakaTak-	KranDha	KataDhaऽ	ऽऽऽऽ	
0				
DhiraDhirakitataka	Takkran	DhaऽKata	Dhaऽkitataka	
3				
Takkran	DhaऽKata	Dha ·kitataka	Takkran	
×				
DhaऽKata	Dhaऽऽऽ,	Dha	Tite	
2				
Kradha	Tite	Gheranage	Tirakita	
0				
NageTira	kitataka	DhaऽGheranage	DhaऽGheranage	
3				
Tirakitataka	Tirakitataka	DhiraDhirakitataka	Takkran	
×				
DhaऽKata	Dhaऽkitataka	Takkran	DhaऽKata	
2				
Dhaऽkitataka	Takkran	DhaऽKata	Dhaऽऽऽ	
0				
ऽऽDhiraDhira	kitatakaTak-	KranDha	KataDhaऽ	
3				
kitatakaTak-	KranDha	KataDhaऽ	kitatakaTak-	
×				
KranDha	KataDhaऽ	ऽऽऽऽ	DhiraDhirakitataka	
2				
Takkran	DhaऽKata	Dhaऽkitataka	Takkran	
0				
DhaऽKata	Dhaऽkitataka	Takkran	DhaऽKata	Dha
3				×

Navahakka of Banaras Gharana

KaTitegi	natiDha,Ka	Titegina	tiDha,KaTi	
×				
Teginati	DhaऽKaTi	teginati	Dha,KaTite	
2				
GinatiDha,	KaTitegi	natiDhaऽ	KaTitegi	
0				
NatiDha,Ka	Titegina	tiDha,KaTi	Teginati	Dha
3				×

Navahakka-2

Titegina ×	DhatiDha,Ti	teginaDha	ti Dha,Tite	
ginaDhati 2	DhaSTite	ginaDhati	Dha,Titegi	
naDhatiDha, 0	Titegina	DhatiDhaS	Titegina	
DhatiDha,Ti 3	teginaDha	ti Dha,Tite	ginaDhati	Dha ×

Navahakka-3

TirakitaTakataS ×	TirakitaDhaSTira	kitaTakataSTira	kitaDhaSTirakita
TakataSTirakita 2	DhaSSSTirakita	TakataSTirakita	DhaSTirakitaTaka
taSTirakitaDhaS 0	TirakitaTakataS	TirakitaDhaSSS	TirakitaTakataS
TirakitaDhaSTira 3	kitaTakataSTira	kitaDhaSTirakita	TakataSTirakita
Dha ×			

Navahakka-4 (starting from 4th Beats)

Dha ×	Dhin	Dhin	GinaTite	
DhaSGina 2	TiteDhaS	GinaTite	DhaSGina	
TiteDhaS 0	GinaTite	DhaSGina	TiteDhaS	
GinaTite 3	DhaSGina	TiteDhaS	GinaTite	Dha ×

Navahakka-5 (starting from 4th Beats)

Dha ×	Dhin	Dhin	DhiraDhirakitataka
DhaSSSDhiraDhira 2	kitatakaDhaSSS	DhiraDhirakitataka	DhaSSSDhiraDhira

kitatakaDhaSSS	DhiraDhirakitataka	DhaSSSDhiraDhira	kitatakaDhaSSS
0			
DhiraDhirakitataka	DhaSSSDhiraDhira	kitatakaDhaSSS	DhiraDhirakitataka
3			
Dha			
×			

9

Composition in Rupaktal

Kayada-1

Dhage	Tete	Tete	Dhage	Tete	KraDha	Tete
0			1		2	
Dhage	Tete	Tete	Dhage	Nage	Tuna	Katta
0			1		2	
Take	Tete	Tete	Take	Tete	KraTa	Tete
0			1		2	
Dhage	Tete	Tete	Dhage	Nage	Dhinna	Katta
0			1		2	

Prastar-1

Dhage	Tete	Tete	Dhage	Tete	KraDha	Tete
0			1		2	
Dhage	Tete	Tete	Dhage	Tete	KraDha	Tete
0			1		2	
Dhage	Tete	Tete	Dhage	Tete	KraDha	Tete
0			1		2	
Dhage	Tete	Tete	Dhage	Nage	Tuna	Katta
0			1		2	
Take	Tete	Tete	Take	Tete	KraTa	Tete
0			1		2	
Take	Tete	Tete	Take	Tete	KraTa	Tete
0			1		2	
Dhage	Tete	Tete	Dhage	Tete	KraDha	Tete
0			1		2	
Dhage	Tete	Tete	Dhage	Nage	Dhinna	Katta
0			1		2	

Prastar-2

Dhage	Tete	Tete	Dhage	Tete	KraDha	Tete
0			1		2	
KraDha	Tete	Tete	KraDha	Tete	KraDha	Tete
0			1		2	
Dhage	Tete	Tete	Dhage	Tete	KraDha	Tete
0			1		2	
Dhage	Tete	Tete	Dhage	Nage	Tuna	Katta
0			1		2	
Take	Tete	Tete	Take	Tete	KraTa	Tete
0			1		2	
KraTa	Tete	Tete	KraTa	Tete	KraTa	Tete
0			1		2	
Dhage	Tete	Tete	Dhage	Tete	KraDha	Tete
0			1		2	
Dhage	Tete	Tete	Dhage	Nage	Dhinna	Katta
0			1		2	

Prastar-3

Dhage	Tete	Tete	KraDha	Tete	KraDha	Tete
0			1		2	
Dhage	Tete	Tete	Dhage	Nage	Tuna	Katta
0			1		2	
Take	Tete	Tete	KraTa	Tete	KraTa	Tete
0			1		2	
Dhage	Tete	Tete	Dhage	Nage	Dhinna	Katta
0			1		2	

Prastar-4

Dhage	Tete	KraDha	Tete	Tete	KraDha	Tete
0			1		2	
Dhage	Tete	Tete	Dhage	Nage	Tuna	Katta
0			1		2	
Take	Tete	KraTa	Tate	Tete	KraTa	Tete
0			1		2	
Dhage	Tete	Tete	Dhage	Nage	Dhinna	Katta
0			1		2	

Prastar-5

Dhage 0	Tete	KraDha	Dha 1	Tete	KraDha 2	Tete
Dhage 0	Tete	Tete	Dhage 1	Nage	Tuna 2	Katta
Take 0	Tete	KraTa	Ta 1	Tete	KraTa 2	Tete
Dhage 0	Tete	Tete	Dhage 1	Nage	Dhinna 2	Katta

Prastar-6

Dha 0	KraDha	Tete	Dha 1	KraDha	Tete 2	Tete
Dhage 0	Tete	Tete	Dhage 1	Nage	Tuna 2	Katta
Ta 0	KraTa	Tete	Ta 1	KraTa	Tete 2	Tete
Dhage 0	Tete	Tete	Dhage 1	Nage	Dhinna 2	Katta

Tihai

Dhage 0	Nage	Dhinna	Katta 1	Dha	Dhage 2	Nage
Dhinna 0	Katta	Dha	Dhage 1	Nage	Dhinna 2	Katta
Dha ×						

Tihai

Dhage 0	Nage	Dhinna	Katta 1	Dha	Katta 2	Dha
Katta 0	Dha	S	Dhage 1	Nage	Dhinna 2	Katta
Dha 0	Katta	Dha	Katta 1	Dha	S 2	Dhage
Nage 0	Dhinna	Katta	Dha 1	Katta	Dha 2	Katta
Dha ×						

Kayada-2

DhaऽKita	TakaTaka	Tirakita	DhaऽTira	Kitataka	Tuna	Kitataka
0			1		2	
Taऽkita	TakaTaka	Tirakita	DhaऽTira	Kitataka	Dhinna	Kitataka
0			1		2	

Prastar-1

Dhaऽkita	TakaTaka	Tirakita	DhaऽTira	Kitataka	DhaऽTira	Kitataka
0			1		2	
Dhaऽkita	TakaTaka	Tirakita	DhaऽTira	Kitataka	Tuna	Kitataka
0			1		2	
Taऽkita	TakaTaka	Tirakita	TaऽTira	Kitataka	TaऽTira	Kitataka
0			1		2	
Dhaऽkita	TakaTaka	Tirakita	DhaऽTira	Kitataka	Dhinna	Kitataka
0			1		2	

Prastar-2

Dhaऽkita	TakaTaka	Tirakita	Dha	Kitataka	TakaTira	Kitataka
0			1		2	
Dhaऽkita	TakaTaka	Tirakita	DhaऽTira	Kitataka	Tuna	Kitataka
0			1		2	
Taऽkita	TakaTaka	Tirakita	Ta	Kitataka	TakaTira	Kitataka
0			1		2	
Dhaऽkita	TakaTaka	Tirakita	DhaऽTira	Kitataka	Dhinna	Kitataka
0			1		2	

Prastar-3

Dhaऽkita	TakaTaka	Tirakita	TakaTira	Kitataka	TakaTira	Kitataka
0			1		2	
Dhaऽkita	TakaTaka	Tirakita	DhaऽTira	Kitataka	Tuna	Kitataka
0			1		2	
Taऽkita	TakaTaka	Tirakita	TakaTira	Kitataka	TakaTira	Kitataka
0			1		2	
Dhaऽkita	TakaTaka	Tirakita	DhaऽTira	Kitataka	Dhinna	Kitataka
0			1		2	

Prastar-4

DhaSkita	TakaTaka	Tirakita	TakaTaka	Tirakita	TakaTaka	Tirakita
0			1		2	
DhaSkita	TakaTaka	Tirakita	DhaSTira	Kitataka	Tuna	Kitataka
0			1		2	
TaSkita	TakaTaka	Tirakita	TakaTaka	Tirakita	TakaTaka	Tirakita
0			1		2	
DhaSkita	TakaTaka	Tirakita	DhaSTira	Kitataka	Dhinna	Kitataka
0			1		2	

Prastar-5

TakaTira	Kitataka	Tirakita	TakaTaka	Tirakita	TakaTaka	Tirakita
0			1		2	
DhaSkita	TakaTaka	Tirakita	DhaSTira	Kitataka	Tuna	Kitataka
0			1		2	
TakaTira	Kitataka	Tirakita	TakaTaka	Tirakita	TakaTaka	Tirakita
0			1		2	
DhaSkita	TakaTaka	Tirakita	DhaSTira	Kitataka	Dhinna	Kitataka
0			1		2	

Prastar-6

Tirakita	TakaTira	Kitataka	Tirakita	TakaTira	Kitataka	Tirakita
0			1		2	
DhaSkita	TakaTaka	Tirakita	DhaSTira	Kitataka	Tuna	Kitataka
0			1		2	
Tirakita	TakaTira	Kitataka	Tirakita	TakaTira	Kitataka	Tirakita
0			1		2	
DhaSkita	TakaTaka	Tirakita	DhaSTira	Kitataka	Dhinna	Kitataka
0			1		2	

Tihai

DhaSTira	Kitataka	Dhinna	Kitataka	Dha	DhaSTira	kitataka
0			1		2	
Dhinna	Kitataka	Dha	DhaSTira	Kitataka	Dhinna	Kitataka
0			1		2	
Dha						
0						

Kayada-3

DhageTite	DhageTraka	Dhinnakita	
0			
DhgenaDha	TrakaDhete	DhageTraka	Tinnakita
1		2	
TakeTita	TakeTraka	Tinnakita	
0			
DhgenaDha	TrakaDhete	DhageTraka	Dhinnakita
1		2	

Prastar-1

DhageTite	DhageTraka	Dhinnakita	
0			
DhageTraka	Dhinnakita	DhageTraka	Dhinnakita
1		2	
DhageTite	DhageTraka	Dhinnakita	
0			
DhgenaDha	TrakaDhete	DhageTraka	Tinnakita
1		2	
TakeTite	TakeTraka	Tinnakita	
0			
TakeTraka	Tinnakita	TakeTraka	Tinnakita
1		2	
DhageTite	DhageTraka	Dhinnakita	
0			
DhgenaDha	TrakaDhete	DhageTraka	Dhinnakita
1		2	

Prastar-2

DhageTite	DhageTraka	Dhinnakita	
0			
DhageTite	DhageTite	DhageTraka	Dhinnakita
1		2	
DhageTite	DhageTraka	Dhinnakita	
0			
DhgenaDha	TrakaDhete	DhageTraka	Tinnakita
1		2	
TakeTite	TakeTraka	Tinnakita	
0			

TakeTite	TakeTite	TakeTraka	Tinnakita
1		2	
DhageTite	DhageTraka	Dhinnakita	
0			
DhgenaDha	TrakaDhete	DhageTraka	Dhinnakita
1		2	

Prastar-3

DhagenaDha	TrakaDhage	naDhaTraka	
0			
DhgenaDha	TrakaDhete	DhageTraka	Tinnakita
1		2	
Takenata	TrakaTake	naTaTraka	
0			
DhgenaDha	TrakaDhete	DhageTraka	Dhinnakita
1		2	

Prastar-4

DhagenaDha	genaDhage	naDhaTraka	
0			
DhgenaDha	TrakaDhete	DhageTraka	Tinnakita
1		2	
Takenata	kenaTake	naTaTraka	
0			
DhgenaDha	TrakaDhete	DhageTraka	Dhinnakita
1		2	

Prastar-5

DhagenaDha	TrakaDhete	DheteDhete	
0			
DhgenaDha	TrakaDhete	DhageTraka	Tinnakita
1		2	
Takenata	TrakaTite	TiteTite	
0			
DhgenaDha	TrakaDhete	DhageTraka	Dhinnakita
1		2	

Prastar-6

DheteDhaTra	kaDheteDha	TrakaDhete	
0			
DhgenaDha	TrakaDhete	DhageTraka	Tinnakita
1		2	

TiteTaTra   kaTiteTa   TrakaTite
0

DhgenaDha   TrakaDhete   DhageTraka   Dhinnakita
1   2

Tihai

DhgenaDha   TrakaDhete   DhageTraka
0

Dhinnakita   Dha   DhgenaDha   TrakaDhete
1   2

DhageTraka   Dhinnakita   Dha
0

DhgenaDha   TrakaDhete   DhageTraka   Dhinnakita
1   2

Dha
0

Kayada–4

DhaSGhera   SnDhage   Tirakita
0

DhaSGhera   SnDhage   Titegina   TunaKatta
1   2

TaSKera   SnDhage   Tirakita
0

DhaSGhera   SnDhage   Titegina   DhinnaKatta
1   2

Prastar-1

DhaSGhera   SnDhaS   DhaSGhera
0

SnDhaS   DhaSGhera   SnDhage   Titegina
1   2

DhaSGhera   nDhage   Tirakita
0

DhaSGhera   SnDhage   Titegina   TunaKatta
1   2

TaSKera   SnTaS   TaSKera
0

SnTaS   TaSKera   SnTake   Titekina
1   2

DhaSGhera	SnDhage	Tirakita	
0			
DhaSGhera	SnDhage	Titegina	DhinnaKatta
1		2	

Prastar-2

DhaSGhera	SnDhaS	GheraSn	
0			
DhaSGhera	SnDhage	Titegina	DhinnaKatta
1		2	
DhaSGhera	SnDhage	Tirakita	
0			
DhaSGhera	SnDhage	Titegina	TunaKatta
1		2	
TaSKera	SnTaS	KeraSn	
0			
TaSKera	SnTake	Titekina	TunaKatta
1		2	
DhaSGhera	SnDhage	Tirakita	
0			
DhaSGhera	SnDhage	Titegina	DhinnaKatta
1		2	

Prastar-3

DhaSGhera	SnDhage	Tirakita	
0			
GheraSn	DhageTira	kitaDhage	Titegina
1		2	
DhaSGhera	SnDhage	Tirakita	
0			
DhaSGhera	SnDhage	Titegina	TunaKatta
1		2	
TaSKera	SnTake	Tirakita	
0			
KeraSn	TakeTira	kitaTake	Titekina
1		2	
DhaSGhera	SnDhage	Tirakita	
0			
DhaSGhera	SnDhage	Titegina	DhinnaKatta
1		2	

Prastar-4

DhaSGhera	SnDhage	Tirakita	
0			
DhageTira	kitaDhage	Tirakita	GheraSn
1		2	
DhaSGhera	SnDhage	Tirakita	
0			
DhaSGhera	SnDhage	Titegina	TunaKatta
1		2	
TaSKera	SnTake	Tirakita	
0			
TakeTira	kitaTake	Tirakita	KeraSn
1		2	
DhaSGhera	SnDhage	Tirakita	
0			
DhaSGhera	SnDhage	Titegina	DhinnaKatta
1		2	

Prastar-5

DhageTira	kitaDhage	Tirakita	
0			
DhaSGhera	SnDhage	Tirakita	GheraSn
1		2	
DhaSGhera	SnDhage	Tirakita	
0			
DhaSGhera	SnDhage	Titegina	TunaKatta
1		2	
TakeTira	kitaTake	Tirakita	
0			
TaSkera	-nTake	Tirakita	KeraSn
1		2	
DhaSGhera	SnDhage	Tirakita	
0			
DhaSGhera	SnDhage	Titegina	DhinnaKatta
1		2	

Prastar-6

DhageTira	kitaDhage	Tirakita	
0			
Gheraऽn	DhageTira	kitaDhage	Tirakita
1		2	
DhaऽGhera	ऽnDhage	Tirakita	
0			
DhaऽGhera	ऽnDhage	Titegina	TunaKatta
1		2	
TakeTira	kitaTake	Tirakita.	
0			
Keraऽn	TakeTira	kitaTake	Tirakita
1		2	
DhaऽGhera	ऽnDhage	Tirakita	
0			
DhaऽGhera	ऽnDhage	Titegina	DhinnaKatta
1		2	

Tihai

DhaऽGhera	ऽnDhage	Titegina	
0			
DhinnaKatta	Dha	DhaऽGhera	ऽnDhage
1		2	
Titegina	DhinnaKatta	Dha	
0			
DhaऽGhera	ऽnDhage	Titegina	DhinnaKatta
1		2	

Bant–1

DhaginaDha	Titegina	Takadhin	
0			
DhaginaDha	Titegina	TakaTin	Tinnakina
1		2	
TakinaTa	Titekina	Takatin	
0			
DhaginaDha	Titegina	Takadhin	Dhinnagina
1		2	

Prastar-1

DhaginaDha	Titegina	DhaginaDha	
0			
Titegina	DhaginaDha	Titegina	Takadhin
1		2	
DhaginaDha	Titegina	Takadhin	
0			
DhaginaDha	Titegina	TakaTin	Tinnakin
1		2	
TakinaTa	Titekina	TakinaTa	
0			
Titekina	TakinaTa	Titekina	TakaTin
1		2	
DhaginaDha	Titegina	Takadhina	
0			
DhaginaDha	Titegina	Takadhin	Dhinnagina
1		2	

Prastar-2

DhaginaDha	Titegina	DhaginaDha	
0			
TiteDhagi	naDhaTite	GinaDhagi	nadhaTite
1		2	
DhaginaDha	Titegina	Takadhin	
0			
DhaginaDha	Titegina	TakaTin	Tinnakina
1		2	
TakinaTa	Titekina	TakinaTa	
0			

TiteTaki	naTaTite	kinaTaki	nataTite
1		2	
DhaginaDha	Titegina	Takadhin	
0			
DhaginaDha	Titegina	Takadhin	Dhinnagina
1		2	

Prastar-3

DhaginaDha	TiteDhagi	naDhaTite	
0			
DhaginaDha	Titegina	TakaTin	Tinnakina
1		2	
TakinaTa	TiteTaki	naTaTite	
0			
DhaginaDha	Titegina	TakaDhin	Dhinnagina
1		2	

Prastar-4

TakaDhin	TakaDhin	Dhinnagina	
0			
DhaginaDha	Titegina	TakaTin	Tinnakina
1		2	
TakaTin	TakaTin	Tinnakina	
0			
DhaginaDha	Titegina	TakaDhin	Dhinnagina
1		2	

Prastar-5

TakaDhin	Dhinnagina	TakaDhin	
0			
DhaginaDha	Titegina	TakaTin	Tinnakina
1		2	
TakaTin	Tinnakina	TakaTin	
0			
DhaginaDha	Titegina	TakaDhin	Dhinnagina
1		2	

Prastar-6

DhinDhinna	ginaDhin	Dhinnagina	
0			

DhaginaDha	Titegina	TakaTin	Tinnakina
1		2	
TinTinna	kinaTin	Tinnakina	
0			
DhaginaDha	Titegina	TakaDhin	Dhinnagina
1		2	

Tihai

DhaginaDha	Titegina	TakaDhin	
0			
Dhinnagina	Dha	DhaginaDha	Titegina
1		2	
TakaDhin	Dhinnagina	Dha	
0			
DhaginaDha	Titegina	TakaDhin	Dhinnagina
1		2	
Dha			
0			

Tihai-Chakradar

DhaginaDha	Titegina	TakaDhin	
0			
Dhinnagina	DhaSTaka	DhinDhina	ginaDhaS
1		2	
TakaDhin	Dhinnagina	DhaSDhagi	
0			
naDhaTite	ginaTaka	DhinDhina	ginaDhaS
1		2	
TakaDhin	Dhinnagina	DhaSTaka	
0			
DhinDhina	ginaDhas	DhaginaDha	Titegina
1		2	
TakaDhina	Dhinnagina	DhaSTaka	
0			
DhinDhinna	ginaDhaS	TakaDhin	Dhinnagina
1		2	
Dha			
0			

Bant–2

Dharagina	Takadhin	Dharagina	
0			
Dhragina	Takadhin	Ginatin	Tarakina
1		2	
Tarakina	Takatin	Tarakina	
0			
Dhragina	Takadhin	Ginadhin	Dharagina
1		2	

Prastar-1

Dharagina	Takadhin	Dharagina	
0			
Takadhin	Dharagina	Takadhin	Dharagina
1		2	
Dharagina	Takadhin	Dharagina	
0			
Dhragina	Takadhin	Ginatin	Tarakina
1		2	
Tarakina	Takatin	Tarakina	
0			
Takatin	Tarakina	Takatin	Tarakina
1		2	
Dharagina	Takadhin	Dharagina	
0			
Dhragina	Takadhin	Ginadhin	Dharagina
1		2	

Prastar-2

Dharagina	Dharagina	Takadhin	
0			
Dharagina	Takadhin	Takadhin	Dharagina
1		2	
Dharagina	Takadhin	Dharagina	
0			
Dhragina	Takadhin	Ginatin	Tarakina
1		2	
Tarakin	Tarakina	Takatin	
0			

Takatin 1	Tarakina	Takatina 2	Tarakina
Dharagina 0	Takadhin	Dharagina	
Dhragina 1	Takadhin	Ginadhin 2	Dharagina

Prastar-3

Takadhin 0	ginadhin	Dharagina	
Dharagina 1	Takadhin	ginadhin 2	Dharagina
Dharagina 0	Takadhin	Dharagina	
Dhragina 1	Takadhin	Ginatin 2	Tarakina
Takatin 0	kinatin	Tarakina	
Tarakina 1	Takatin	kinatin 2	Tarakina
Dharagina 0	Takadhin	Dharagina	
Dhragina 1	Takadhin	Ginatdhin 2	Dharagina

Prastar-4

Takadhin 0	ginadhin	Dharagina	
Takadhin 1	Takadhin	ginadhin 2	Dharagina
Dharagina 0	Takadhin	Dharagina	
Dhragina 1	Takadhin	Ginatina 2	Tarakina
Takatin 0	kinatin	Tarakina	
Takatin 1	Takatin	kinatin 2	Tarakina

Dharagina	Takadhin	Dharagina		
0				
Dhragina	Takadhin	Ginadhin	Dharagina	|
1		2		

Prastar-5

Takadhin	ginaTaka	dhingina		
0				
Takadhin	Takadhin	ginatin	Tarakina	
1		2		
Takatina	KinaTak	Tinkina		
0				
Takadhin	Takadhin	Ginadhin	Dharagina	|
1		2		

Prastar-6

TạkaDhin	ginadhin	TakaTaka		
0				
Takadhin	ginadhin	ginatin	Tarakina	
1		2		
Takatina	kinatin	TakaTaka		
0				
Takadhina	ginadhin	Ginadhin	Dharagina	|
1		2		

Tihai

Takadhin	ginadhin	ginadhin			
0					
Dharagina	Dha	Takadhin	ginadhin		
1		2			
ginadhin	Dharagina	Dha			
0					
Takadhin	ginadhin	ginadhin	Dharagina	|	Dha
1		2			0

Tihai

Takadhin	ginadhin	ginadhin		
0				
Dharagina	Dhaऽdhin	Dharagina	Dhaऽdhin	|
1		2		

Dharagina	Dha	S		
0				
Takadhin	ginadhin	ginadhin	Dharagina	
1		2		
DhaSdhina	Dharagina	DhaSdhin		
0				
Dharagin	DhaS	Takadhin		
1		2		
ginadhin	ginadhin	Dharagina		
0				
DhaSdhin	Dharagina	DhaSdhin	Dharagina	Dha
1		2		0

Navahakka

TirakitaDhaSTiS	DhaSSSTirakita	DhaSTiDhaSSS	
0			
TirakitaDhaSTiS	Dha	TirakitaDhaSTiS	DhaSSSTirakita
1		2	
DhaSTiDhaSSS	TirakitaDhaSTiS	Dha	
0			
TirakitaDhaSTiS	DhaSSSTirakita	DhaSTiDhaSSS	TirakitaDhaSTiS
1		2	
Dha			
0			

Chakradar

DhirDhirkitataka	TakitadhaSSS	DhetSDhirDhir	
0			
KitataktaSSS	KitatakaTirakita	DhaSSS Kitataka	TirakitaDhaSSS
1		2	
KitatakaTirakita	DhaSSS	KitatakaTirakita	
0			
DhaSSS kitataka	TirakitaDhaSSS	KitatakaTirakita	DhaSSS
1		2	
KitatakaTirakita	DhaSSSKitataka	TirakitaDhaSSS	
0			
KitatakaTirakita	DhaSSS	DhirDhirkitataka	TakitadhaSSS
1		2	

DhetSDhirDhir	KitataktaSSS	KitatakaTirakita	
0			
DhaSSSKitataka	TirakitaDhaSSS	KitatakaTirakita	DhaSSS
1		2	
KitatakaTirakita	DhaSSSKitataka	TirakitaDhaSSS	
0			
KitatakaTirakita	DhaSSS	KitatakaTirakita	DhaSSSKitataka
1		2	
TirakitaDhaSSS	KitatakaTirakita	DhaSSS	
0			
DhirDhirkitataka	TakitadhaSSS	DhetSDhirDhir	KitataktaSSS
1		2	
KitatakaTirakita	DhaSSSkitataka	TirakitaDhaSSS	
0			
KitatakaTirakita	DhaSSS	KitatakaTirakita	DhaSSSKitataka
1		2	
TirakitaDhaSSS	KitatakaTirakita	DhaSSS	
0			
KitatakaTirakita	DhaSSSkitataka	TirakitaDhaSSS	KitatakaTirakita
1		2	
Dha			
0			

Chakradar (Ada Laya)

DhatiS	DhatiS	DhatiDha	Tirkittak	Tirkittak	Tirkittak	TaSS
0			1		2	
DhirDhirkit	DhaSkra	DhaSn	DhaSS	DhirDhirkit	DhaSkra	DhaSn
0			1		2	
DhaSSDhir	Dhirkit	DhaSkra	DhaSn	Dha	DhatiS	DhatiS
0			1		2	
DhatiDha	Tirkittak	Tirkittak	Tirkittak	TaSS	DhirDhirkit	DhaSkra
0			1		2	
DhaSn	DhaSS	DhirDhirkit	DhaSkra	DhaSn	DhaSSDhir	Dhirkit
0			1		2	
DhaSkra	DhaSn	Dha	DhatiS	DhatiS	DhatiDha	Tirkittak
0			1		2	

Tirkittak	Tirkittak	Tass	DhirDhirkit	Dha-kra	Dhasn	DhaSS
0			1		2	
DhirDhirkit	DhaSkra	DhaSn	DhaSSDhir	Dhirkit	DhaSkra	DhaSn
0			1		2	
Dha						
0						

Chakradar

DhaSgina	DhaginaDha	Titegina	TiteTite	ginaTite	DhaginaDha	Titegina
0			1		2	
DhaSTiS	Dha	ginaTite	DhaginaDha	Titegina	DhaSTiS	Dha
0			1		2	
ginaTite	DhaginaDha	Titegina	DhaSTiS	Dha	DhaSgina	DhaginaDha
0			1		2	
Titegina	TiteTite	ginaTite	DhaginaDha	Dha	Titegina	DhaSTiSDha
0			1		2	
ginaTite	DhaginaDha	Titegina	DhaSTiS	Dha	ginaTite	DhaginaDha
0			1		2	
Titegina	DhaSTiS	Dha	DhaSgina	DhaginaDha	Titegina	TiteTite
0			1		2	
ginaTite	DhaginaDha	Titegina	DhaSTiS	Dha	ginaTite	DhaginaDha
0			1		2	
Titegina	DhaSTiS	Dha	ginaTite	DhaginaDha	Titegina	DhaSTiS
0			1		2	
Dha						
0						

Chakradar

DhaSTite	KradhaTite	KitatakadinS	
0			
NaNaTite	KataDhaS	KaTiteDha	SKraDhati
1		2	
DhaSSTi	DhaSTite	KataDhaS	
0			
KaTiteDha	SKraDhati	DhaSSTi	DhaSTite
1		2	
KataDhaS	KaTiteDha	SKraDhati	
0			

DhaSSTi	Dha	DhaSTite	KradhaTite	
1		2		
KitatakadinS	NaNaTite	KataDhaS		
0				
KaTiteDha	SKraDhati	DhaSSTi	DhaSTite	
1		2		
KataDhaS	KaTiteDha	SKraDhati		
0				
DhaSSTi	DhaSTite	KataDhaS	KaTiteDha	
1		2		
SKraDhati	DhaSSTi	Dha		
0				
DhaSTite	KradhaTite	KitatakadinS	NaNaTite	
1		2		
KataDhaS	KaTiteDha	SKraDhati		
0				
DhaSSTi	DhaSTite	KataDhaS	KaTiteDha	
1		2		
SKraDhati	DhaSSTi	DhaSTite		
0				
KataDhaS	KaTiteDha	SKraDhati	DhaSSTi	Dha
1		2		0

10

Composition in Jhaptal

Kayada–1

Dhage	Tirakita	Dhage	naDha	Tirakita	Dhage	Tirakita	Dhage	Tinna	kina
×		2			0		3		
Take	Tirakita	Take	naTa	Tirakita	Dhage	Tirakita	Dhage	Dhinna	gina
×		2			0		3		

Prastar-1

Dhage	Tirakita	Dhage	naDha	Tirakita	Dhage	Tirakita	Dhage	naDha	Tirakita
×		2			0		3		
Dhage	Tirakita	Dhage	naDha	Tirakita	Dhage	Tirakita	Dhage	Tinna	kina
×		2			0		3		
Take	Tirakita	Take	naTa	Tirakita	Take	Tirakita	Take	naTa	Tirakita
×		2			0		3		
Dhage	Tirakita	Dhage	naDha	Tirakita	Dhage	Tirakita	Dhage	Dhinna	gina
×		2			0		3		

Prastar-2

Dhage	Tirakita	Dhage	naDha	Tirakita	DhaDha	Tirakita	Dhage	naDha	Tirakita
×		2			0		3		
Dhage	Tirakita	Dhage	naDha	Tirakita	Dhage	Tirakita	Dhage	Tinna	kina
×		2			0		3		
Take	Tirakita	Take	naTa	Tirakita	TaTa	Tirakita	Take	naTa	Tirakita
×		2			0		3		
Dhage	Tirakita	Dhage	naDha	Tirakita	Dhage	Tirakita	Dhage	Dhinna	gina
×		2			0		3		

Prastar-3

Dhage	Tirakita	Dhage	naDha	Tirakit	DhaDha	Tirakita	Dhaऽtira	kitaDha	Tirakita
×		2			0		3		
Dhage	Tirakita	Dhage	naDha	Tirakita	Dhage	Tirakita	Dhage	Tinna	kina
×		2			0		3		

Take Tirakita	Take naTa Tirakita	TaTa Tirakita	Taऽtira kitaTa Tirakita
×	2	0	3
Dhage Tirakita	Dhage naDha Tirakita	Dhage Tirakita	Dhage Dhinna gina
×	2	0	3

Prastar-4

Dhage Tirakita	Dhage Tirakita Dhage	naDha Tirakita	Dhage naDha Tirakita
×	2	0	3
Dhage Tirakita	Dhage naDha Tirakita	Dhage Tirakita	Dhage Tinna kina
×	2	0	3
Take Tirakita	Take Tirakita Take	naTa Tirakita	Take naTa Tirakita
×	2	0	3
Dhage Tirakita	Dhage naDha Tirakita	Dhage Tirakita	Dhage Dhinna gina
×	2	0	3

Prastar-5

Dhage Tirakita	Dhage naDha gena	Dhage Tirakita	Dhage naDha gena
×	2	0	3
Dhage Tirakita	Dhage naDha Tirakita	Dhage Tirakita	Dhage Tinna kina
×	2	0	3
Take Tirakita	Take naTa kena	Take Tirakita	Take naTa kena
×	2	0	3
Dhage Tirakita	Dhage naDha Tirakita	Dhage Tirakita	Dhage Dhinna gina
×	2	0	3

Prastar-6

TirakitaDhage	naDha Tirakita Dhage	naDha Tirakita	Dhage naDha Tirakita
×	2	0	3
Dhage Tirakita	Dhage naDha Tirakita	Dhage Tirakita	Dhage Tinna kina
×	2	0	3
Tirakita Take	naTa Tirakita Take	naTa Tirakita	Take naTa Tirakita
×	2	0	3
Dhage Tirakita	Dhage naDha Tirakita	Dhage Tirakita	Dhage Dhinna gina
×	2	0	3

Tihai

Dhage naDha	Tirakita Dhage Dhinna	gina Dha	Dhage naDha Tirakita
×	2	0	3
Dhage Dhinna	gina Dha Dhage	naDha Tirakita	Dhage Dhinna gina
×	2	0	3
Dha			
×			

Kayada-2

Dha	Tite	KraDhe	Tite	gina	Dha	gina	Dhage	Tinna	kina
×		2			0		3		
Ta	Tite	Krate	Tite	kina	Dha	gina	Dhage	Dhinna	gina
×		2			0		3		

Prstar-1

Dha	Tite	KraDhe	Tite	gina	Dha	Tite	KraDhe	Tite	gina
×		2			0		3		
Dha	Tite	KraDhe	Tite	gina	Dha	gina	Dhage	Tinna	kina
×		2			0		3		
Ta	Tite	Krate	Tite	kina	Ta	Tite	Krate	Tite	kina
×		2			0		3		
Dha	Tite	KraDhe	Tite	gina	Dha	gina	Dhage	Dhinna	gina
×		2			0		3		

Prstar-2

Dha	Tite	KraDhe	Tite	gina	Tite	KraDhe	Tite	Tite	gina
×		2			0		3		
Dha	Tite	KraDhe	Tite	gina	Dha	gina	Dhage	Tinna	kina
×		2			0		3		
Ta	Tite	Krate	Tite	kina	KraTe	Tite	Tite	Tite	kina
×		2			0		3		
Dha	Tite	KraDhe	Tite	gina	Dha	gina	Dhage	Dhinna	gina
×		2			0		3		

Prstar-3

Dha	Tite	KraDhe	Tite	KraDhe	Tite	KraDhe	Tite	Tite	gina
×		2			0		3		
Dha	Tite	KraDhe	Tite	gina	Dha	gina	Dhage	Tinna	kina
×		2			0		3		
Ta	Tite	Krate	Tite	KraTe	Tite	KraTe	Tite	Tite	kina
×		2			0		3		
Dha	Tite	KraDhe	Tite	gina	Dha	gina	Dhage	Dhinna	gina
×		2			0		3		

Prastar-4

Dha	Tite	KraDhe	Tite	Tite	Dha	gina	Dhage	Dhinna	gina
×		2			0		3		
Dha	Tite	KraDhe	Tite	gina	Dha	gina	Dhage	Tinna	kina
×		2			0		3		

Ta	Tite	KraTe	Tite	Tite	Ta	kina	Take	Tinna	kina
×		2			0		3		
Dha	Tite	KraDhe	Tite	gina	Dha	gina	Dhage	Dhinna	gina
×		2			0		3		

Prastar-5

Dha	Tite	KraDhe	Tite	Tite	KraDhe	Tite	Dhage	Dhinna	gina
×		2			0		3		
Dha	Tite	KraDhe	Tite	gina	Dha	gina	Dhage	Tinna	kina
×		2			0		3		
Ta	Tite	KraTe	Tite	Tite	KraTe	Tite	Take	Tinna	kina
×		2			0		3		
Dha	Tite	KraDhe	Tite	gina	Dha	gina	Dhage	Dhinna	gina
×		2			0		3		

Prstar-6

Dha	gina	Dhage	Dhinna	gina	Dha	gina	Dhage	Dhinna	gina
×		2			0		3		
Dha	Tite	KraDhe	Tite	gina	Dha	gina	Dhage	Tinna	kina
×		2			0		3		
Ta	kina	Take	Tinna	kina	Ta	kina	Take	Tinna	kina
×		2			0		3		
Dha	Tite	KraDhe	Tite	gina	Dha	gina	Dhage	Dhinna	gina
×		2			0		3		

Tihai

KraDhe	Tite	gina	Dhage	Dhinna	gina	Dha	KraDhe	Tite	gina
×		2			0		3		
Dhage	Dhinna	gina	Dha	KraDhe	Tite	gina	Dhage	Dhinna	gina
×		2			0		3		
Dha									
×									

Kayada-3

Dha	Gheranage	Tirakita	TakTak	Tirakita
×		2		
Dha	Gheranage	Tirakita	Tuna	Kitatak
0		3		
Ta	Keranake	Tirakita	TakTak	Tirakita
×		2		
Dha	Gheranage	Tirakita	Dhinna	Kitatak
0		3		

Prastar-1

Dha	Gheranage	Tirakita	TakTak	Tirakita
×		2		
Dha	Gheranage	Tirakita	TakTak	Tirakita
0		3		
Dha	Gheranage	Tirakita	TakTak	Tirakita
×		2		
Dha	Gheranage	Tirakita	Tuna	Kitatak
0		3		
Ta	Keranake	Tirakita	TakTak	Tirakita
×		2		
Ta	Keranake	Tirakita	TakTak	Tirakita
0		3		
Dha	Gheranage	Tirakita	TakTak	Tirakita
×		2		
Dha	Gheranage	Tirakita	Dhinna	Kitatak
0		3		

Prastar-2

Dha	Gheranage	Dha	Gheranage	Tirakita
×		2		
Dha	Gheranage	Tirakita	Dhinna	Kitatak
0		3		
Dha	Gheranage	Tirakita	TakTak	Tirakita
×		2		
Dha	Gheranage	Tirakita	Tuna	Kitatak
0		3		
Ta	Keranake	Ta	Keranake	Tirakita
×		2		

Ta	Keranake	Tirakita	Tuna	Kitatak
0		3		
Dha	Gheranage	Tirakita	TakTak	Tirakita
×		2		
Dha	Gheranage	Tirakita	Dhinna	Kitatak
0		3		

Prastar-3

Dha	Gheranage	Dha-Ghera	nageTira	kitataka
×		2		
Dha	Gheranage	Tirakita	Dhinna	Kitatak
0		3		
Dha	Gheranage	Tirakita	TakTak	Tirakita
×		2		
Dha	Gheranage	Tirakita	Tuna	Kitatak
0		3		
Ta	Keranake	Ta-Kera	nakeTira	kitataka
×		2		
Ta	Keranake	Tirakita	Tuna	Kitatak
0		3		
Dha	Gheranage	Tirakita	TakTak	Tirakita
×		2		
Dha	Gheranage	Tirakita	Dhinna	Kitatak
0		3		

Prastar-4

Dha	Gheranage	Tirakita	Dhinna	Kitatak
×		2		
Dhinna	Kitatak	Tirakita	Dhinna	Kitatak
0		3		
Dha	Gheranage	Tirakita	TakTak	Tirakita
×		2		
Dha	Gheranage	Tirakita	Tuna	Kitatak
0		3		
Ta	Keranake	Tirakita	Tuna	Kitatak
×		2		
Tuna	Kitatak	Tirakita	Tuna	Kitatak
0		3		

Dha ×	Gheranage	Tirakita 2	TakTak	Tirakita
Dha 0	Gheranage	Tirakita 3	Dhinna	Kitatak

Prastar-5

Tirakita ×	Dhinna	Tirakita 2	Dhinna	Kitatak
Tirakita 0	Dhinna	Tirakita 3	Dhinna	Kitatak
Dha ×	Gheranage	Tirakita 2	TakTak	Tirakita
Dha 0	Gheranage	Tirakita 3	Tuna	Kitatak
Tirakita ×	Tuna	Tirakita 2	Tuna	Kitatak
Tirakita 0	Tuna	Tirakita 3	Tuna	Kitatak
Dha ×	Gheranage	Tirakita 2	TakTak	Tirakita
Dha 0	Gheranage	Tirakita 3	Dhinna	Kitatak

Tihai

Tirakita ×	Dhinna	Kitatak 2	Tirakita	Dhinna
Kitatak 0	Dha	Tirakita 3	Dhinna	Kitatak
Tirakita ×	Dhinna	Kitatak 2	Dha	Tirakita
Dhinna 0	Kitatak	Tirakita 3	Dhinna	Kitatak
Dha ×				

Chakradar-Tihai

Tirakita ×	Dhinna	Kitatak 2	Tirakita	Dhinna
Kitatak 0	Dha	Dhinna 3	Kitatak	Dha

Dhinna	Kitatak	Dha	ऽ	Tirakita
×		2		
Dhinna	Kitatak	Tirakita	Dhinna	Kitatak
0		3		
Dha	Dhinna	Kitatak	Dha	Dhinna
×		2		
Kitatak	Dha	ऽ	Tirakita	Dhinna
0		3		
Kitatak	Tirakita	Dhinna	Kitatak	Dha
×		2		
Dhinna	Kitatak	Dha	Dhinna	Kitatak
0		3		
Dha				
×				

Kayada–4

TakaDin	TakaTaka	Dinataka	TakaTin	Tinnakita
×		2		
TakaTin	TakaTaka	Dinataka	TakaDhin	Dhinnakita
0		3		

Prastar-1

TakaDin	TakaTaka	Dinataka	Dinataka	TakaDin
×		2		
TakaDin	TakaTaka	Dinataka	TakaTin	Tinnakita
0		3		
TakaTin	TakaTaka	TinTaka	TinTaka	TakaTin
×		2		
TakaTin	TakaTaka	Dinataka	TakaDhin	Dhinnakita
0		3		

Prastar-2

TakaDin	TakaDin	TakaTaka	TakaDin	TakaTaka
×		2		
TakaDin	TakaTaka	Dinataka	TakaTin	Tinnakita
0		3		
TakaTin	TakaTin	TakaTaka	TakaTin	TakaTaka
×		2		
TakaTin	TakaTaka	Dinataka	TakaDhin	Dhinnakita
0		3		

Prastar-3

TakaDin	TakaDin	TakaDin	TakaTaka	TakaTaka
×		2		
TakaDin	TakaTaka	Dinataka	TakaTin	Tinnakita
0		3		
TakaTin	TakaTin	TakaTin	TakaTaka	TakaTaka
×		2		
TakaTin	TakaTaka	Dinataka	TakaDhin	Dhinnakita
0		3		

Prastar-4

TakaTaka	DinaTaka	TakaDin	TakaTaka	DinaTaka
×		2		
TakaDin	TakaTaka	Dinataka	TakaTin	Tinnakita
0		3		

TakaTaka	TinaTaka	TakaTin	TakaTaka	TinaTaka
×		2		
TakaTin	TakaTaka	Dinataka	TakaDhin	Dhinnakita
0		3		

Prastar-5

TakaTaka	TakaTaka	TakaTaka	TakaDin	TakaDin
×		2		
TakaDin	TakaTaka	Dinataka	TakaTin	Tinnakita
0		3		
TakaTaka	TakaTaka	TakaTaka	TakaTin	TakaTin
×		2		
TakaTin	TakaTaka	Dinataka	TakaDhin	Dhinnakita
0		3		

Prastar-6

TakaDhin	Dhinnakita	TakaDhin	TakaDhin	Dhinnakita
×		2		
TakaDin	TakaTaka	Dinataka	TakaTin	Tinnakita
0		3		
TakaTin	Tinnakita	TakaTin	TakaTin	Tinnakita
×		2		
TakaTin	TakaTaka	Dinataka	TakaDhin	Dhinnakita
0		3		

Tihai

TakaDhin	TakaDhin	Dhinnakita	DhaऽTaka	Dhin Taka
×		2		
DhinDhinna	kita Dhaऽ	TakaDhin	TakaDhin	Dhinnakita
0		3		
Dha				
×				

Bant

Gina	Tite	DhaTi	teDhe	Tite	Gina	Tite	Dhage	Tinna	kita
×		2			0		3		
Kina	Tite	TaTi	teTe	Tite	Gina	Tite	Dhage	Dhinna	kita
×		2			0		3		

Prastar-1

Gina	Tite	DhaTi	teDhe	Tite	Gina	Tite	DhaTi	teDhe	Tite
×		2			0		3		
Gina	Tite	DhaTi	teDhe	Tite	Gina	Tite	Dhage	Tinna	kita
×		2			0		3		
Kina	Tite	TaTi	teTe	Tite	Kina	Tite	TaTi	teTe	Tite
×		2			0		3		
Gina	Tite	DhaTi	teDhe	Tite	Gina	Tite	Dhage	Dhinna	kita
×		2			0		3		

Prastar-2

Gina	Tite	DhaTi	teDhe	Tite	Tite	Gina	DhaTi	teDhe	Tite
×		2			0		3		
Gina	Tite	DhaTi	teDhe	Tite	Gina	Tite	Dhage	Tinna	kita
×		2			0		3		
Kina	Tite	TaTi	teTe	Tite	Tite	kina	TaTi	teTe	Tite
×		2			0		3		
Gina	Tite	DhaTi	teDhe	Tite	Gina	Tite	Dhage	Dhinna	kita
×		2			0		3		

Prastar-3

Gina	Tite	Gina	Tite	DhaTi	teDhe	Tite	DhaTi	teDhe	Tite
×		2			0		3		
Gina	Tite	DhaTi	teDhe	Tite	Gina	Tite	Dhage	Tinna	kita
×		2			0		3		
Kina	Tite	Kina	Tite	Tati	teTe	Tite	Tati	teTe	Tite
×		2			0		3		
Gina	Tite	DhaTi	teDhe	Tite	Gina	Tite	Dhage	Dhinna	kita
×		2			0		3		

Prastar-4

Gina	Tite	DhaTi	teDhe	Tite	Dhite	Dhite	DheTi	teDhe	Tite
×		2			0		3		
Gina	Tite	DhaTi	teDhe	Tite	Gina	Tite	Dhage	Tinna	kita
×		2			0		3		

Kina	Tite	TaTi	teTe	Tite	Tite	Tite	TeTi	teTe	Tite
×		2			0		3		
Gina	Tite	DhaTi	teDhe	Tite	Gina	Tite	Dhage	Dhinna	kita
×		2			0		3		

Prastar-5

Gina	Tite	Dhage	Tinna	Kita	Kina	Tite	Dhage	Dhinna	Kita
×		2			0		3		
Gina	Tite	Dhage	Tinna	Kita	Kina	Tite	Dhage	Dhinna	Kita
×		2			0		3		

Prastar-6

Gina	Tite	Tite	Gina	Tite	Gina	Tite	Dhage	Tinna	kita
×		2			0		3		
Kina	Tite	Tite	Kina	Tite	Gina	Tite	Dhage	Dhinna	kita
×		2			0		3		

Prastar-7

Dhage	Dhinna	Dhage	Tinna	kita	Take	Tinna	Dhage	Dhinna	kita
×		2				0		3	
Dhage	Dhinna	Dhage	Tinna	kita	Take	Tinna	Dhage	Dhinna	kita
×		2				0		3	

Tihai

Dhage	Dhinna	kita	Dhage	Dhinna	
×		2			
kita	Dha	Dhage	Dhinna	kita	
0		3			
Dhage	Dhinna	kita	Dha	Dhage	
×		2			
Dhinna	kita	Dhage	Dhinna	kita	Dha
0		3			×

Bant–2

DhaTrakaDhe	Titegina	Dhaऽgina	Dharagina	Tunnakatta
×		2		
TaTrakaTe	Titekina	Dhaऽgina	Dharagina	Dhinnakatta
0		3		

Prastar-1

DhaTrakaDhe	Titegina	DhaTrakaDhe	Titegina	Dha·gina
×		2		
DhaTrakaDhe	Titegina	Dhaऽgina	Dharagina	Tunnakatta
0		3		
TaTrakaTe	Titekina	TaTrakaTe	Titekina	Taऽkina
×		2		
Dha TrakaDhe	Titegina	Dhaऽgina	Dharagina	Dhinnakatta
0		3		

Prastar-2

DhaTrakaDhe	Titegina	Dharagina	Titegina	Dharagina
×		2		
DhaTrakaDhe	Titegina	Dhaऽgina	Dharagina	Tunnakatta
0		3		
TaTrakaTe	Titekina	Tarakina	Titekina	Tarakina
×		2		
DhaTrakaDhe	Titegina	Dhaऽgina	Dharagina	Dhinnakatta
0		3		

Prastar-3

DhaTrakaDhe	Titegina	Dhaऽgina	Titegina	Dhaऽgina
×		2		
DhaTrakaDhe	Titegina	Dhaऽgina	Dharagina	Tunnakatta
0		3		
TaTrakaTe	Titekina	Taऽkina	Titekina	Taऽkina
×		2		
DhaTrakaDhe	Titegina	Dhaऽgina	Dharagina	Dhinnakatta
0		3		

Prastar-4

DhaTrakaDhe	Titegina	Dhaऽgina	Dha·gina	Dhaऽgina
×		2		
DhaTrakaDhe	Titegina	Dhaऽgina	Dharagina	Tunnakatta
0		3		

TaTrakaTe	Titekina	TaऽKina	TaऽKina	TaऽKina
×		2		
DhaTrakaDhe	Titegina	Dhaऽgina	Dharagina	Dhinnakatta
0		3		

Prastar-5

Dharagina	Tunnakatta	Dharagina	Dharagina	Tunnakatta
×		2		
Tarakina	Tunnakatta	Dharagina	Dharagina	Dhinnakatta
0		3		

Prastar-6

GinaDhara	GinaTunna	KattaGina	Dharagina	Tunnakatta
×		2		
KinaTara	kinaTunna	KattaGina	Dharagina	Dhinnakatta
0		3		

Tihai-1

KattaGina	Dharagina	Dhinnakatta	DhaऽKatta	GinaDhara
×		2		
GinaDhinna	KattaDha	KattaGina	Dharagina	Dhinnakatta
0		3		
Dha				
×				

Tihai-2

Dharagina	Dharagina	Dhinnakatta	DhaऽDhara	GinaDhara
×		2		
GinaDhinna	KattaDhaऽ	Dharagina	Dharagina	Dhinnakatta
0		3		
Dha				
×				

Chakradar-Tihai

Dharagina	Dharagina	Dhinnakatta	DhaऽDhinna	KattaDhaऽ
×		2		
Dhinnakatta	Dha	Dharagina	Dharagina	Dhinnakatta
0		3		
DhaऽDhinna	KattaDhaऽ	Dhinnakatta	Dha	Dharagina
×		2		
Dharagina	Dhinnakatta	DhaऽDhinna	KattaDhaऽ	Dhinnakatta
0		3		
Dha				
×				

Chakradar-Tukra

DhageTite	DhaginaDha	KraDhaTuna	KatऽTite	TiteDinऽ
×		2		
NaNaTite	TiteKraDha	ऽnaKata	DhaऽTite	KraDhaऽna
0		3		
KateDhaऽ	TiteKraDha	ऽnaKata	DhaऽDhage	TiteDhagi
×		2		
NaDhakradha	Tunakata	TiteTite	DinऽNaNa	TiteTie
0		3		
KraDhaऽna	KateDhaऽ	TiteKraDha	ऽnaKata	DhaऽTite
×		2		
KraDhaऽna	KateDhaऽ	DhageTite	DhaginaDha	KraDhaTuna
0		3		
KatऽTite	TiteDinऽ	NaNaTite	TiteKraDha	ऽnaKata
×				
DhaऽTite	KraDhaऽna	KateDhaऽ	TiteKraDha	naKata
0		3		
Dha				
×				

Chakradar-Tukra

DhaऽGhera	nagetira	Kitataka	TaऽTite	katagadi
×		2		
GanaDhaऽ	naDhaऽna	DhaऽGadi	GanaDhaऽ	naDhaऽna
0		3		
DhaऽGadi	GanaDhaऽ	naDhaऽna	DhaऽDhaऽ	Gheranage
×		2		
Tirakita	takaTaऽ	Titekata	Gadigana	DhaऽnaDha
0		3		
ऽnaDhaऽ	Gadigana	DhaऽnaDha	ऽnaDhaऽ	Gadigana
×		2		
DhaऽnaDha	ऽnaDhaऽ	DhaऽGhera	nagetira	Kitataka
0		3		
TaऽTite	katagadi	GanaDhaऽ	naDhaऽna	DhaऽGadi
×		2		
GanaDhaऽ	naDhaऽna	DhaऽGadi	GanaDhaऽ	naDhaऽna
0		3		
Dha				
×				

Chakradar-Tukra

KitatakaTaSSS ×	KitatakaTaSSS	
Tunakitataka 2	Ta-tirakitataka	DhetS,DhiraDhira
kitatakaDhetS 0	DhiraDhirakitataka	
Dha-tirakitataka 3	Dha	KitatakaTaSSS
DhiraDhirakitataka ×	DhaS,DhiraDhira	
kitatakaDhaS 2	DhiraDhirakitataka	Dha
KitatakaTaSSS 0	DhiraDhirakitataka	
DhaS,DhiraDhira 3	kitatakaDhaS	DhiraDhirakitataka
Dha ×	KitatakaTaSSS	
DhiraDhirakitataka 2	DhaS,DhiraDhira	kitatakaDhaS
DhiraDhirakitataka 0	Dha	
KitatakaTaSSS 3	KitatakaTaSSS	Tunakitataka
Ta-tirakitataka ×	DhetS,DhiraDhira	
kitatakaDhetS 2	DhiraDhirakitataka	Dha-tirakitataka
Dha 0	KitatakaTaSSS	
DhiraDhirakitataka 3	DhaS,DhiraDhira	kitatakaDhaS
DhiraDhirakitataka ×	Dha	
KitatakaTaSSS 2	DhiraDhirakitataka	DhaS,DhiraDhira

kitatakaDhaS	DhiraDhirakitataka	
0		
Dha	KitatakaTaSSS	DhiraDhirakitataka
3		
DhaS,DhiraDhira	kitatakaDhaS	
×		
DhiraDhirakitatak	Dha	KitatakaTaSSS
2		
KitatakaTaSSS	Tunakitataka	
0		
Ta-tirakitataka	DhetS,DhiraDhira	kitatakaDhetS
3		
DhiraDhirakitataka	Dha-tirakitataka	
×		
Dha	KitatakaTaSSS	DhiraDhirakitataka
2		
DhaS,DhiraDhira	kitatakaDhaS	
0		
DhiraDhirakitatak	Dha	KitatakaTaSSS
3		
DhiraDhirakitataka	DhaS,DhiraDhira	
×		
kitatakaDhaS	DhiraDhirakitatak	Dha
2		
KitatakaTaSSS	DhiraDhirakitataka	
0		
DhaS,DhiraDhira	kitatakaDhaS	DhiraDhirakitatak
3		
Dha		
×		

Farmaishi Chakradar-Tukra

DheTite	Dhagina	DhaSGi	naTite	DhaTinS
×		2		
NaTite	KaTite	Katakra	DhaSna	DhaSna
0		3		
DhaSkra	DhaSna	DhaSna	DhaSkra	DhaSna
×		2		

DhaSna 0	Dha	DheTite 3	Dhagina	DhaSGi
naTite ×	DhaTiS	NaTite 2	KaTite	Katakra
DhaSna 0	DhaSna	DhaSkra 3	DhaSna	DhaSna
DhaSkra ×	DhaSna	DhaSna 2	Dha	DheTite
Dhagina 0	DhaSGi	naTite 3	DhaTinS	NaTite
KaTite ×	Katakra	DhaSna 2	DhaSna	DhaSkra
DhaSna 0	DhaSna	DhaSkra 3	DhaSna	DhaSna
Dha ×				

Navahakka

KraDhaTite ×	DhaS	SKraDha 2	TiteDhaS	SS
KraDhaTite 0	Dha	KraDhaTite 3	DhaS	SKraDha
Tite DhaS ×	SS	KraDhaTite 2	Dha	KraDhaTite
DhaS 0	SKraDha	Tite DhaS 3	SS	KraDhaTite
Dha ×				

11

Composition in Ektal

Kayada–1

DhaTi	teDha	Gina	Dhage	Tinna	Kina
×		0		2	
TaTi	teTa	kina	Dhage	Dhinna	Gina
0		3		4	

Prastar-1

DhaTi	teDha	Gina	DhaTi	teDha	Gina
×		0		2	
DhaTi	teDha	Gina	Dhage	Tinna	Kina
0		3		4	
TaTi	teTa	kina	TaTi	teTa	kina
×		0		2	
DhaTi	teDha	Gina	Dhage	Dhinna	Gina
0		3		4	

Prastar-2

DhaTi	teDha	Tite	DhaTi	teDha	Gina
×		0		2	
DhaTi	teDha	Gina	Dhage	Tinna	Kina
0		3		4	
TaTi	teTa	Tite	TaTi	teTa	kina
×		0		2	
DhaTi	teDha	Gina	Dhage	Dhinna	Gina
0		3		4	

Prastar-3

DhaTi	teDha	Tite	Tite	Tite	Tite
×		0		2	
DhaTi	teDha	Gina	Dhage	Tinna	Kina
0		3		4	
TaTi	teTa	Tite	Tite	Tite	Tite
×		0		2	
DhaTi	teDha	Gina	Dhage	Dhinna	Gina
0		3		4	

Prastar-4

Gina	Dha	Gina	Dhage	Dhinna	Gina
×		0		2	
DhaTi	teDha	Gina	Dhage	Tinna	Kina
0		3		4	
Kina	Ta	Kina	Take	Tinna	Kina
×		0		2	
DhaTi	teDha	Gina	Dhage	Dhinna	Gina
0		3		4	

Prastar-5

Dhage	Dhinna	Gina	Dhage	Dhinna	Gina
×		0		2	
DhaTi	teDha	Gina	Dhage	Tinna	Kina
0		3		4	
Take	Tinna	Kina	Take	Tinna	Kina
×		0		2	
Dha	Ti teDha	Gina	Dhage	Dhinna	Gina
0		3		4	

Prastar-6

Dhage	Dhinna	Dhage	Dhinna	Dhage	Dhinna
×		0		2	
DhaTi	teDha	Gina	Dhage	Tinna	Kina
0		3		4	
Take	Tinna	Take	Tinna	Take	Tinna
×		0		2	
DhaTi	teDha	Gina	Dhage	Dhinna	Gina
0		3		4	

Tihai

DhaTi ×	teDha	Gina 0	Dhage	Dhinna 2	Gina
Dha 0	ऽ	ऽ 3	DhaTi	teDha 4	Gina
Dhage ×	Dhinna	Gina 0	Dha	ऽ 2	ऽ
DhaTi 0	teDha	Gina 3	Dhage	Dhinna 4	Gina
Dha ×					

Chakradar-Tihai

DhaTi ×	teDha	Gina 0	Dhage	Dhinna 2	Gina
Dha 0	ऽ	Gina 3	Dhage	Dhinna 4	Gina
Dha ×	ऽ	Gina 0	Dhage	Dhinna 2	Gina
Dha 0	ऽ	ऽ 3	DhaTi	teDha 4	Gina
Dhage ×	Dhinna	Gina 0	Dha	ऽ 2	Gina
Dhage 0	Dhinna	Gina 3	Dha	ऽ 4	Gina
Dhage ×	Dhinna	Gina 0	Dha	ऽ 2	ऽ
DhaTi 0	teDha	Gina 3	Dhage	Dhinna 4	Gina
Dha ×	ऽ	Gina 0	Dhage	Dhinna 2	Gina
Dha 0	ऽ	Gina 3	Dhage	Dhinna 4	Gina
Dha ×					

Kayada-2

DhaSTirakitataka	DhageTirakita	TakDhaSTirakita	DhaSTirakitataka
×		0	
DhageTirakita	TunaKitataka	TaSTirakitataka	TakeTirakita
2		0	
TakTaSTirakita	DhaSTirakitataka	DhageTirakita	Dhinnakitataka
3		4	

Prastar-1

DhaSTirakitataka	DhageTirakita	TakDhaSTirakita	DhaSTirakitataka
×		0	
DhageTirakita	TakDhSTirakita	DhaSTirakitataka	DhageTirakita
2		0	
TakDhaSTirakita	DhaSTirakitataka	DhageTirakita	TunaKitataka
3		4	
TaSTirakitataka	TakeTirakita	TakTaSTirakita	TaSTirakitataka
×		0	
TakeTirakita	TakTaSTirakita	DhaSTirakitataka	DhageTirakita
2		0	
TakDhaSTirakita	DhaSTirakitataka	DhageTirakita	Dhinnakitataka
3		4	

Prastar-2

DhaSTirakitataka	DhageDhaSTira	kitatakaDhage	DhaSTirakitataka
×		0	
DhageTirakita	TakDhaSTirakita	DhaSTirakitataka	DhageTirakita
2		0	
TakDhaSTirakita	DhaSTirakitataka	DhageTirakita	TunaKitataka
3		4	
TaSTirakitataka	TakeTaSTira	kitatakaTake	TaSTirakitataka
×		0	
TakeTirakita	TakTaSTirakita	DhaSTirakitataka	DhageTirakita
2		0	
TakDhaSTirakita	DhaSTirakitataka	DhageTirakita	Dhinnakitataka
3		4	

Prastar-3

DhaTirakitataka	Dhage Tirakita	TakDhaSTirakita	DhageTirakita
×		0	
DhageTirakita	TakDhaSTirakita	DhaSTirakitataka	DhageTirakita
2		0	

TakDhaऽTirakita	DhaऽTirakitataka	DhageTirakita	TunaKitataka
3		4	
TaऽTirakitataka	TakeTirakita	TakTaऽTirakita	TakeTirakita
×		0	
TakeTirakita	TakTaऽTirakita	DhaऽTirakitataka	DhageTirakita
2		0	
TakDhaऽTirakita	DhaऽTirakitataka	DhageTirakita	Dhinnakitataka
3		4	

Prastar-4

Dhage Tirakita	TakDhaऽTirakita	DhageTirakita	TakDhaऽTirakita
×		0	
DhageTirakita	TakDhaऽTirakita	DhaऽTirakitataka	DhageTirakita
2		0	
TakDhaऽTirakita	DhaऽTirakitataka	DhageTirakita	TunaKitataka
3		4	
TakeTirakita	TakTaऽTirakita	TakeTirakita	TakTaऽTirakita
×		0	
TakeTirakita	TakTaऽTirakita	DhaऽTirakitataka	DhageTirakita
2		0	
TakDhaऽTirakita	DhaऽTirakitataka	DhageTirakita	Dhinnakitataka
3		4	

Prastar-5

TirakitaTakDhaऽ	TirakitatakaTira	kitatakaTirakita	DhaऽTirakitataka
×		0	
DhageTirakita	TunaKitataka	TirakitatakaTaऽ	TirakitatakaTira
2		0	
kitatakaTirakita	DhaऽTirakitataka	DhageTirakita	Dhinnakitataka
3		4	

Prastar-6

TirakitaDhinna	kitatakaTirakita	Dhinnakitataka	Dha ·Tirakitataka
×		0	
DhageTirakita	TunaKitataka	TirakitataTuna	kitatakaTirakita
2		0	
TunaKitataka	Dha ·Tirakitataka	DhageTirakita	Dhinnakitataka
3		4	

Tihai

DhaSTirakitataka ×	DhageTirakita	Dhinnakitataka 0	Dha SSS
SSDhaSTira 2	KitatakaDhage	TirakitataDhinna 0	kitatakaDhaS
SSSS 3	DhaSTirakitataka	DhageTirakita 4	Dhinnakitataka
Dha ×			

Kayada-3

Tirakita	DhageTite	Gheranage	Tirakita	Tuna	Kitataka
×		0		2	
Tirakita	TakeTite	Keranake	Tirakita	Dhinna	Kitataka
0		3		4	

Prastar-1

Tirakita	DhageTite	Gheranage	Tirakita	DhageTite	Gheranage
×		0		2	
Tirakita	DhageTite	Gheranage	Tirakita	Tuna	Kitataka
0		3		4	
Tirakita	TakeTite	Keranake	Tirakita	TakeTite	Keranake
×		0		2	
Tirakita	DhageTite	Gheranage	Tirakita	Dhinna	Kitataka
0		3		4	

Prastar-2

Tirakita	DhageTite	Gheranage	DhageTite	DhageTite	Gheranage
×		0		2	
Tirakita	DhageTite	Gheranage	Tirakita	Tuna	Kitataka
0		3		4	
Tirakita	TakeTite	Keranake	TakeTite	TakeTite	Keranake
×		0		2	
Tirakita	DhageTite	Gheranage	Tirakita	Dhinna	Kitataka
0		3		4	

Prastar-3

Tirakita	DhageTite	Gheranage	TiteGhera	nageTite	Gheranage
×		0		2	
Tirakita	DhageTite	Gheranage	Tirakita	Tuna	Kitataka
0		3		4	
Tirakita	TakeTite	Keranake	TiteKera	nakeTite	Keranake
×		0		2	
Tirakita	DhageTite	Gheranage	Tirakita	Dhinna	Kitataka
0		3		4	

Prastar-4

DhageTite	Gheranage	DhageTite	Gheranage	DhageTite	Gheranage
×		0		2	
Tirakita	DhageTite	Gheranage	Tirakita	Tuna	Kitataka
0		3		4	

TakeTite	Keranake	TakeTite	Keranake	TakeTite	Keranake
×		0		2	
Tirakita	DhageTite	Gheranage	Tirakita	Dhinna	Kitataka
0		3		4	

Prastar-5

Tirakita	Dhinna	Kitataka	Tirakita	Dhinna	Kitataka
×		0		2	
Tirakita	DhageTite	Gheranage	Tirakita	Tuna	Kitataka
0		3		4	
Tirakita	Tuna	Kitataka	Tirakita	Tuna	Kitataka
×		0		2	
Tirakita	DhageTite	Gheranage	Tirakita	Dhinna	Kitataka
0		3		4	

Prastar-6

Tirakita	Dhinna	Tirakita	Dhinna	Tirakita	Dhinna
×		0		2	
Tirakita	DhageTite	Gheranage	Tirakita	Tuna	Kitataka
0		3		4	
Tirakita	Tuna	Tirakita	Tuna	Tirakita	Tuna
×		0		2	
Tirakita	DhageTite	Gheranage	Tirakita	Dhinna	Kitataka
0		3		4	

Tihai

Tirakita	Dhinna	Kitataka	DhaS	STira	KitaDhin
×		0		2	
NaKita	takaDha	SS	Tirakita	Dhinna	Kitataka
0		3		4	
Dha					
×					

Kayada-4

DhaऽTirakitataka	DhirDhirKitataka	DhaऽGheranage	DhirDhirKitataka
×		0	
DhaऽTirakitataka	TuऽNaaऽKitataka	TaऽTirakitataka	TiraTiraKitataka
2		0	
DhaऽGheranage	DhirDhirKitataka	DhaऽTirakitataka	DhinnaaKitataka
3		4	

Prastar-1

DhaऽTirakitatak	DhirDhirKitataka	DhaऽGheranage	DhaऽTirakitataka
×		0	
DhirDhirKitataka	DhaऽGheranage	DhaऽTirakitataka	DhirDhirKitataka
2		0	
DhaऽGheranage	DhirDhirKitataka	DhaऽTirakitataka	TuऽNaaऽKitataka
3		4	
TaऽTirakitataka	TiraTiraKitataka	TaऽKeranake	TaऽTirakitataka
×		0	
TiraTiraKitataka	TaऽKeranake	DhaऽTirakitataka	DhirDhirKitataka
2		0	
DhaऽGheranage	DhirDhirKitataka	DhaऽTirakitataka	DhinnaaKitataka
3		4	

Prastar-2

DhaऽTirakitataka	DhirDhirKitataka	DhirDhirKitataka	DhaऽTirakitataka
×		0	
DhirDhirKitataka	DhirDhirKitataka	DhaऽTirakitataka	DhirDhirKitataka
2		0	
DhaऽGheranage	DhirDhirKitataka	DhaऽTirakitataka	TuऽNaaऽKitataka
3		4	
TaऽTirakitataka	TiraTiraKitataka	TiraTiraKitataka	TaऽTirakitataka
×		0	
TiraTiraKitataka	TiraTiraKitataka	DhaऽTirakitataka	DhirDhirKitataka
2		0	
DhaऽGheranage	DhirDhirKitataka	DhaऽTirakitataka	DhinnaaKitataka
3		4	

Prastar-3

DhaऽTirakitataka	DhirDhirKitataka	DhaऽGheranage	DhirDhirKitataka
×		0	

DhaऽGheranage	DhirDhirKitataka	DhaऽTirakitataka	DhirDhirKitataka
2		0	
DhaऽGheranage	DhirDhirKitataka	DhaऽTirakitataka	Tu ·Naa ·Kitataka
3		4	
TaऽTirakitataka	TiraTiraKitataka	TaऽKeranake	TiraTiraKitataka
×		0	
TaऽKeranake	TiraTiraKitataka	DhaऽTirakitataka	DhirDhirKitataka
2		0	
DhaऽGheranage	DhirDhirKitataka	DhaऽTirakitataka	DhinnaaKitataka
3		4	

Prastar-4

DhaऽTirakitataka	DhirDhirKitataka	Dha	GheranageDhirDhir
×		0	
KitatakaGheranage	DhirDhirKitataka	DhaऽTirakitataka	DhirDhirKitataka
2		0	
DhaऽGheranage	DhirDhirKitataka	DhaऽTirakitataka	TuऽNaaऽKitataka
3		4	
TaऽTirakitataka	TiraTiraKitataka	Ta	KeranakeTiraTira
×		0	
KitatakaKeranake	TiraTiraKitataka	DhaऽTirakitataka	DhirDhirKitataka
2		0	
DhaऽGheranage	DhirDhirKitataka	DhaऽTirakitataka	DhinnaaKitataka
3		4	

Prastar-5

GheranageDhirDhir	KitatakaGheranage	DhirDhirKitataka	DhirDhirKitataka
×		0	
DhaऽTirakitataka	TuऽNaaऽKitataka	KeranakeTiraTira	kitatakaKeranake
2		0	
DhirDhirKitataka	DhirDhirKitataka	DhaऽTirakitataka	DhinnaaKitataka
3		4	

Prastar-6

GheranageGheranag	DhirDhirKitataka	GheranageGheranage	DhirDhirKitataka
×		0	
DhaऽTirakitataka	TuऽNaaऽKitataka	KeranakeKeranake	TiraTirakitataka
2		0	
GheranageGheranag	DhirDhirKitataka	DhaऽTirakitataka	DhinnaaKitataka
3		4	

Tihai

DhirDhirKitataka	DhaSTirakitataka	DhinnaaKitataka	DhaS
×		0	
SDhirDhir	KitatakaDhaSTira	KitatakaDhinna	KitatakaDha
2		0	
SS	DhirDhirKitataka	DhaSTirakitataka	DhinnaaKitataka
3		4	

Bant-1

DhaSTite	TiteGhera	NageTaka	Tirakita	Takatin	Tinnakina
×		0		2	
TaSTite	Titekera	NageTaka	Tirakita	TakaDhin	Dhinnagina
0		3		4	

Prastar-1

DhaSTite	TiteGhera	NageTaka	Tirakita	NageTaka	Tirakita
×		0		2	
DhaSTite	TiteGhera	NageTaka	Tirakita	Takatin	Tinnakina
0		3		4	
TaSTite	TiteKera	NakeTaka	Tirakita	NakeTaka	Tirakita
×		0		2	
DhaSTite	TiteGhera	NageTaka	Tirakita	TakaDhin	Dhinnagina
0		3		4	

Prastar-2

DhaSTite	TiteGhera	NageTaka	Tirakita	DhaSSS	Gheranage
×		0		2	
DhaSTite	TiteGhera	NageTaka	Tirakita	Takatin	Tinnakina
0		3		4	
TaSTite	TiteKera	NakeTaka	Tirakita	TaSSS	Keranake
×		0		2	
DhaSTite	TiteGhera	NageTaka	Tirakita	TakaDhin	Dhinnagina
0		3		4	

Prastar-3

DhaSTite	TiteGhera	NageTaka	Tirakita	DhaSTite	TiteGhera
×		0		2	
NageTaka	Tirakita	NageTaka	Tirakita	Takatin	Tinnakina
0		3		4	
TaSTite	TiteKera	NakeTaka	Tirakita	TaSTite	TiteKera
×		0		2	
NageTaka	Tirakita	NageTaka	Tirakita	TakaDhin	Dhinnagina
0		3		4	

Prastar-4

DhaSTite	TiteGhera	NageTaka	Tirakita	GheraNage	TakaTira
×		0		2	
KitaGhera	NageTaka	Tirakita	TakaTin	Takatin	Tinnakina
0		3		4	
TaSTite	TiteKera	NakeTaka	Tirakita	KeraNake	TakaTira
×		0		2	
KitaGhera	NageTake	Tirakita	TakaDhin	TakaDhin	Dhinnagina
0		3		4	

Prastar-5

DhaSTite	TiteGhera	NageTite	Titegina	Takatin	Tinnakina
×		0		2	
TaSTite	TiteKera	NakeTite	Titegina	TakaDhin	Dhinnagina
0		3		4	

Prastar-6

Gheranage	TiteGhera	NageTite	Titegina	Takatin	Tinnakina
×		0		2	
Keranake	TiteKera	NakeTite	Titegina	TakaDhin	Dhinnagina
0		3		4	

Prastar-7

Takatin	Takatin	Tinnakina	TakaDhina
×		0	
TakaDhin	Dhinnagina	Takatin	Takatin
2		0	
Tinnakina	TakaDhin	TakaDhin	Dhinnagina
3		4	

Tihai

TakaDhin	TakaDhin	Dhinnagina	DhaS	
×		0		
STaka	DhinTaka	DhinDhinna	ginaDha	
2		0		
SS	TakaDhin	TakaDhin	Dhinnagina	Dha
3		4		×

Bant-2

Dhaऽ	KraDhe	Tite	Dhar	Dhatin	Nar
×		0		2	
Taऽ	KraTe	Tite	Dhar	DhaDhin	Nar
0		3		4	

Prastar-1

Dhaऽ	KraDhe	Tite	Dhaऽ	KraDhe	Tite
×		0		2	
Dha	KraDhe	Tite	Dhar	Dhatin	Nar
0		3		4	
Taऽ	KraTe	Tite	Taऽ	KraTe	Tite
×		0		2	
Dhaऽ	KraDhe	Tite	Dhar	DhaDhin	Nar
0		3		4	

Prastar-2

Dhaऽ	KraDhe	Tite	Tite	KraDhe	Tite
×		0		2	
Dhaऽ	KraDhe	Tite	Dhar	Dhatin	Nar
0		3		4	
Taऽ	KraTe	Tite	Tite	KraTe	Tite
×		0		2	
Dhaऽ	KraDhe	Tite	Dhar	DhaDhin	Nar
0		3		4	

Prastar-3

Dhaऽ	KraDhe	Tite	Dhar	Dhar	Dhar
×		0		2	
Dhaऽ	KraDhe	Tite	Dhar	Dhatin	Nar
0		3		4	
Taऽ	KraTe	Tite	Tar	Tar	Tar
×		0		2	
Dhaऽ	KraDhe	Tite	Dhar	DhaDhin	Nar
0		3		4	

Prastar-4

KraDhe	Tite	Tite	Dhar	DhaDhin	Nar
×		0		2	
DhaS	KraDhe	Tite	Dhar	Dhatin	Nar
0		3		4	
KraTe	Tite	Tite	Tar	Tatin	Nar
×		0		2	
DhaS	KraDhe	Tite	Dhar	DhaDhin	Nar
0		3		4	

Prastar-5

Dhar	Dhar	DhaDhin	Nar	DhaDhin	Nar
×		0		2	
DhaS	KraDhe	Tite	Dhar	Dhatin	Nar
0		3		4	
Tar	Tar	Tatin	Nar	Tatin	Nar
×		0		2	
DhaS	KraDhe	Tite	Dhar	DhaDhin	Nar
0		3		4	

Prastar-6

DheTi	teDhe	Tite	Dhar	Dhar	Dhar
×		0		2	
DhaS	KraDhe	Tite	Dhar	Dhatin	Nar
0		3		4	
TeTi	teTe	Tite	Tara	Tar	Tar
×		0		2	
DhaS	KraDhe	Tite	Dhar	DhaDhin	Nar
0		3		4	

Prastar-7

DhaS	KraDhe	Tite	Dhar	DhaDhin	Nar
×		0		2	
Dhar	DhaDhin	Nar	Dhar	Dhatin	Nar
0		3		4	
TaS	Krate	Tite	Tar	Tatin	Nar
×		0		2	
Dhar	DhaDhin	Nar	Dhar	DhaDhin	Nar
0		3		4	

Tihai

Dha	KraDhe	Tite	Dhara	DhaDhin	Nara
×		0		2	
Dha	ऽ	ऽ	Dha	KraDhe	Tite
0		3		4	
Dhara	DhaDhin	Nara	Dha	ऽ	ऽ
×		0		2	
Dha	KraDhe	Tite	Dhara	DhaDhin	Nara
0		3		4	
Dha					
×					

Tihai-Chakradar

Dha	KraDhe	Tite	Dhara	DhaDhin	Nara
×		0		2	
Dha	ऽ	Tite	Dhara	DhaDhin	Nara
0		3		4	
Dha	ऽ	Tite	Dhara	DhaDhin	Nara
×		0		2	
Dha	ऽ	ऽ	Dha	KraDhe	Tite
0		3		4	
Dhara	DhaDhin	Nara	Dha	ऽ	Tite
×		0		2	
Dhara	DhaDhin	Nara	Dha	ऽ	Tite
0		3		4	
Dhara	DhaDhin	Nara	Dha	ऽ	ऽ
×		0		2	
Dha	KraDhe	Tite	Dhara	DhaDhin	Nara
0		3		4	
Dha	ऽ	Tite	Dhara	DhaDhin	Nara
×		0		2	
Dha	ऽ	Tite	Dhara	DhaDhin	Nara
0		3		4	
Dha					
×					

Navahakka (in Ada Laya)

DhatiDha	ऽDhati	DhaऽDha	tiDhaऽ	ऽDhati	DhaऽDha
×		0		2	
tiDhaऽ	DhatiDha	ऽऽDha	tiDhaऽ	DhatiDha	ऽDhati
0		3		4	
Dha					
×					

Chakradar

DhirDhirkitataka	TakitaDha-	DhirDhirkitataka	TakitaDha-
×		0	
TakitaDha-	TakitaDha-	DhirDhirkitataka	TakitaDha-
2		0	
Kat-DhirDhir	kitatakaDhirDhir	kitatakaTakita	Dha-kat-
3		4	
DhirDhirkitataka	DhirDhirkitataka	TakitaDha-	Kat-DhirDhir
×		0	
kitatakaDhirDhir	kitatakaTakita	Dha	ऽ
2		0	
ऽ	DhirDhirkitataka	TakitaDha-	DhirDhirkitataka
3		4	
TakitaDha-	TakitaDha-	TakitaDha-	DhirDhirkitataka
×		0	
TakitaDha-	Kat-DhirDhir	kitatakaDhirDhir	kitatakaTakita
2		0	
Dha-kat-	DhirDhirkitataka	DhirDhirkitataka	TakitaDha-
3		4	
Kat-DhirDhir	kitatakaDhirDhir	kitatakaTakita	Dha
×		0	
ऽ	ऽ	DhirDhirkitataka	TakitaDha-
2		0	
DhirDhirkitataka	TakitaDha-	TakitaDha-	TakitaDha-
3		4	
DhirDhirkitataka	TakitaDha-	Kat-DhirDhir	kitatakaDhirDhir
×		0	
kitatakaTakita	Dha-kat-	DhirDhirkitataka	DhirDhirkitataka
2		0	

TakitaDha-	Kat-DhirDhir	kitatakaDhirDhir	kitatakaTakita
3		4	
Dha			
×			

Chakradar

DhaऽtirakitaTaka	Taऽ,Dha tira	kitaTakaTa-	Dhettaऽ
×		0	
Dhikkata	ऽnaDhaऽ	TirakitaTakataऽ	ऽDhaऽTa
2		0	
Dha	Dhikkata	ऽnaDhaऽ	TirakitaTakataऽ
3		4	
ऽDhaऽTa	Dha	Dhikkata	ऽnaDhaऽ
×		0	
TirakitaTakataऽ	ऽDhaऽTa	Dha	ऽऽऽऽ
2		0	
ऽऽऽऽ	Dhaऽtirakitataka	Taऽ,Dhaऽtira	KitaTakaTa-
3		4	
Dhettaऽ	Dhikkata	ऽnaDhaऽ	TirakitaTakataऽ
×		0	
ऽDhaऽTa	Dha	Dhikkata	ऽnaDhaऽ
2		0	
TirakitaTakataऽ	ऽDhaऽTa	Dha	Dhikkata
3		4	
ऽnaDhaऽ	TirakitaTakataऽ	ऽDhaऽTa	Dha
×		0	
ऽऽऽऽ	ऽऽऽऽ	Dhaऽtirakitataka	Taऽ,Dhaऽtira
2		0	
KitaTakaTa-	Dhettaऽ	Dhikkata	ऽnaDhaऽ
3		4	
TirakitaTakataऽ	ऽDhaऽTa	Dha	Dhikkata
×		0	
ऽnaDhaऽ	TirakitaTakataऽ	ऽDhaऽTa	Dha
2		0	
Dhikkata	ऽnaDhaऽ	TirakitaTakataऽ	ऽDhaऽTa
3		4	
Dha			
×			

Chakradar-Paran

DheteDhete ×	DhageTite	Kradhetite 0	Dhagetite
KradheSDhe 2	TiteDhage	Titekata 0	Gadigana
DhaSDhaS 3	DhaSSDhe	TiteDhage 4	Titekata
Gadigana ×	DhaSDhaS	DhaSSDhe 0	TiteDhage
Titekata 2	Gadigana	DhaSDhaS 0	DhaSSS
SSDhete 3	DheteDhage	Titekradhe 4	TiteDhage
Titekradhe ×	SDheTite	DhageTite 0	katagadi
GanaDhaS 2	DhaSDhaS	SDheTite 0	DhageTite
Katagadi 3	GanaDhaS	DhaSDhaS 4	SDheTite
DhageTite ×	Katagadi	GanaDhaS 0	DhaSDhaS
SSSS 2	DheteDhete	DhageTite 0	Kradhetite
Dhagetite 3	KradheSDhe	TiteDhage 4	Titekata
Gadigana ×	DhaSDhaS	DhaSSDhe 0	TiteDhage
Titekata 2	Gadigana	DhaSDhaS 0	DhaSSDhe
TiteDhage 3	Titekata	Gadigana 4	DhaSDhaS
Dha ×			

Chakradar–Paran

DhaTrakaDhe ×	Titekata	Gadigana 0	NageTite	KitaDhet- 2	TaSkata
Gadigana 0	NageTite	KitaDhet- 3	Taginna	DhaSDhaS 4	DhaSKita

Dhet-Tagi ×	SnDhaS	DhaSDhaS 0	KitaDhet-	Taginna 2	DhaSDhaS
Dha 0	S	S 3	DhaTrakaDhe	Titekata 4	Gadigana
NageTite ×	KitaDhet-	TaSkata 0	Gadigana	NageTite 2	KitaDhet-
Taginna 0	DhaSDhaS	DhaSKita 3	Dhet-Tagi	SnDhaS 4	DhaSDhaS
KitaDhet- ×	Taginna	DhaSDhaS 0	Dha	S 2	S
DhaTrakaDhe 0	Titekata	Gadigana 3	NageTite	KitaDhet- 4	TaSkata
Gadigana ×	NageTite	KitaDhet- 0	Taginna	DhaSDhaS 2	DhaSKita
Dhet-Tagi 0	SnDhaS	DhaSDhaS 3	KitaDhet-	Taginna 4	DhaSDhaS
Dha ×					

12

Composition in Adachartal

Kayada-1

DhageTraka	Dhinagina	Dhagenage	Dhinagina	DhaSgina	Dhagenage
×		2		0	
Tinakina,	TakeTraka	Tinakina	Takenake	Tinakina	DhaSgina
3		0		4	
Dhagenage	Dhinagina				
0					

Prastar-1

DhageTraka	Dhinagina	Dhagenage	Dhinagina	DhaSgina	DhaSgina
×		2		0	
DhaSgina,	DhageTraka	Dhinagina	Dhagenage	Dhinagina	DhaSgina
3		0		4	
Dhagenage	Tinakina				
0					
TakeTraka	Tinakina	Takenake	Tinakina	TaSkina	TaSkina
×		2		0	
TaSkina ,	DhageTraka	Dhinagina	Dhagenage	Dhinagina	DhaSgina
3		0		4	
Dhagenage	Dhinagina				
0					

Prastar-2

DhageTraka	Dhinagina	TrakaDhina	ginaTraka	Dhinagina	Dhagenage
×		2		0	
Dhinagina,	DhageTraka	Dhinagina	Dhagenage	Dhinagina	DhaSgina
3		0		4	
Dhagenage	Tinakina				
0					

TakeTraka	Tinakina	TrakaTina	kinaTraka	Tinakina	Takenakea
×		2		0	
Tinakina,	DhageTraka	Dhinagina	Dhagenage	Dhinagina	Dhaऽgina
3		0		4	
Dhagenage	Dhinagina				
0					

Prastar-3

DhageTraka	DhageTraka	DhageTraka	Dhinagina	Dhaऽgina	Dhagenage
×		2		0	
Tinakina,	TakeTraka	TakeTraka	TakeTraka	Dhinagina	Dhaऽgina
3		0		4	
Dhagenage	Dhinagina				
0					

Prastar-4

DhageTraka	Dhaऽgina	Dhagenage	Dhinagina	Dhaऽgina	Dhagenage
×		2		0	
Tinakina,	TakeTraka	Taऽkina	TakeNake	Tinakina	Dhaऽgina
3		0		4	
Dhagenage	Dhinagina				
0					

Prastar-5

DhageTraka	Dhinagina	Dhagenage	Dhinagina	Dhaऽgina	Dhagenage
×		2		0	
Tinakina,	TakeTraka	Tinakina	Takenake	Tinakina	Dhaऽgina
3		0		4	
Dhagenage	Dhinagina				
0					

Tihai

Dhaऽgina	Dhaऽgina	Dhagenage	Dhinagina	Dhaऽऽऽ	Dhaऽgina
×		2		0	
Dhaऽgina,	Dhagenage	Dhinagina	Dhaऽऽऽ	Dhaऽgina	Dhaऽgina
3		0		4	
Dhagenage	Dhinagina				
0					
Dha					
×					

Kayada-2

Dhaऽtirakitataka	DhiraDhirakitataka	Dhaऽऽऽkitataka	DhiraDhirakitataka
×		2	
Dhaऽtirakitataka	Dhaऽtirakitataka	Tinnakitataka,	Taऽtirakitataka
0		3	
TiraTirakitataka	Taऽऽऽkitataka	TiraTirakitataka	Dhaऽtirakitataka
0		4	
Dhaऽtirakitataka	Dhinnakitataka		
0			

Prastar-1

Dhaऽtirakitataka	DhiraDhirakitataka	Dhaऽtirkitataka	DhiraDhirakitataka
×		2	
Dhaऽtirakitataka	DhiraDhirakitataka	Dhaऽऽऽkitataka ,	Dhaऽtirakitataka
0		3	
DhiraDhirakitataka	Dhaऽऽऽkitataka	DhiraDhirakitataka	Dhaऽtirakitataka
0		4	
Dhaऽtirakitataka	Tinnakitataka		
0			
Taऽtirakitataka	TiraTirakitataka	Taऽtirakitataka	TiraTirakitataka
×		2	
Taऽtirakitataka	TiraTirakitataka	Taऽऽऽkitataka	Dhaऽtirakitataka
0		3	
DhiraDhirakitataka	Dhaऽऽऽkitataka	DhiraDhirakitataka	Dhaऽtirakitataka
0		4	
Dhaऽtirakitataka	Dhinnakitataka		
0			

Prastar-2

Dhaऽtirakitataka	DhiraDhirakitataka	Dhaऽऽऽkitataka	Dhaऽऽऽkitataka
×		2	
DhiraDhirakitataka	Dhaऽtirakitataka	Tinnakitataka	Taऽtirakitataka
0		3	
TiraTirakitataka	Taऽऽऽkitataka	Taऽऽऽkitataka	DhiraDhirakitataka
0		4	
Dhaऽtirakitataka	Dhinnakitataka		
0			

Prastar-3

DhaStirakitataka	DhiraDhirakitataka	DhiraDhirakitataka	DhiraDhirakitataka
×		2	
DhaSSSkitataka	Dha ·tirakitataka	Tinnakitataka	TaStirakitataka
0		3	
TiraTirakitataka	TiraTirakitataka	TiraTirakitataka	DhaSSSkitataka
0		4	
DhaStirakitataka	Dhinnakitataka		
0			

Prastar-4

DhiraDhirakitataka	Dha ·tirakitataka	DhaSSSkitataka	DhiraDhirakitataka
×		2	
DhiraDhirakitataka	DhaStirakitataka	Tinnakitataka	TiraTirakitataka
0		3	
TaStirakitataka	TaSSSkitataka	TiraTirakitataka	DhirDhirkitataka
0		4	
DhaStirakitataka	Dhinnakitataka		
0			

Tihai

DhiraDhirakitataka	DhaSSSkitataka	DhaStirakitataka	Dhinnakitataka
×		2	
DhaSSS	DhiraDhirakitataka	DhaSSSkitataka	DhaStirakitataka
0		3	
Dhinnakitataka	DhaSSS	DhiraDhirakitataka	DhaSSSkitataka
0		4	
DhaStirakitataka	Dhinnakitataka		
0			
Dha			
×			

Kayada-3

GenageTa	kitaGena	Titekita	Genatite	Titegina	TakaDhin
×		2		0	
Tunakata,	KenakeTa	kitakena	Titekita	kenaTite	TiteGina
3		0		4	
TakaDhina	Dhinnakata				
0					

Prastar-1

GenageTa	kitaGena	Genage	Ta kitaGena	GenageTa	kitaGena
×		2		0	
Titekita	GenageTa	kitaGena	Titekita	Genatite	Titegina
3		0		4	
TakaDhina	Tunakata	KenakeTa	kitakena	KenakeTa	kitakena
0		×		2	
KenakeTa	kitakena	Titekita	GenageTa	kitaGena	Titekita
0		3		0	
Genatite	Titegina	TakaDhin	Dhinnakata		
4		0			

Prastar-2

GenageTa	kitaGena	Titegina	Titegina	Titegina	TakaDhin
×		2		0	
Tunakata,	KenakeTa	kitakena	Titekina	Titekina	Titegina
3		0		4	
TakaDhin	Dhinnakata				
0					

Prastar-3

GenageTa	kitaGena	TiteTite	Titegina	Titegina	TakaDhin
×		2		0	
Tunakata,	KenakeTa	kitakena	TiteTite	Titekina	Titegina
3		0		4	
TakaDhina	Dhinnakata				
0					

Prastar-4

GenageTa	kitaGena	Titekita	Genatite	kitataka	TakaDhin
×		2		0	
Tunakata,	KenakeTa	kitakena	Titekita	kenatite	Titegina
3		0		4	
TakaDhin	Dhinnakata				
0					

Prastar-5

Genatite ×	kitataka	TakaDhin 2	Dhinnakata
TakaDhin 0	TakaDhin	Tunakata, 3	Kenatite
Kitataka 0	Takatin	Tunakata 4	TakaDhin
TakaDhin 0	Dhinnakata		

Prastar-6

TakaDhin ×	Dhinnakata	TakaDhin 2	Dhinnakata
TakaDhin 0	TakaDhin	Tunakata, 3	Takatin
Tunakata 0	Takatin	Tunakata 4	TakaDhin
TakaDhin 0	Dhinnakata		

Tihai

TakaDhin ×	TakaDhin	TakaDhin 2	Dhinnakata	
DhaSSS 0	TakaDhin	TakaDhin 3	TakaDhin	
Dhinnakata 0	DhaSSS	TakaDhin 4	TakaDhin	
TakaDhin 0	Dhinnakata			Dha ×

Kayada-4 (Adalaya)

Dhatite	Dhagina	DhaTite	DheTite	Dhagina	DhageTin
×		2		0	
nakina,	Tatite	Takina	TaTite	TeTite	Dhagina
3		0		4	
DhageDhin	nagina				
0					

Prastar-1

Dhatite	Dhagina	Dhatite	Dhagina	Dhatite	Dhagina
×		2		0	
Dhatite,	Dhatite	Dhagina	Dhatite	DheTite	Dhagina
3		0		4	
Dhage	Tin nakina				
0					
Tatite	Takina	Tatite	Takina	Tatite	Takina
×		2		0	
Tatite ,	Dhatite	Dhagina	Dhatite	DheTite	Dhagina
3		0		4	
Dhage	Dhin nagina				
0					

Prastar-2

Dhatite	Dhagina	Dhatite	DheTite	Dhatite	DheTite
×		2		0	
Dhagina,	Dhatite	Dhagina	Dhatite	DheTite	Dhagina
3		0		4	
DhageTin	nakina				
0					
Tatite	Takina	Tatite	TeTite	Tatite	TeTite
×		2		0	
Takina ,	Dhatite	Dhagina	Dhatite	DheTite	Dhagina
3		0		4	
DhageDhin	nagina				
0					

Prastar-3

Dhatite	Dhagina	Dhatite	Dhatite	Dhatite	DheTite
×		2		0	
Dhagina ,	Dhatite	Dhagina	Dhatite	DheTite	Dhagina
3		0		4	
DhageTin	nakina				
0					

Tatite	Takina	Tatite	Tatite	Tatite	TeTite
×		2		0	
Takina ,	Dhatite	Dhagina	Dhatite	DheTite	Dhagina
3		0		4	
DhageDhin	nagina				
0					

Prastar-4

Dhatite	Dhagina	Dhatite	DheTite	DheTite	DheTite
×		2		0	
Dhagina ,	Dhatite	Dhagina	Dhatite	DheTite	Dhagina
3		0		4	
DhageTin	nakina				
0					

Tatite	Takina	Tatite	TeTite	TeTite	TeTite
×		2		0	
Takina ,	Dhatite	Dhagina	Dhatite	DheTite	Dhagina
3		0		4	
DhageDhin	nagina				
0					

Prastar-5

Dhatite	Dhagina	DhiteDhi	teDhite	Dhagina	DhageDhin
×		2		0	
nagina ,	Dhatite	Dhagina	Dhatite	DheTite	Dhagina
3		0		4	
DhageTin	nakina				
0					

Tatite	Takina	TiteTi	teTite	Takina	TakeTin
×		2		0	
nakina ,	Dhatite	Dhagina	Dhatite	DheTite	Dhagina
3		0		4	
DhageDhin	nagina				
0					

Tihai-1

DheTite	Dhagina	Dhagedhin	nagina	DhaSSS	DheTite
×		2		0	
Dhagina	Dhagedhin	nagina	DhaSSS	DheTite	Dhagina
3		0		4	

DhageDhin	nagina				
0					
Dha					
×					

Tihai-2

DhaTite	Dhagina	Dhatite	DheTite	DhaSSS	DhaTite
×		2		0	
Dhagina	Dhatite	DheTite	DhaSSS	DhaTite	Dhagina
3		0		4	
Dhatite	DheTite				
0					
Dha					
×					

Bant–1

Gina	Dhar	DhaऽTite	Titegina	Takadhin	Takatinऽ
×		2		0	
nara ,	Kina	Tar	TaऽTite	Titegina	Takadhin
3		0		4	
Takadhinऽ	Dhar				
0					

Prastar-1

Gina	Dhar	DhaऽTite	Titegina	DhaऽTite	Titegina
×		2		0	
Takadhin	Gina	Dhar	DhaऽTite	Titegina	Takadhin
3		0		4	
TakaTinऽ	nar				
0					
Kina	Tar	TaऽTite	Titekina	TaऽTite	Titekina
×		2		0	
TakaTin,	Gina	Dhar	DhaऽTite	Titegina	Takadhin
3		0		4	
TakaDhinऽ	Dhar				
0					

Prastar-2

Gina	Dhar	Gina	Dhar	DhaऽTite	Titegina
×		2		0	
Takadhin,	Gina	Dhar	DhaऽTite	Titegina	Takadhin
3		0		4	
TakaTinऽ	nar				
0					
Kina	Tar	Kina	Tar	TaऽTite	Titekna
×		2		0	
TakaTin,	Gina	Dhar	DhaऽTite	Titegina	Takadhin
3		0		4	
TakaDhinऽ	Dhar				
0					

Prastar-3

Dha·Tite	Titegina	TakaDhinS	nar	Takadhin	Takatin
×		2		0	
nar,	TaSTite	Titekina	TakaTinS	nar	TakaDhinS
3		0		4	
TakaDhinS	nar				
0					

Prastar-4

TakaDhinS	nar	TakaDhinS	narS	TakaDhin	TakaDhinS
×		2		0	
nar	DhaSTite	Titegina	TakaDhinS	nar	Takadhin
3		0		4	
TakatinS	nar				
0					

TakatinS	nar	TakatinS	nar	TakatinS	TakatinS
×		2		0	
nar	DhaSTite	Titegina	TakaDhinS	nar	Takadhin
3		0		4	
TakaDhinS	nar				
0					

Prastar-5

TakaDhinS	nar	TakaDhinS	nar	TakaDhinS	TakaDhin
×		2		0	
nar,	TakatinS	nar	TakatinS	nar	Takadhin
3		0		4	
TakaDhinS	nar				
0					

Prastar-6

Takadhina	Takadhina	TakaDhinS	nar	TakaDhin	TakatinS
×		2		0	
nar,	TakatinS	nar	TakatinS	nar	Takadhin
3		0		4	
TakaDhinS	nar				
0					

Tihai

Takadhin	Takadhin	TakaDhinऽ	nar	Dha	Takadhin
×		2		0	
Takadhin	Takadhin	naraDha	Takadhina	Takadhin	
3		0		4	
Takadhin	nar				
0					
Dha					
×					

Tihai

Takadhin	Takadhin	TakaDhinऽ	nar	Dha	nar
×		2		0	
Dha	nar	Dha	ऽ	Takadhin	Takadhin
3		0		4	
TakaDhinऽ	nar				
0					
Dha	nar	Dha	nar	Dha	ऽ
×		2		0	
Takadhin	Takadhin	TakaDhinऽ	nar	Dha	nar
3		0		4	
Dha	nar				
0					
Dha					
×					

Bant–2

DhaSSGhe	TageDhina	DhaSGhe	TageDhina
×		2	
DhaSSGhe	TageTina	Tarakina,	TaSSKe
0		3	
Taketina	TaSSKe	Taketina	DhaGhe
0		4	
TageDhina	Dharagina		
0			

Prastar-1

DhaSSSSGhe	TageDhina	SSSGhe	TageDhina
×		2	
SSSGhe	TageDhina	Dharagina ,	DhaSSGhe
0		3	
TageDhina	DhaSSGhe	TageDhina	DhaSSGhe
0		4	
Tagetina	Tarakina		
0			

TaSSKe	TakeTina	SSSke	TakeTina
×		2	
SSSke	TakeTina	Tarakina,	DhaSSGhe
0		3	
TageDhina	DhaSSGhe	TageDhina	DhaSSGhe
0		4	
TageDhina	Dharagina		
0			

Prastar-2

DhaSSGhe	TageDhina	GheTageGhe	TageDhina
×		2	
DhaSSGhe	TageDhina	Tarakina,	TaSSKe
0		3	
TakeTina	KetakeKe	TakeTina	DhaSSGhe
0		4	
TageDhina	Dharagina		
0			

Prastar-3

TageDhina ×	TageDhina		GheTageGhe 2	TageDhina
DhaSSGhe 0	TageDhina		Tarakina , 3	TakeTina
TakeTina 0	KetakeKe		TakeTina 4	DhaSSGhe
TageDhina 0	Dharagina			

Prastar-4

GheTageGhe ×	TageDhina		GheTageGhe 2	TageDhina
DhaSSGhe 0	TageDhina		Tarakina, 3	KetakeKe
TakeTina 0	KetakeKe		TakeTina 4	DhaSSGhe
TageDhina 0	Dharagina			

Prastar-5

GheTageGhe ×	TageDhina		TageDhina 2	TageDhina
GheTageGhe 0	TageTina		Tarakina , 3	KetakeKe
TakeTina 0	TakeTina		TakeTina 4	GheTageGhe
TageDhina 0	Dharagina			

Prastar-6

TakeTina ×	Tarakina		TageDhina 2	Dharagina
TakeTina 0	TakeTina		Tarakina, 3	TakeTina
Tarakina 0	TageDhina		Dharagina 4	TageDhina
TageDhina 0	Dharagina			

Tihai

TakeTina ×	Tarakina	TageDhina 2	Dharagina
Dha 0	TakeTina	Tarakina 3	TageDhina
Dharagina 0	Dha	TakeTina 4	Tarakina
TageDhina 0	Dharagina		
Dha ×			

Chakradar

DhageTite ×	TiteDhage	TiteTite 2	DhageTite	Gadigana 0	NageTite
Gadigana 3	NageTite	KitaDhet 0	TaSkita	Dhetta 4	KitaDhet
Taginna 0	DhaSkita				
DhetTagi ×	SnaDhaS	KitaDhet 2	Taginna	Dha 0	DhageTite
TiteDhage 3	TiteTite	DhageTite 0	Gadigana	NageTite 4	Gadigana
NageTite 0	KitaDhet				
TaSkita ×	Dhetta	KitaDhet 2	Taginna	DhaSkita 0	DhetTagi
SnaDhaS 3	KitaDhet	Taginna 0	Dha	DhageTite 4	TiteDhage
TiteTite 0	DhageTite				
Gadigana ×	NageTite	Gadigana 2	NageTite	KitaDhet 0	TaSkita
Dhetta 3	KitaDhet	Taginna 0	DhaSkita	DhetTagi 4	SnaDhaS
KitaDhet 0	Taginna	Dha ×			

Navahakka

Gadigana ×	DhaऽGadi	GanaDhaऽ 2	Gadigana	Dha 0	Gadigana
DhaऽGadi 3	GanaDhaऽ	Gadigana 0	Dha	Gadigana 4	DhaऽGadi
GanaDhaऽ 0	Gadigana				
Dha ×					

Chakradar

Dhaऽtirakitataka ×	Dhaऽtirakitataka	DhirDhirkitataka 2	Dhaऽtirakitataka
DhirDhirkitataka 0	DhaऽऽऽDhirDhir	kitatakaDhaऽऽऽ 3	DhirDhirkitataka
Dha 0	DhirDhirkitataka	DhaऽऽऽDhirDhir 4	kitatakaDhaऽऽऽ
DhirDhirkitataka 0	Dha	DhirDhirkitataka ×	DhaऽऽऽDhirDhir
kitatakaDhaऽऽऽ 2	DhirDhirkitataka	Dha 0	Dhaऽtirakitataka
Dhaऽtirakitataka 3	DhirDhirkitataka	Dhaऽtirakitatak 0	DhirDhirkitataka
DhaऽऽऽDhirDhir 4	kitatakaDhaऽऽऽ	DhirDhirkitataka 0	Dha
DhirDhirkitataka ×	DhaऽऽऽDhirDhir	kitatakaDhaऽऽऽ 2	DhirDhirkitataka
Dha 0	DhirDhirkitataka	DhaऽऽऽDhirDhir 3	kitatakaDhaऽऽऽ
DhirDhirkitataka 0	Dha	Dhaऽtirakitataka 4	Dhaऽtirakitataka
DhirDhirkitataka 0	Dhaऽtirakitataka	DhirDhirkitataka ×	DhaऽऽऽDhirDhir
kitatakaDhaऽऽऽ 2	DhirDhirkitataka	Dha 0	DhirDhirkitataka
DhaऽऽऽDhirDhir 3	kitatakaDhaऽऽऽ	DhirDhirkitataka 0	Dha
DhirDhirkitataka 4	DhaऽऽऽDhirDhir	kitatakaDhaऽऽऽ 0	DhirDhirkitataka
Dha ×			

Chakradar-Paran

TrakaDhet	TaSTraka	Dhetta	TrakaDhet	DheteDhete	DhageTite
×		2		0	
KraDheTite	DhageTite	katagadi	ganaDhet	TaraSna	DhaSkata
3		0		4	
DhaSDhet	TaraSna				
0					

DhaSkata	DhaSDhet	TaraSna	DhaSkata	Dha	TrakaDhet
×		2		0	
TaSTraka	Dhetta	TrakaDhet	DheteDhete	DhageTite	KraDheTite
3		0		4	
DhageTite	katagadi				
0					

ganaDhet	TaraSna	DhaSkata	DhaSDhet	TaraSna	DhaSkata
×		2		0	
DhaSDhet	TaraSna	DhaSkata	Dha	TrakaDhet	TaSTraka
3		0		4	
Dhetta	TrakaDhet				
0					

DheteDhete	DhageTite	kradheTite	DhgeTite	katagadi	ganaDhet
×		2		0	
TaraSna	DhaSkata	DhaSDhet	TaraSna	DhaSkata	DhaSDhet
3		0		4	
TaraSna	DhaSkata	Dha			
0		×			

Chakradar-Paran

DhageTite	KradhaTite	KradhaTite	TiteDhage	TitekraDhe	TiteDha,kra
×		2		0	
dheTiteDha	KradhaTite	DhaSDhage	TetekraDhe	TiteDha,kra	dheTiteDha
3		0		4	
KradheTite	DhaSDhage				
0					

TitekraDhe	TiteDha,kra	dheTiteDha	KradheTite	Dha	DhageTite
×		2		0	
KradhaTite	KradhaTite	TiteDhage	TitekraDhe	TiteDha,kra	dheTiteDha
3		0		4	
KradhaTite	DhaSDhage				
0					

TitekraDhe	TiteDha,kra	dheTiteDha	KradheTite	DhaऽDhage	TitekraDhe
×		2		0	
TiteDha,kra	dheTiteDha	KradhaTite	Dha	DhageTite	KradhaTite
3		0		4	
KradhaTite	TiteDhage				
0					

TitekraDhe	TiteDha,kra	dheTiteDha	KradhaTite	DhaऽDhage	TitekraDhe
×		2		0	
TiteDha,kra	dheTiteDha	KradheTite	DhaऽDhage	TitekraDhe	TiteDha,kra
3		0		4	
dheTiteDha	KradheTite				
0					
Dha					
×					

13

Paran in Sultal

Paran in Sultal-1

DhetDhet ×	TrakDhet	DheteDhete 0	DhageTite	
Dhetekradhe 2	TiteDhage	Titekata 3	Gadigana	
DhaऽDhaऽ 0	DhaऽDhete	KradheTite ×	DhageTite	
Katagadi 0	ganaDhaऽ	DhaऽDhaऽ 2	Dhetekradhe	
TiteDhage 3	Titekata	Gadigana 0	DhaऽDhaऽ	Dha ×

Paran-2

DheteDhete ×	KradheTite	DhageTite 0	DhageTite	
KradheTite 2	Katagadi	GanaNage 3	Titekata	
TakitaTa 0	ऽnDhiki	taTaऽn ×	DhaऽTite	
KataTaki 0	taTaऽn	DhikitaTa 2	ऽnDhaऽ	
Titekata 3	TakitaTa	ऽnDhiki 0	taTaऽn	Dha ×

Paran-3

TrakaDhet ×	Dhet-Dhet	DheteDhete 0	DhageTite

KradheTite	DhageTite	Gadigana	NageTite	
2		3		
KaTiteTa	ginaTaka	Titekata	gadigana	
0		×		
DhaऽDhaऽ	DhaऽTite	katagadi	ganaDhaऽ	
0		2		
DhaऽDhaऽ	Titekata	gadigana	DhaऽDhaऽ	Dha
3		0		×

Paran-4

Dhaऽkita	takaDhaऽ	kitataka	DhaऽDhaऽ	kitataka	Titekata
×		0		2	
Gadigana	Dhaऽऽऽ	Dhaऽऽऽ	Dhaऽkita	takaTite	katagadi
3		0		×	
GanaDhaऽ	ऽऽDhaऽ	ऽऽDhaऽ	Kitataka	Titekata	Gadigana
0		2		3	
Dhaऽऽऽ	Dhaऽऽऽ				
0					
Dha					
×					

Paran in Chartal-1

DheteDhete ×	DhageTite	KradhaTite 0	KradhaTite	
DhageTite 2	TiteDhage	Titekata 0	Gadigana	
KradhaTite 3	DhaऽKradha	TiteDhaऽ 4	KradhaTite	
DhaऽKata ×	gadigana	KradhaTite 0	DhaऽKradha	
TiteDhaऽ 2	KradhaTite	DhaऽKata 0	Gadigana	
KradhaTite 3	DhaऽKradha	TiteDha 4	KradhaTite	Dha ×

Paran-2

DhageTite ×	DhageTite	TageTite 0	TageTite	
DheteDhete 2	DhageTite	DheteDhete 0	DhageTite	
KradheऽDhe 3	TiteDhage	Titekata 4	Gadigana	
Dha ×	Dha	Dha 0	Titekata	
Gadigana 2	Dha	Dha 0	Dha	
Titekata 3	Gadigana	Dha 4	Dha	Dha ×

Paran-3

DhaऽGadi ×	ganaDhaऽ	Gadigana 0	DhaऽDhaऽ
DhaऽGadi 2	ganaNage	DhetऽDhara 0	ऽnDhaऽ
Gadigana 3	DhaऽGadi	ganaDhaऽ 4	Gadigana
DhaऽDhaऽ ×	DhaऽGadi	ganaDhaऽ 0	Gadigana

DhaSGadi 2	ganaDhaS	DhaSDhaS 0	Gadigana	
DhaSGadi 3	ganaDhaS	Gadigana 4	DhaSDhaS	Dha ×

Paran–4

DhageTite ×	KradhaTite	DhageTite 0	KradhaTite	
DhageTite 2	TiteDhage	TiteTite 0	KradhaTite	
DhageTite 3	Katagadi	GanaDhaS 4	naDhaSna	
DhaSSS ×	KradhaTite	DhageTite 0	Katagadi	
GanaDhaS 2	naDhaSna	DhaSSS 0	KradhaTite	
DhageTite 3	Katagadi	GanaDhaS 4	naDhaSna	Dha ×

14

Mukhara or Mohara

4 Beats (matras) for Teental

	3				×
1.	Kitataka	Tirakita	TaktaS	Tirakita	Dha
2.	Tirakita	TaktaS	Tirakita	Dhati	Dha
3.	Tirakita	Dhagi	nadha	Tirakita	Dha
4.	Dhagi	nadha	Tite	Dhati	Dha
5.	Dhage	Tirakita	taka,Taka	Tirakita	Dha
6.	Kran	Tirakita	TaktaS	Tirakita	Dha
7.	Tirakita	Kran	Kitataka	Tirakita	Dha
8.	KitadhaS	Tirakita	Kran	Kitataka	Dha
9.	Takkran	SSTira	Kitataka	Kran	Dha
10.	Tirakita	TakDhir	Kitataka	Dhati	Dha
11.	Kitataka	Tirakita	TakDhir	Kitataka	Dha
12.	Tirakita	DhetS	DhirDhir	Kitataka	Dha
13.	Gheranage	DhirDhir	Kitataka	Tirakita	Dha
14.	DhirDhir	KatS	DhirDhir	Kitataka	Dha
15.	Dhete	Kradhe	Tite	Kata	Dha
16.	KaTi	teDha	Tuna	Kata	Dha

8 Beats (matras)

1.	KaTi	teDhe	Tite	Gina	Tite	Tite	Gina	Nati	Dha
	0				3				×
2.	Kradhe	Tite	KaTi	teTa	Sn	TaSS	Kra	Dhati	Dha
	0				3				×

3.	KaS	TaDhe	Tite	Kradhe	Tite	KaTi	teTa	Sn	Dha
	0				3				×
4.	Tirakita	taka,Taka	Tirakita	dhati	Dha	Dhati	Dha	Dhati	Dha
	0				3				×
5.	Dha	Kitataka	TaStira	kitataka	Tirakita	takaDhir	Dhirkita	Dhati	Dha
	0				3				×
6.	Tirakita	takaTaka	Tirakita	DhaStira	Kitataka	Tirakita	taka	Tak kran	Dha
	0				3				×
7.	DhirDhir	KatS	DhirDhir	Kitataka	DhaStira	kitataka	DhaS	Kata	Dha
	0				3				×
8.	Dhagi	naDha	Tite	Gina	Tite	Dhagi	naDha	Tite	Dha
	0				3				×
9.	Tirakita	takaDha	Tirakita	Kran	Dha	Kran	Dha	Kran	Dha
	0				3				×
10.	Gheranage	Tirakita	takaTaS	Tirakita	Dhati	DhaS	naDha	Sna	Dha
	0				3				×
11.	Tirakita	TakataS	Skra	Dhati	Dhakra	Dhati	Dhakra	Dhati	Dha
	0				3				×
12.	Dhage	Tite	Dhagi	nadha	KraDha	Tuna	Skra	Dhati	Dha
	0				3				×

13.	KradheTite	KaTitedhe	Titekata	DhaSKati	
	0				
	tedheTite	KataDhaS	KaTitedhe	Titekata	Dha
	3				×
14.	DhetDhet	TrakaDhet	Taginna	DhaSTraka	
	0				
	DhetTagi	SnaDha	TrakaDhet	Taginna	Dha
	3				×
15.	DhirDhir	Kitataka	Ta	Kitataka	
	0				
	Tirakita	DhaSTira	kitaDhaS	Tirakita	Dha
	3				×
16.	Gheranage	Tirakita	Dhati	DhaS	
	0				
	KraDha	TiDha	SKra	Dhati	Dha
	3				×

Tal Kaharawa
Theka (main Bol of Tal)

Matras	-	1	2	3	4	5	6	7	8
Theka	-	Dha	Ge	Na	Tin	Na	Ke	Dhee	Na
Symbol	-	×				0			

VARIATION OF THEKA (Tal-Kaharawa)

	×				0			
1.	Dha	Dhi	Na	Ti	Na	Ke	Dhee	Na
2.	Dha	Dhi	Na	Ti	Na	Ti	Dha	Ta
3.	Dha	Ge	Na	Ti	Na	Na	Dhee	Na
4.	Dha	Dha	Ge	Ti	Na	Tit	Dha	Ta
5.	Dha	Dhin	Na	Kran	Na	Tit	Dha	Ta
6.	Dha	Tin	Na	Kina	Na	Tit	Dha	Ta
7.	Dha	Dhee	Ge	Tee	Na	Dhee	Ge	Dhee
8.	Dhin	S	Dha	Dhee	Ge	Ti	Na	Kra
9.	Dha	Gege	Nage	tin	Na	Kran	Dhee	Na
10.	Dha	Gena	Nage	tin	Na	Na	Dhee	Na
11.	Dha	SKra	Dha	tin	Na	Kran	Dhee	Nana
12.	DhaTi	tege	Nage	tin	Na	Kran	Dhee	Nana
13.	Dhadha	Gina	Tin	Nana	Nati	Gina	Dhin	Nati
14.	Dhatra	keDhi	Nage	tin	Nake	Traka	Dhina	Gina
15.	DhaTi	teDhi	Nane	kina	Na	Traka	Dhina	Gina
16.	Dhage	Traka	Tina	kina	Na	Traka	Dhina	Gina
17.	Dha	Kradhi	Nage	tin	Na	Kradhi	Nage	Dhin
18.	Gina	Dhati	Geti	Nana	Kina	Tadhi	Gedhi	Nana
19.	Dha	SGe	Nage	tin	Nana	Tite	Dhin	Nana
20.	Dha	SGe	Nage	tin	Na	Kradhi	Nage	Dhin
21.	Dha	Tirakita	Dhage	tin	NaStir	KitadhiS	SNa	Tirakita
22.	Dha	Gina	Nati	Keti	Na	Traka	Dhina	Traka
23.	DhaStira	kitaDhi	SNage	tintin	NaStir	kitaDhiS	Nage	dhintin
24.	Dha	Tirakita	Dhati	keti	Ta	Tirakita	Nadhi	Gedhi
25.	Tirakita	Dhadhi	Geti	Nake	Tirakita	Tadhi	Gedhi	Nage

Varieties of Tal Teental

1.

Dha	Dheena	DhinDhin	Dhati	Dha	Dheena	DhinDhin	Dhati
×				2			
Dha	Teena	TinTin	Tati	Ta	Dheena	DhinDhin	Dhati
0				3			

2.

Dha	Tirakita	DhinDhin	Dhakra	Dha	Tirakita	DhinDhin	Dhakra
×				2			
Dha	Tirakita	TinTin	Takra	Ta	Tirakita	DhinDhin	Dhakra
0				3			

3.

DhaStira	kitaDhinS	Skra	Dhati	DhaStira	kitaDhinS	Skra	Dhati
×				2			
DhaStira	kitaTinS	Skra	Tati	TaStira	kitaDhinS	Skra	Dhati
0				3			

4.

DhaSTite	Dhina	TiteDhin	DhaSTite
×			
DhaSTite	Dhina	TiteDhin	DhaSTite
2			
DhaSTite	Tina	TiteTin	TaSTite
0			
TaSTite	Dhina	TiteDhin	DhaSTite
3			

5.

DhaSTite	DhinSTite	DhinDhin	NaNaTite
×			
DhaSTite	DhinSTite	DhinDhin	NaNaTite
2			
DhaSTite	TinSTite	TinTin	NaNaTite
0			
TaSTite	DhinSTite	DhinDhin	NaNaTite
3			

6.

DhaSTite	DhinSSkra	Dhina	GinaTite
×			
DhaSTite	DhinSSkra	Dhina	GinaTite
2			
DhaSTite	TinSSkra	Tina	kinaTite
0			
TaSTite	DhinSSkra	Dhina	GinaTite
3			

7.	DhaSTite	DhinSnana	TiteDhin	NaNaTite
	×			
	DhaSTite	DhinSnana	TiteDhin	NaNaTite
	2			
	DhaSTite	TinSnana	TiteTin	NaNaTite
	0			
	TaSTite	DhinSnana	TiteDhin	NaNaTite
	3			
8.	DhaSTraka	DhinSSkra	DhinSSS	DhageTraka
	×			
	DhaSTraka	DhinSSkra	DhinSSS	DhageTraka
	2			
	DhaSTraka	TinSSkra	TinSSS	TakeTraka
	0			
	TaSTraka	DhinSSkra	DhinSSS	DhageTraka
	3			
9.	DhaSgina	Tirakita	DhiSgina	Nagetete
	×			
	DhaSgina	Tirakita	DhiSgina	Nagetete
	2			
	DhaSgina	Tirakita	TiSkina	Naketete
	0			
	Taketete	DhiSgina	Tete DhiS	ginaTete
	3			

15

Talas of Tabla are Used in Light and Classical Music

Tal-Dadara (6 Beats)

6 Beats (matra), 2 Vibhag, Tali (clap) on First matra, Khali on 4th matra:

Theka

Matra		2	3	4	5	6
Bol of Theka	Dha	Dhi	Na	Dha	Tu	Na
Symbol	×			0		

Tal-Kaharawa (8 Beats)

8 Beats (matra), 2 Vibhag ,Tali (clap) on First matra, Khali on 5th matra:

Theka

Matra	1	2	3	4	5	6	7	8
Bol of Theka	Dha	Ge	Na	Ti	Na	Ke	Dhi	Na
Symbol	×				0			

Tal-Dhumali (8 Beats)

There are two types in Tal Dhumali
First: 8 Beats (matra), 2 Vibhag, Tali (clap) on First matra, Khali on 5th matra:

Theka

Matra	1	2	3	4	5	6	7	8
Bol of Theka	Dhin	Dhin	Dha	Tin	Traka	Dhin	Dhage	Traka
Symbol	×				0			

Second: 8 Beats (matra), 4 Vibhag ,Tali (clap) on First matra, 3rd matra and 7th matra, Khali on 5th matra:

Theka

Matra	1	2	3	4	5	6	7	8
Bol of Theka	Dhin	Dhin	Dha	Tin	Traka	Dhin	Dhage	Traka
Symbol	×		2		0		3	

Tal-Khemta (12 Beats)

12 Beats (matra), 4 Vibhag, Tali (clap) on First matra, 4th matra and 10th matras, Khali on 7th matra.

Theka

Matra	1	2	3	4	5	6	7	8	9	10	11	12
Bol of Theka	Dha	Te	Dhi	Na	Ti	Na	Ta	Te	Dhi	Na	Dhi	Na
Symbol	×			2			0			3		

Tal-Pashto (7 Beats)

7 Beats (matra), 3 Vibhagas, Khali on First matra, Tali (clap) on 4th and 6th matras.

Theka (as per first opinion)

Matra	1	2	3	4	5	6	7
Bol of Theka	Tin	S	Traka	Dhin	S	Dha	Ge
Symbol	×			2		3	

Theka (as per second opinion)

Matra	1	2	3	4	5	6	7
Bol of Theka	Tin	S	Traka	Dhin	S	Dha	Ge
Symbol	0			1		2	

Tal-Rupak (7 Beats)

Tal Rupak is used in Semi classical and classical music both. There are two opinions for its presentation. As per the opinion of olden times, there is a tradition of showing 'Khali' on its 'Sum' i.e. 1st matra, but according to second opinion there is no 'Khali' in this Tal, hence, 'Tali' (clap) is shown on its 'Sum'. This Tal contains 7 Beats (matra), 3 Vibhagas, Khali on First matra, Tali (clap) on 4th and 6th matras.

Theka (as per first opinion)

Matra	1	2	3	4	5	6	7
Bol of Theka	Tee	Tee	Na	Dhi	Na	Dhi	Na
Symbol	0			1		2	

Theka (as per second opinion)

Matra	1	2	3	4	5	6	7
Bol of Theka	Tee	Tee	Na	Dhi	Na	Dhi	Na
Symbol	×			2		3	

Tal-Jhaptal (10 Beats)

10 Beats (matra), 4 Vibhag , Tali (clap) on First matra, 3rd matra and 8th matras, Khali on 6th matra.

Theka

Matra	1	2	3	4	5	6	7	8	9	10
Bol of Theka	Dhi	Na	Dhi	Dhi	Na	Ti	Na	Dhi	Dhi	Na
Symbol	×		2			0				3

Tal-Teental (16 Beats)

16 Beats (matra), 4 Vibhag, Tali (clap) on First matra, 5th matra and 13th matras, Khali on 9th matra.

Theka

Matra	1	2	3	4	5	6	7	8
Bol of Theka	Dha	Dhin	Dhin	Dha	Dha	Dhin	Dhin	Dha
Symbol	×				2			
Matra	9	10	11	12	13	14	15	16
Bol of Theka	Dha	Tin	Tin	Ta	Ta	Dhin	Dhin	Dha
Symbol	0				3			

Tal-Tilwara (16 Beats)

16 Beats (matra), 4 Vibhag, Tali (clap) on First matra, 5th matra and 13th matras, Khali on 9th matra.

Theka

Matra	1	2	3	4	5	6	7	8
Bol of Theka	Dha	Tirakita	Dhin	Dhin	Dha	Dha	Tin	Tin
Symbol	×				2			
Matra	9	10	11	12	13	14	15	16
Bol of Theka	Ta	Tirakita	Dhin	Dhin	Dha	Dha	Dhin	Dhin
Symbol	0				3			

Tal-Addha (16 Beats)

16 Beats (matra), 4 Vibhag, Tali (clap) on First matra, 5th matra and 13th matras, Khali on 9th matra.

Theka

Matra	1	2	3	4	5	6	7	8
Bol of Theka	Dha	SDhi	SGe	Dha	Dha	SDhi	SGe	Dha
Symbol	×				2			
Matra	9	10	11	12	13	14	15	16
Bol of Theka	Dha	STi	SKe	Ta	Ta	SDhi	Ge	Dha
Symbol	0				3			

Tal-Sitarkhani (16 Beats)

16 Beats (matra), 4 Vibhag, Tali (clap) on First matra, 5th matra and 13th matras, Khali on 9th matra.

Theka

Matra	1	2	3	4	5	6	7	8
Bol of Theka	Dha	Dhin	S	Dha	Dha	Dhin	S	Dha
Symbol	×				2			

Matra	9	10	11	12	13	14	15	16
Bol of Theka	Dha	Tin	S̱	Ta	Ta	Dhin	S̱	Dha
Symbol	0				3			

Tal-Tappa (16 Beats)

16 Beats (matra), 4 Vibhag, Tali (clap) on First matra, 5th matra and 13th matras, Khali on 9th matra.

Theka

Matra	1	2	3	4	5	6	7	8
Bol of Theka	Dha	Dhin	S̱Ta	Dhin	Dha	Dhin	S̱Ta	Dhin
Symbol	×				2			

Matra	9	10	11	12	13	14	15	16
Bol of Theka	Ta	Kat	Ke	S̱Ta	Ta	Dhin	S̱Ta	Dhin
Symbol	0				3			

Tal-Panjabi (16 Beats)

16 Beats (matra), 4 Vibhag, Tali (clap) on First matra, 5th matra and 13th matras, Khali on 9th matra.

Theka

Matra	1	2	3	4	5	6	7	8
Bol of Theka	Dha	SDhin	SNa	Dha	Dha	SDhin	SNa	Dha
Symbol	×				2			

Matra	9	10	11	12	13	14	15	16
Bol of Theka	Dha	STi	Sna	Ta	Ta	SDhin	Sna	Dha
Symbol	0				3			

Tal-Ektal (12 Beats)

12 Beats (matra), 6 Vibhag, Tali (clap) on First, 5th, 9th and 11th matras, Khali on 3rd and 7th matra.

Theka

Matra	1	2	3	4	5	6
Bol of Theka	Dhin	Dhin	Dhage	Tirakita	Tu	na
Symbol	×		0		2	

Matra	7	8	9	10	11	12
Bol of Theka	Kat	Ta	Dhage	Tirakita	Dhi	Na
Symbol	0		3		4	

Tal-Adachartal (14 Beats)

14 Beats (matra), 7 Vibhag, Tali (clap) on First, 3rd, 7th and 11th matras, Khali on 5th, 9th and 13th matra.

Theka

Matra	1	2	3	4	5	6	7	8
Bol of Theka	Dhin	Tirakita	Dhi	Na	Tu	Na	Kat	Ta
Symbol	×		2		0		3	
Matra	9	10	11	12	13	14		
Bol of Theka	Tirakita	Dhi	Na	Dhi	Dhi	Na		
Symbol	0		4		0			

Tal-Jhoomara (14 Beats)

14 Beats (matra), 4 Vibhag, Tali (clap) on First, 4th and 11th matras, Khali on 8th matra.

Theka

Matra	1	2	3	4	5	6	7
Bol of Theka	Dhin	SDha	Tirakita	Dhin	Dhin	Dhage	Tirakita
Symbol	×			2			
Matra	8	9	10	11	12	13	14
Bol of Theka	Tin	STa	Tirakita	Dhin	Dhin	Dhage	Tirakita
Symbol	0			3			

Tal-Deepchandi (14 Beats)

This Tal is known as 'Chanchar' also. It is mainly used in Thumri, Chaiti etc.

14 Beats (matra), 4 Vibhag, Tali (clap) on First, 4th and 11th matras, Khali on 8th matra.

Theka

Matra	1	2	3	4	5	6	7
Bol of Theka	Dha	Dhin	S	Dha	Dha	Tin	S
Symbol	×			2			
Matra	8	9	10	11	12	13	14
Bol of Theka	Ta	Tin	S	Dha	Dha	Dhin	S
Symbol	0			3			

Tal-Jata (16 Beats)

16 Beats (matra), 4 Vibhag, Tali (clap) on First, 5th and 13th matras, Khali on 9th matra.

Theka

Matra	1	2	3	4	5	6	7	8
Bol of Theka	Dha	S	Dhin	S	Dha	Dha	Tin	S
Symbol	×				2			
Matra	9	10	11	12	13	14	15	16
Bol of Theka	Ta	S	Tin	S	Dha	Dha	Dhin	S
Symbol	0				3			

Tal-Dhamar (14 Beats)

14 Beats (matra), 4 Vibhag, Tali (clap) on First, 6th and 11th matras, Khali on 8th matra.

Theka-1

Matra	1	2	3	4	5	6	7
Bol of Theka	Ka	Dhi	Te	Dhi	Te	Dha	S̱
Symbol	×					2	
Matra	8	9	10	11	12	13	14
Bol of Theka	Ga	Di	Na	Di	Na	Ta	S̱
Symbol	0			3			

Theka-2

Matra	1	2	3	4	5	6	7
Bol of Theka	Ka	Dhi	Te	Dhi	Te	Dha	S̱
Symbol	×					2	
Matra	8	9	10	11	12	13	14
Bol of Theka	Ga	Ti	Te	Ti	Te	Ta	S̱
Symbol	0			3			

Tal-Chartal (12 Beats)

12 Beats (matra), 6 Vibhag, Tali (clap) on First, 5th, 9th and 11th matras, Khali on 3th and 7th matra.

Theka

Matra	1	2	3	4	5	6
Bol of Theka	Dha	Dha	Din	Ta	Kita	Dha
Symbol	×		0		2	
Matra	7	8	9	10	11	12
Bol of Theka	Din	Ta	Tite	Kata	Gadi	Gana
Symbol	0		3		4	

Tal-Sooltal (10 Beats)

10 Beats (matra), 5 Vibhag, Tali (clap) on 1st, 5th and 7th matras, Khali on 3rd and 9th matra.

Theka-1

Matra	1	2	3	4	5	6
Bol of Theka	Dha	Dha	Din	Ta	Kita	Dha
Symbol	×		0		2	
Matra	7	8	9	10		
Bol of Theka	Tite	Kata	Gadi	Gana		
Symbol	3		0			

Theka-2

Matra	1	2	3	4	5	6
Bol of Theka	Dha	Ghera	Nage	Dee	Ghera	nage
Symbol	×		0		2	

Matra	7	8	9	10
Bol of Theka	Gad-	Dee	Ghera	Nage
Symbol	3		0	

Tal-Teevara (7 Beats)

7 Beats (matra), 3 Vibhag, Tali (clap) on First, 4th, and 6th matras.

Theka

Matra	1	2	3	4	5	6	7
Bol of Theka	Dha	Dhin	Ta	Tite	Kata	Gadhi	Gana
Symbol	×			2		3	

Tal-Rudra (11 Beats)

11 Beats (matra), 11 Vibhag, Tali (clap) on First, 3rd, 4th, 5th, 7th 8th, 9th and 10th matras, Khali on 2nd, 6th and 11th matras.

Theka

Matras	1	2	3	4	5	6	7
Bol of Theka	Dha	Tat	Dha	Tirakita	Dhi	Na	Tirakita
Symbol	×	0	2	3	4	0	5

Matras	8	9	10	11
Bol of Theka	Tu	Na	Kat	Ta
Symbol	6	7	8	0

Tal-Leelawati (13 Beats)

13 Beats (matra), 4 Vibhag, Tali (clap) on 1st matra, 5th matra 9th matras and 12th matra.

Theka

Matras	1	2	3	4	5	6	7	8
Bol of Theka	Dhin	Dhin	Dha	Trak	Dhin	S	Tin	Tin
Symbol	×				2			

Matras	9	10	11	12	13
Bol of Theka	Ta	Trak	Dhin	Dhin	S
Symbol	3			4	

Tal-Pancham Sawari (15 Beats)

15 Beats (matra), 4 Vibhag, Tali (clap) on 1st matra, 4th matra and 12th matras, Khali on 8th matra.

Theka-1

Matras	1	2	3	4	5	6	7	
Bol of Theka	Dhin	Na	Dhidhi	Kat	Dhidhi	Nadhi	Dhina	
Symbol	×			2				
Matras	8	9	10	11	12	13	14	15
Bol of Theka	Tikra	Tina	Tirakita	Tuna	Katta	Dhidhi	Nadhi	Dhina
Symbol	0				3			

Theka-2

Matras	1	2	3	4	5	6	7	
Bol of Theka	Dha	Dhin	Dhage	Nage	Tinkra	Tina	Tina	
Symbol	×			2				
Matras	8	9	10	11	12	13	14	15
Bol of Theka	Tina	Katta	DhiDhi	Nadhi	Dhina	DhaKra	DhinDhin	Dhati
Symbol	0				3			

Tal-Brahma (14 Beats)

14 Beats (matra), 14 Vibhag, Tali (clap) on 1st, 3rd, 4th, 6th, 7th 8th, 9th, 10th, 11th, 12th and 13th matras, Khali on 2nd, 5th, 9th and 14th matras.

Theka

Matras	1	2	3	4	5	6	7	8
Bol of Theka	Dha	Tat	Dhet	Dhina	naka	Dhet	Dhet	Dhina
Symbol	×	0	2	3	0	4	5	6
Matras	9	10	11	12	13	14		
Bol of Theka	Naka	Dhage	Tete	Kata	Gadi	Gana		
Symbol	0	7	8	9	10	0		

Tal-Brahma (28 Beats)

(28 Beats matra), 14 Vibhag, Tali (clap) on 1st, 5th, 7th 11th, 13th, 15th, 19th, 21st, 23rd and 25th matras, Khali on 3rd, 9th, 17th and 27th matras.

Theka

Matras	1	2	3	4	5	6	7	8	9	10
Bol of Theka	Dha	ऽ	Ta	ऽ	Dha	ऽ	Di	Na	Ta	ऽ
Symbol	×		0		2		3		0	
Matras	11	12	13	14	15	16	17	18	19	20
Bol of Theka	Ki	ta	Dha	ऽ	Din	ऽ	Ta	ऽ	Dha	ऽ
Symbol	4		5		6		0		7	
Matras	21	22	23	24	25	26	27	28		
Bol of Theka	Ti	te	ka	ta	Ga	Din	Ga	Na		
Symbol	8		9		10		0			

Tal-Gajjhampa (15 Beats)

15 Beats (matra), 4 Vibhag, Tali (clap) on 1st matra, 5th matra and 12th matras, Khali on 9th matra.

Theka

Matras	1	2	3	4	5	6	7	8
Bol of Theka	Dha	Dhina	Nage	Taka	Dha	Dhina	Nage	Taka
Symbol	×				2			
Matras	9	10	11	12	13	14	15	
Bol of Theka	Tina	nake	Taka	Tete	Katta	Gadi	Gana	
Symbol	0			3				

Tal-Basant (9 Beats)

9 Beats (matra), 9 Vibhag, Tali (clap) on 1st matra, 2nd, 3rd, 4th, 6th and 8th matras, Khali on 5th, 7th and 9th matras.

Theka

Matras	1	2	3	4	5	6	7	8	9
Bol of Theka	Dha	Dhin	Ta	Dhet	Ta	Tete	Kata	Gadi	Gana
Symbol	×	2	3	4	0	5	0	6	0

Tal-Matta (18 Beats)

18 Beats (matra), 9 Vibhag, Tali (clap) on First matra, 5th, 7th, 11th, 13th and 15th matras, Khali on 3rd, 9th and 17th matras.

Theka-1

Matras	1	2	3	4	5	6	7	8	9	10
Bol of Theka	Dha	S̱	Ghe	Ra	Na	Ka	Ghe	Ra	Na	Ka
Symbol	×		0		2		3		0	
Matras	11	12	13	14	15	16	17	18		
Bol of Theka	Te	Te	Ka	Ta	Ga	Di	Ga	Na		
Symbol	4		5		6		0			

Theka-2

Matras	1	2	3	4	5	6	7	8	9	10
Bol of Theka	Dhin	S̱	Na	S̱	Dhin	Tirakita	Dhi	Na	Tu	Na
Symbol	×		0		2		3		0	
Matras	11	12	13		14	15	16	17	18	
Bol of Theka	Kat	Ta	Tirakita		Dhi	Na	Dhi	Dhi	Na	
Symbol	4		5			6		0		

Tal-Laxmi (18 Beats)

18 Beats (matra), 18 Vibhag, Tali (clap) on 1st matra, 2nd, 3rd, 5th, 6th, 7th, 9th, 10th, 11th, 12th, 13th, 14th, 15th, 16th and 17th matras, Khali on 4th, 8th and 18th matras.

Theka-1

Matras	1	2	3	4	5	6
Bol of Theka	Dhinna	Dhindha	Tirakita	Dhinna	Dhindha	Tirakita
Symbol	×	2	3	0	4	5

Matras	7	8	9	10	11	12
Bol of Theka	DhaDha	Tirakita	DhaDha	Tirakita	Dhinna	Dhindha
Symbol	6	0	7	8	9	10

Matras	13	14	15	16	17	18
Bol of Theka	Tirakita	Tuna	Kidanaka	Tage	Ta	Tirakita
Symbol	11	12	13	14	15	0

Theka-2

Matras	1	2	3	4	5	6	7	8
Bol of Theka	Dha	S̲	Dhet	Dhet	Dha	S̲	Traka	Dhet
Symbol	×	2	3	0	4	5	6	0

Matras	9	10	11	12	13	14	15
Bol of Theka	Dha	S̲	Dhet	Dha	Traka	Dhet	Dhedhe
Symbol	7	8	9	10	11	12	13

Matras	16	17	18
Bol of Theka	S̲Dha	S̲Na	Dhet
Symbol	14	15	0

Tal-Shikhara (17 Beats)

17 Beats (matra), 5 Vibhag, Tali (clap) on 1st matra, 5th, 9th, 12th and 14th matras.

Theka

Matras	1	2	3	4	5	6	7	8
Bol of Theka	Dha	Traka	Dhina	Naka	Thoon	Ga	Dhina	Naka
Symbol	×				2			

Matras	9	10	11	12	13
Bol of Theka	Dhuma	Kita	Taka	Dhet	Dha
Symbol	3			4	

Matras	14	15	16	17
Bol of Theka	Tete	Kata	Gadhi	Gana
Symbol	5			

Tal-Ashtmangal (11 Beats)

11 Beats (matra), 11 Vibhag, Tali (clap) on 1st matra, 3rd, 4th, 6th, 7th, 9th, 10th and 11th matras, Khali on 2nd, 5th and 8th matras.

Theka

Matras	1	2	3	4	5	6	7	8
Bol of Theka	Dhi	Na	Dhi	Dhi	Na	Dhi	Dhi	Na
Symbol	×	0	2	3	0	4	5	0

Matras	9	10	11
Bol of Theka	Dhage	naDha	Traka
Symbol	6	7	8

Tal-Ashtmangal (22 Beats)

22, beats, 11 vibhag, Tali (Clap) on Ist matra, 5th, 7th, 11th, 13th, 17th, 19th and 21st matras, khali on 3rd, 9th and 15th matras.

Theka

Matra	1	2	3	4	5	6	7	8	9	10	11	12
Bol of Theka	Dha	S	Ki	Ta	Ta	Ka	Dhu	Ma	Ki	Ta	Ta	Ka
Symbol	×		0		2		3		0		4	

Matra	13	14	15	16	17	18	19	20	21	22
Bol of Theka	Dhe	S	Ta	S	Ta	Ka	Dha	Di	Ga	Na
Symbol	5	0		6		7		8		

Tal-Shesha (19 Beats)

19 beats, 7 vibhag, Tali (clap) on Ist, 5th, 9th, 11th, 13th, 17th and 18th Matras.

Theka

Matra	1	2	3	4	5	6	7	8	9	10
Bol of Theka	Dha	S	Ki	ta	Ta	Ka	Dhu	Ma	Ki	ta
Symbol	×				2				3	

Matra	11	12	13	14	15	16	17	18	19
Bol of Theka	Ta	Ka	Dha	S	Ta	S	Dha	GaDi	Gana
Symbol	4		5				6	7	

Tal-Shiva (19 Beats)

19 beats, 5 vibhag, Tali (clap) on Ist, 5th, 13th and 17th Matras, Khali on 9th Matras.

Theka

Matra	1	2	3	4	5	6	7	8
Bol of Theka	Dha	S	Dhin	S	Dha	Ge	Na	Ge
Symbol	×				2			

Matra	9	10	11	12	13	14	15	16
Bol of Theka	Tira	Kita	Tu	Na	Kat	Ta	Dhi	Na
Symbol	0				3			

Matra	17	18	19
Bol of Theka	Dhi	Dhi	Na
Symbol	4		